D0969035

HC   Hansen, Niles M.
107
.A165 The border economy
H36

DATE			

© THE BAKER & TAYLOR CO.

The Border Economy

The Border Economy
Regional Development in the Southwest

by Niles Hansen

University of Texas Press, Austin

Library of Congress Cataloging in Publication Data
Hansen, Niles M
    The border economy.
    Bibliography: p.
    Includes index.
    1. Southwest, New—Economic conditions. 2. Mexicans
in the United States. 3. Mexican Americans—Southwest, New.
I. Title.
HC107.A165H36   330.979   80-25134
ISBN 0-292-75061-7
ISBN 0-292-75063-3 (pbk.)

To Karen, Eric, and Laura, with affection

Contents

Preface   ix

1. Regional Development Issues in the Southwest Borderlands: A Preliminary Overview   3

2. The Nature of Border Regions   19

3. Subregions of the Southwest Borderlands   35

4. Regional Development: Structure and Change of Employment and Earnings   53

5. The Role of Mexican Labor in Southwestern Economic Development   77

6. Undocumented Mexican Immigration: What Are the Issues? What Are the Alternatives?   103

7. Mexican Americans: The Human Connection   127

8. Summary and Conclusions   155

Appendixes   167

Notes   185

Bibliography   207

Index   221

Preface

This book has its origins in research that I carried out in 1975–1977 at the International Institute for Applied Systems Analysis in Laxenburg, Austria. Increasing international economic integration in Western Europe has led to a proliferation of studies and policy debates concerning border region problems; a significant portion of my research at IIASA was devoted to critical analyses of European border region theories and policies. Upon returning to my home institution, the University of Texas at Austin, I was pleased to find a newly created Mexico–United States Border Research Program. The realization of my interest in pursuing border region research in the North American context was made possible by the encouragement of the program's coordinator, Professor Stanley Ross, and by the financial support of the Andrew W. Mellon Foundation.

Among the issues that have made the United States and Mexico increasingly interdependent are the movement of large numbers of persons from both countries to the borderlands, undocumented Mexican immigration to the United States, the use of Mexico's massive oil and gas reserves, and growing trade between the two countries. Problems and opportunities arising from increasing interdependence are most clearly and intensely evident in the borderlands.

The Mexico–United States border area is unique. Nowhere else in the world do two neighboring countries have so great a disparity in their respective per capita income levels. Nevertheless, research focused only on the Mexico–United States borderlands would run the risk of producing a parochial case study. Thus, while underscoring the special attributes of this region, I also have attempted to provide a broader international perspective in dealing with the theoretical, empirical, and policy issues that are discussed. For example, major attention is given to a wide range of border region theories (chapter 2), to the significance of the new international division of labor (chapter 5), and to European guest worker experiences (chapter 6), all of which have relevance to the Mexico–United States borderlands.

Regional development issues on both sides of the border also are examined in the respective national contexts of Mexico and the United States. However, as the title of this volume suggests, primary attention is given to the U.S. side, partly because of my greater familiarity with the United States and because relevant data are more available for this country for recent years. More important, though, is the fact that my research was formulated and carried out as part of a larger collaborative undertaking with Professor Clark Reynolds of Stanford University. He has been analyzing the Mexican side in depth and will report his findings in a separate volume.

In addition to examining the role of Mexican workers in southwestern economic development, detailed consideration is given in this study to Mexican Americans, whose influence continues to grow in the southwest as well as in the nation as a whole. In keeping with common practice, distinctions are made between Mexican Americans and Anglos; unless otherwise indicated, the term "Anglo" is used for the sake of simplicity to designate all white persons, as defined by the U.S. Bureau of the Census, who are not Mexican American.

The first chapter of this book introduces regional development issues in the southwest borderlands and critically examines some of the assumptions underlying recent development policies for the region. Chapter 2 presents a general evaluation of economic theories concerning border regions and specifically considers their relevance to the U.S.-Mexican border. Chapter 3 describes the subregions of the southwest borderlands; their recent economic development in terms of employment and earnings is discussed in some detail in chapter 4. The next three chapters deal with various aspects of the Mexican connection: the historical role of Mexican labor in the southwest, the nature and significance of undocumented Mexican immigration, and the status and prospects of Mexican Americans. The final chapter summarizes the principal findings and conclusions of the study.

Parts of some chapters are revised portions of material previously published in the *Journal of Regional Science*, the *Annals of Regional Science*, and *Growth and Change: A Journal of Regional Development*. For their valuable help I am indebted to Milton Adams, Ellen Brennan, Frank Call, Gilbert Cardenas, Efrain Conrique, Ernie Cortés, Kenneth Horowitz, Michael McAndrew, James Miller, Michael Miller, William Mitchell, Clark Reynolds, Robert Rivera,

Koren Sherrill, Ellwyn Stoddard, and Sidney Weintraub. I am particularly grateful to Benjamin Chinitz, Lay James Gibson, and Stanley Ross for their detailed comments and suggestions, and to Marilyn Norton for the high quality of the secretarial and administrative support she provided.

The Border Economy

1. Regional Development Issues in the Southwest Borderlands: A Preliminary Overview

In the nineteenth century both the United States and Mexico regarded the present borderlands area as a remote frontier. Increasing contacts between the two frontier societies were strongly marked by confrontation and conflict because neither really understood the history, customs, beliefs, or political and legal institutions of the other. Conflicts and misunderstandings have not disappeared, but interdependencies between Mexican and U.S. border communities have resulted in many examples of trans-boundary cooperation—frequently informal in nature to avoid unrealistic bureaucratic rigidities created and maintained in Mexico City and Washington.

Clearly many border cities have pressing economic and social difficulties. Rapid population growth and slums typical of many Third World cities plague the Mexican side, and the three poorest metropolitan areas in the nation are found on the U.S. side. Nevertheless, the boundary has created a zone of attraction for people in both countries. Today about 4 million people live on each side in territory that was still very sparsely populated early in the present century. The large Mexican-heritage population living in U.S. border communities provides much of the continuity between neighboring Mexican and U.S. border cities. Moreover, in the southwest borderlands distinctions between Mexican Americans (U.S. citizens) and Mexican nationals are somewhat artificial because both groups play a similar role in establishing the Mexican connection with the United States. The U.S. government has only recently made serious efforts to obtain complete and accurate data on the Mexican American population, and information concerning undocumented (illegal) Mexicans residing in the United States is limited to widely varying guesses. Similarly, the U.S. government has belatedly attempted to deal comprehensively with border region issues by creating the Southwest Border Regional Commission. This agency has had too little time and insufficient funds to warrant an evaluation of its achievements, but the assumptions underlying its establishment do merit consideration because they reflect common—and often er-

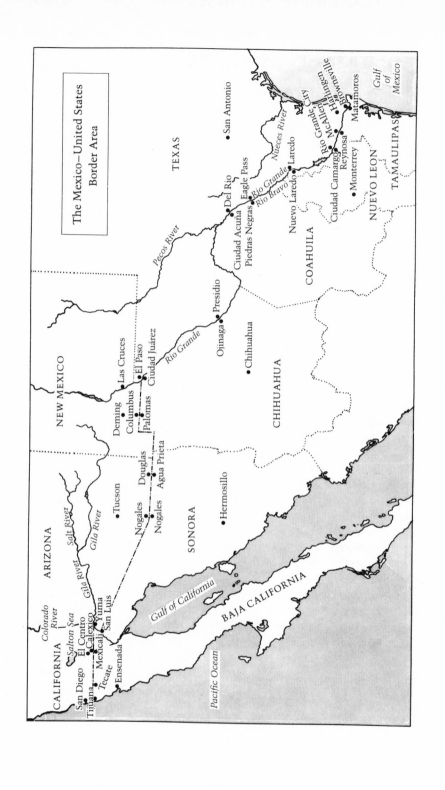

The Mexico–United States Border Area

roneous—views of the southwest borderlands. Before examining these policy assumptions, brief attention will be given to the recent historical background of joint federal-state multistate regional development planning efforts, as well as to the related issue of the definition of the southwest borderlands for the purposes of the present study.

The National Regional Policy Context

Large-scale federal efforts to deal with multistate regional development problems have been based primarily on legislation passed in 1965, during the heyday of President Johnson's Great Society programs. There had, of course, been a number of prior experiments in regional development legislation. For example, during the 1930s such New Deal programs as the Tennessee Valley Authority, rural electrification, and the Civilian Conservation Corps were based on public works and resource development and conservation. In the early 1960s renewed interest in assisting depressed areas led to the Area Redevelopment Act and the Accelerated Public Works Act, both of which provided for public works in declining or stagnating communities. However, funds were not sufficient to overcome basic problems, planning was carried out on too small a scale, and little attention was given to human resource development. Although a public works bias was carried over in the 1965 legislation, the two regional development acts passed in that year—the Appalachian Regional Development Act (ARDA) and the Public Works and Economic Development Act (PWEDA)—represented an unprecedented attempt to deal comprehensively with regional problems characterized by high unemployment and low per capita income.

The institutional mechanisms created to implement these initiatives are too complex to examine here in any detail.[1] For present purposes it will suffice to note that the ARDA created the Appalachian Regional Development Commission, whose function has been to formulate and implement strategies to promote the development of an area involving the entire state of West Virginia and portions of twelve other states. The PWEDA created the Economic Development Administration, which has given developmental assistance to numerous substate areas, and it authorized the designation of multistate regional commissions modeled on the Appalachian program. In 1966 and 1967, regional commissions were established for New England, the Ozarks (comprising 134 counties in Arkansas, Oklahoma, Missouri, and Kansas), the Four Corners Region (consisting of 92 counties in Arizona, Colorado, New Mexico, and Utah), the Atlantic Coastal Plains (made up of 159 tidewater counties in Georgia and the Carolinas), and the Upper Great Lakes (comprising 119 counties in northern Minnesota, Wisconsin, and Michigan).

Most of the regional commission areas have experienced economic and demographic growth in recent years after relatively long periods of stagnation or decline.[2] Regional development programs have no doubt been a positive force in some places, by helping to induce growth or by orchestrating growth that has taken place "spontaneously." However, few observers would go so far as to credit these programs with the major responsibility for the regional turnarounds. The agencies involved have had too little money, too little time, and little in the way of coherent and systematic strategies for development. Nevertheless, the regional commission approach to development issues still has widespread support in Congress and among many state governors; in addition, it has increasingly been regarded as a potential vehicle for coordinating a much wider array of programs within the federal system. While the precise role that regional commissions should have continues to be debated,[3] they have expanded steadily in geographic terms. The original commissions, with the exception of that for New England, covered areas that are largely nonmetropolitan in character. The addition of three new commissions and the territorial expansion of previously existing commissions have given the relevant areas a more heteroge-

Table 1.1. Standard Metropolitan Statistical Area (SMSA) and Nonmetropolitan Population of Southwest Border Regional Commission Counties, 1975

	Border	California
Total population	4,068,531	2,197,933
SMSA	3,467,887	2,113,657
SMSA proportion (%)	85.2	96.2
Non-SMSA	600,644	84,276
Non-SMSA proportion (%)	14.8	3.8

SOURCE: U.S. Bureau of the Census, *County and City Data Book, 1977*, table 2, pp. 42, 54, 66, 318, 438, 450, 462, 474.

neous nature. The commissions now include most of the nation's territory, though less than half of the total population.

Defining the Borderlands

The most recent addition was the Southwest Border Regional Commission, which was designated in 1976 and organized in 1977. For the most part, the data used in the present study are organized in terms of the counties included in this commission area as of July 1, 1980 (twenty-four Texas counties were added later in 1980; see appendix A). With one minor exception—Real County, Texas—all of the commission counties either are on the border or else are adjacent to counties on the border. Special attention is given to the Standard Metropolitan Statistical Areas (SMSAs)[4] within this region because, as the data in table 1.1 indicate, they account for over 85 percent of the total border population.[5] It could be argued that the commission counties do not necessarily represent appropriate units for economic analyses because they were designated on political grounds—and even the political criteria may have varied from state to state. Three points may be made in response to this issue.

First, nothing seems to provoke more controversy among social scientists—and particularly geographers—than the definition of a region. One attempt to delimit the "Hispanic-American Borderland" as a cultural region includes most of Texas, nearly all of New Mexico, about half of California and Arizona, and most of southern Colorado.[6] A *Washington Post* editor recently maintained that

	Arizona	New Mexico	Texas
	601,471	166,938	1,102,189
	443,958	0	910,272
	73.8	0	82.6
	157,513	166,938	191,917
	26.2	100	17.4

states' boundaries do not reflect how the United States really works. He divided the country into nine "nations," which include neighboring areas in Canada, Mexico, and the Caribbean Islands. One of these is MexAmerica, which extends from south of Monterrey, Mexico, to well north of the U.S.-Mexico border, including such cities as Houston, Dallas, Fort Worth, Santa Fe, Phoenix, and Los Angeles.

> Somewhere around the border town of Houston, maybe half way to Beaumont, the grits give way to refried beans and the pines give way to earth shades of red and brown. You know you're out of Dixie and into MexAmerica.
> This strip nation runs for half a continent 200 or 300 miles north of the border with Mexico. It is a nation that is now what the United States in the '80s will be—one in which the biggest minority is not blacks, but Hispanics.[7]

There can be little doubt that "The American Southwest has become a vast social and economic laboratory in which Mexico and the U.S. may learn to live together harmoniously."[8] But the distinctive social and economic phenomena found in this laboratory are most clearly in evidence along the border, where U.S.-Mexican interrelations are the most pervasive and intense. It therefore seems appropriate to limit an investigation of the economic development of the southwest borderlands to an area smaller than that where some degree of hispanic cultural influence may be present.

A related reason for using the regional commission definition of the borderlands is precisely the political element involved. Public policies are neither formulated nor implemented by or for cultural areas; they are made by political entities for political entities. The federal government and the respective border states have the joint capability to implement policies, programs, and projects in the commission area. Thus, the policy implications of a study such as the present one can be acted upon within an existing institutional framework.

Finally, for economic reasons the use of regional commission counties as geographic units of analysis will be supplemented by the use of functional economic areas along the border. Over a decade ago, Karl Fox argued that the delineation of spatial units for regional economic analysis should take account of the functional relations involved in such processes as services delivery and journey-to-work patterns.[9] The notion of a functional economic area recognizes that a large number of services and a large share of regional employment opportunities are located in the core (or nodal) city of a region but that the region's outer perimeter is defined in terms of journey-to-work flows from outlying areas to the core city. Thus, functional economic areas are extended urban fields, with peripheral towns acting as service centers for nearby residents in much the same way as do suburban shopping centers in a large metropolitan area.

In 1969, a nationally exhaustive set of 173 functional economic areas was delineated by the Bureau of Economic Analysis, U.S. Department of Commerce. Regional boundaries were determined by identifying urban cores—usually SMSAs—and then selecting the counties most closely linked to the respective cores. In other words, after the 173 cores were selected, each of the approximately 2,600 counties that did not fall within a core was studied to determine the core to which it was most tied.[10]

Changes in the regional distribution of population and economic activity and changes in commuting patterns—caused in large measure by the expansion of the Interstate Highway System—made it necessary to revise the 1969 BEA region delineations in 1977. Boundary changes were made primarily on the basis of journey-to-work data from the 1970 population census, newspaper circulation data for 1972, and 1975 intercounty commuting data derived from Social Security Administration and Internal Revenue Service records.

The present study uses data for the revised BEA borderlands regions, which are here defined to be San Diego, Tucson, El Paso, San Antonio, and Brownsville. It should be emphasized that while the BEA regions have the names of their respective urban cores, they are usually much larger than the core areas. The counties included in the borderlands BEA regions are listed in appendix B.

The choice of borderlands BEA regions needs some justification. Selection of the San Diego, Tucson, El Paso, and Brownsville regions was relatively straightforward. In each case the core SMSA is on the border with Mexico. The Phoenix and San Angelo BEA regions were *excluded* even though they touch the Mexican border—the only other BEA regions that do so. With the exception of the five counties in the Tucson BEA region, the Phoenix BEA region covers the entire state of Arizona. But only one county in the Phoenix region borders Mexico and only three others are in the second tier of counties from the border. The situation of the San Angelo BEA region is similar;

only one of its sixteen counties is on the border and only two others are in the second tier of counties from the border.

The *inclusion* of the San Antonio BEA region may seem the most problematic decision in view of the fact that the core SMSA is 150 miles from the border. The SMSA cores of the excluded Phoenix and Corpus Christi regions are about the same distance from the border. Three considerations strongly supported San Antonio's inclusion. First, the Corpus Christi BEA region has no border counties and, as already mentioned, the Phoenix region has only one border county. The San Antonio region includes five border counties (one of which is Webb County—the Laredo SMSA) as well as seven counties in the second tier of counties from the border. Second, large numbers of Mexican residents shop in the San Antonio BEA region and not just in the border towns. Many Mexicans from as far away as Monterrey shop in the city of San Antonio. This is not the case for Corpus Christi, which has no pretensions in this regard, or for Phoenix, which is very remote from significant population centers in Mexico. Finally, the city of San Antonio has a strongly Mexican flavor. In the 1970 census, persons of Spanish heritage accounted for 52.2 percent of its total population; the corresponding proportion for Corpus Christi was 40.6 percent and for Phoenix only 14.0 percent.[11]

Policy Assumptions concerning the Borderlands: A Critique

Having defined for present purposes the geographic extent of the borderlands, it is now necessary to consider briefly the issues that make this laboratory unique. In 1976 the governors of the respective border states requested that the Secretary of Commerce create the Southwest Border Regional Commission. Their application refrained from making specific policy proposals, but it did set forth some explicit and implicit assumptions concerning the borderlands. Some of them no doubt continue to influence policy discussions. One of the principal tasks of the present study is to evaluate widely held but not necessarily correct assumptions about the nature and significance of borderlands problems, so that policy issues can be addressed within a context that reflects the social and economic realities of the borderlands. It should be noted here that the governors' rationale for the creation of a regional commission for the southwest borderlands was no doubt influenced in part by the legislation authorizing the designation of regional commissions. To the extent that this is the case, the criticisms of the governors' application set forth in the remainder of this chapter and in the following chapter are applicable to present federal regional development legislation insofar as it relates to the borderlands. In the forward to the governors' application it is stated that:

> Historically the United States–Mexico border has been a conflict and poverty ridden area. This is explained by the existence of many innate friction-laden features chief among which is the greatest disparity in per capita income between any two bordering nations in the world. This disparity has led to an ever growing imbrogliation of the region's economy. Undocumented workers (illegal aliens) and commuters contribute heavily to the increasing levels of domestic unemployment.
>
> Over the years there have been attempts at cooperative Mexican-American efforts to solve common border problems; but unfortunately, positive efforts have often been hampered by insufficient attention and commitment from the national level. The limited resources at the disposal of the municipalities in the proposed region have seriously diminished their ability to solve problems in areas such as San Diego–Tijuana, El Paso–Juarez, and Brownsville–Matamoros.
>
> Traditional, individualistic, ad hoc approaches to such matters as protectionism, immigration, smuggling, crime, unemployment, industrialization, transportation, pollution, energy, water, tourism, education, etc., are woefully obsolete in today's complicated environment. The economic health of the region is, and has been on the decline and constitutes a pernicious drain on the overall economies of our four states; ergo the scope of the border problems demand [sic] a regional approach and the establishment of a regional structure as provided for under Title V of the Public Works and Economic Development Act PL 94-188.
>
> The region's problems are of common economic and social characteristics and extend across jurisdictional boundaries. Efforts of a single state (within the proposed four state region) to improve its own border area without corresponding efforts by the other three sister states would be highly difficult and just possibly overwhelming and ineffectual.

In 1975, Congress explicitly recognized the uniqueness and severity of a wide spectrum of socioeconomic problems in those states. An amendment to Title V provides for the establishment and funding of a Regional Planning Action Commission, specifically for "the region along the border with Mexico in the States of Texas, New Mexico, Arizona, and California."[12]

Many of the problems enumerated in this statement can be found in other parts of the United States. What makes them qualitatively different in the borderlands is the economic disparity between the United States and Mexico. In 1977, per capita income in the United States was \$8,720; the corresponding figure for Mexico was only \$1,130.[13] The push represented by poor social and economic conditions in much of Mexico and the pull of potential economic opportunity in the United States have contributed greatly to rapid population growth on both sides of the border in this century and no doubt will continue to do so for the foreseeable future. However, the implications of these phenomena are not always as evident as they may at first seem, as will be discussed in detail in subsequent chapters. To anticipate, a few comments are in order here with respect to the passage just cited.

Whatever may be meant by "an ever growing imbrogliation of the region's economy," it is true that domestic unemployment in some local U.S. labor markets is relatively high due to the presence of significant numbers of Mexican commuters and undocumented workers. But in many instances United States citizens are no longer willing to take the low-pay, low-status jobs that are now held by Mexicans. Moreover, many local economies in the southwest borderlands are highly dependent on the expenditures of Mexican migrants and commuters.

In a related vein, it is frequently argued that the unemployment rates of Mexican Americans are particularly affected by competing Mexican labor. This probably is true—though the degree is not certain—because the border labor market areas with relatively high unemployment rates also have relatively high proportions of Hispanics in their populations. In the third quarter of 1978, when the national unemployment rate was hovering around 6 percent, the corresponding rates in Texas border SMSAs ranged from 9.4 percent in Brownsville to 13.2 percent in McAllen.[14] In these same SMSAs, the proportion of the total population accounted for by "persons of Spanish heritage" ranged from 56.9 percent in El Paso to 85.6 percent in Laredo in 1970.[15] In contrast, the unemployment rate for the third quarter of 1978 in San Diego was 7.4 percent and that in Tucson was only 5.2 percent.[16] The proportion of the San Diego SMSA's 1970 population accounted for by persons of Spanish heritage was only 12.8 percent, and the corresponding figure for the Tucson SMSA was only 23.6 percent.[17] In the light of such evidence it might seem that Mexican American interest groups would side with those U.S. labor union leaders who favor stricter controls on the entry of Mexican workers into the United States. But this often has not been the case because when crackdowns take place on undocumented Mexican workers, Mexican Americans also have tended to be subjected to harassment. In addition, most Mexican Americans are either themselves immigrants from Mexico or the descendents of relatively recent immigrants from Mexico; there were few Mexicans or Mexican Americans in the United States at the beginning of this century. Thus, large numbers of Mexican Americans still have close ties to Mexico. Immigrants from Mexico and their descendents have typically improved their economic circumstances over what they were or would be in Mexico, even though their economic status may still be relatively low by U.S. standards. The point is not that high unemployment or low income should be passively tolerated but that historical and international perspectives need to be maintained in examining economic conditions in the borderlands.

The contention in the governors' application that the economic health of the southwest borderlands "is, and has been on the decline and constitutes a pernicious drain on the overall economies of our four states" also needs to be examined critically. The demographic data presented in table 1.2 show that during the 1960s the rate of population growth in both the San Diego and Tucson SMSAs greatly exceeded that for the United States; between 1970 and 1975 the rate of population growth in the United States declined, but there was an acceleration of growth during this period in the San Diego and Tucson SMSAs. (It should be kept in mind that the columns in table 1.2 compare a rate of change over a ten-year period with a rate of change over a five-year period.) Laredo's population growth rate increased slightly during the 1970–1975 period. McAllen, which experienced practically no growth during the 1960s, and Brownsville, which had an absolute decline in population during the 1960s, both had growth rates in excess of 20 percent between 1970 and 1975. The rate of net inmigration to the San Diego SMSA increased during the 1970–1975 period and the corresponding rate for Tucson was higher than during the entire 1960–1970 period. All four Texas SMSAs experienced net

Table 1.2. Population Change (%) and Net Migration (%) in Borderlands SMSAs and the United States, 1960–1970 and 1970–1975

	Population Change (%)		Net Migration (%)	
	1960–1970	1970–1975	1960–1970	1970–1975
San Diego	31.4	16.9	16.2	12.4
Tucson	32.4	25.5	17.9	19.9
El Paso	14.4	15.4	−9.4	5.1
Laredo	12.5	7.2	−15.0	−4.9
McAllen	0.3	21.6	−23.9	8.4
Brownsville	−7.1	20.6	−29.8	8.7
U.S.	13.4	4.8	1.8	1.2

SOURCE: U.S. Bureau of the Census, *County and City Data Book, 1977*, table 3, pp. 2, 548, 558, 568, 578, 588.

outmigration during the 1960s, but during the first half of the 1970s three had net inmigration and in the other, Laredo, the rate of net outmigration was considerably lowered. In demographic terms, the southwest borderlands clearly have not been in decline.

Personal income data for the borderlands SMSAs are presented in table 1.3 for the years 1969 and 1977. During this interval, the average annual rate of growth in total personal income in every borderlands SMSA exceeded the national rate of 9.4 percent. Per capita income in San Diego exceeded the corresponding national figure in both 1969 and 1977. In the other five SMSAs it was lower than the national level in both years. However, the percentage change in per capita income over the 1969–1977 period was well above the national growth rate in Laredo, McAllen, and Brownsville, the three poorest SMSAs in the nation. The rate of change in Tucson was about the same as the national rate. Only in El Paso was the growth rate significantly below the national rate.

Demographic and personal income data for the borderlands Bureau of Economic Analysis functional economic regions are shown in table 1.4. The years—1971 and 1976—are the earliest and latest, respectively, for which data are given in the source document. The rate of population growth in each of the regions exceeded that of the United States as a whole during the period in question; the five-year growth rate ranged from 7.7 percent in the San Antonio region to 22.0 percent in the Brownsville region. Per capita personal income

Table 1.3. Personal Income Data for Borderlands SMSAs and the United States, 1969–1977

	Average Annual % Change in Total Personal Income	Per Capita Personal Income 1969	1977	% Change in Per Capita Annual Income, 1969–1977
San Diego	12.0	$3,893	$7,070	81.6
Tucson	12.2	3,317	6,317	90.4
El Paso	10.1	2,805	5,071	80.8
Laredo	11.2	1,896	3,898	105.6
McAllen	14.8	1,664	3,859	131.9
Brownsville	13.3	1,997	4,253	113.0
U.S.	9.4	3,667	7,026	91.6

SOURCE: U.S. Department of Commerce, Bureau of Economic Analysis, Regional Economic Measurement Division, "County and Metropolitan Area Personal Income," *Survey of Current Business* 59, no. 4 (April 1979), pp. 27–29.

in the San Diego region was higher than U.S. per capita personal income in both 1971 and 1976. In the other regions it was lower than the U.S. figure in both years. The percentage change in per capita personal income between 1971 and 1976 was about the same in the El Paso region as in the United States as a whole. The corresponding growth rates for the higher-income borderlands regions—San Diego and Tucson—were below the national rate of increase. However, the corresponding growth rate in the San Antonio region was higher than the national growth rate, and the Brownsville region's 61.0 percent increase was the highest among all the borderlands regions.

In sum, the evidence indicates that there is a great deal of variation among the subregions of the borderlands. The Texas regions and the New Mexico counties economically linked to El Paso have relatively low levels of per capita income, but as a group they have, in relation to the rest of the United States, both rapidly growing population and per capita income. The San Diego SMSA and the San Diego BEA region both have rapid population growth, but their per capita income growth rate is below that of the nation and that of the rest of the borderlands as a whole. The Tucson SMSA and the Tucson BEA region have very high rates of population growth. Per capita income growth in the Tucson SMSA is about the same as that in the

Table 1.4. Population Change (%) and Per Capita Personal Income
Change (%) in Borderlands BEA Regions, 1971–1976

	Population (in thousands)		% Change 1971–	Per Capita Personal Income		% Change 1971–
	1971	1976	1976	1971	1976	1976
San Diego	1,477	1,705	15.4	$4,412	$6,426	45.6
Tucson	484	578	19.4	3,846	5,552	44.4
El Paso	634	717	13.1	3,146	4,852	54.2
San Antonio	1,239	1,335	7.7	3,329	5,299	59.2
Brownsville	368	449	22.0	2,159	3,475	61.0
U.S.	206,206	214,648	4.1	4,132	6,396	54.8

SOURCE: U.S. Department of Commerce, Bureau of Economic Analysis, *Local Area Personal Income 1971–1976*, volume 1, Summary, pp. 1, 224, 225, 226, 240, 250.

nation, but the corresponding growth rate in the Tucson BEA region is somewhat below the national rate. Despite this rather mixed picture, the overall tendency is one of growth rather than decline.

Do the borderlands constitute "a pernicious drain on the overall economies" of the border states, as the governors' application maintains? There is no direct evidence for this contention in the application itself, and only a detailed analysis of the public finance situation within each of the relevant states can decide this question. Nevertheless, there is enough evidence at hand to cast doubt on the notion that the regional commission counties are a net drain on the economies of the border states.

Per capita personal income in San Diego County is above that for the nation as a whole and the cost of living is somewhat less than the national average.[18] But because California is a very prosperous state, San Diego County ranked eighteenth among the state's fifty-eight counties in terms of per capita personal income in 1977. Riverside County ranked thirty-sixth and Imperial County ranked fifty-third. If the California borderlands counties were treated as a single unit, it would rank in the top half of all the state's counties because of the weight of San Diego County, which accounts for nearly three-fourths of the area's total population. Viewed in this light, it is by no means clear why the border area should be a drain on the state of California. It might be argued that undocumented Mexican aliens are a fiscal burden, but the evidence in this regard is quite to the contrary; the social services they consume represent only a small fraction of the money they contribute to the support of local public services.[19]

In New Mexico, three of the five regional commission counties—Grant, Hidalgo, and Otero—rank among the top ten of the state's thirty-two counties in terms of per capita personal income. Luna County ranks thirteenth and Dona Ana County ranks seventeenth. Thus, the tax base of the border counties is higher than that of the rest of New Mexico, indicating that they should not be a drain on the state as a whole.

Arizona has fourteen counties. With respect to per capita personal income, the four regional commission counties rank among the top nine counties: Pima County ranks third; Santa Cruz County, seventh; Yuma County, eighth; and Cochise County, ninth. However, Pima County—the Tucson SMSA—accounts for nearly three-fourths of the total regional commission area population, so taken as a whole the regional commission area has a higher tax base than the rest of Arizona.

In 1977, per capita personal income in Texas was $6,827, but it was below this level in every one of the state's twenty-four regional commission counties. The range among the latter was from $2,515 in Starr County to $6,658 in Terrell County. It would appear that at least in Texas the borderlands are a net burden on the state—yet this is not the case, because Texas has the strongest home rule system in the United States. Texas has no state-local revenue sharing. "Cities therefore receive virtually nothing from the state, and they accept that as the trade-off for limited state-level involvement in their affairs. In return, the Texas legislature has expected cities to provide for themselves."[20] Among the nation's forty-eight largest cities, El Paso ranks third—behind Dallas and Houston—in reliance on local revenues.[21] It might be argued that Texas should do more to alleviate poor economic conditions in its borderlands, but this is a separate issue. In fact, present institutional arrangements prevent the borderlands from being a drain on the rest of the state.

It should be apparent by now that there is yet another questionable assumption in the governors' application, namely, that "The region's problems are of common economic and social characteristics." Rather, within the borderlands as a whole (however defined) there are numerous subregions; each has, in kind or in degree, its own characteristics and problems. Preliminary evidence in this regard was presented earlier in this chapter and more will be presented in subsequent chapters. First, however, it is necessary to consider the general issue of the nature of border regions. More specifically, to what extent does the conceptual and theoretical literature on border regions provide policy-relevant guidance for dealing with problems of border regions in general and those of the United States–Mexico border area in particular?

2. The Nature of Border Regions

This chapter critically examines a representative body of the literature on border regions to ascertain whether there are general principles or empirical regularities that may be used to elucidate the nature and significance of the development of the U.S.-Mexican borderlands. For present purposes border regions may be defined as subnational areas whose economic and social life is directly and significantly affected by proximity to an international boundary.[1] Small nations often have many of the attributes of border regions, but the primary concern here is the border region in the larger context of its own nation, as well as its international setting.

The Concept of a Border: A Historical Overview

In antiquity, as among some primitive tribes today, the territories associated with distinctive groups were delimited by boundaries having a spiritual or mythological character, rather than a political or economic connotation. Because of their sacred nature, borders were generally respected by the peoples concerned. For the Chinese and Roman empires, the notion of a border had the sense of a limit of civilization. Despite the walls erected in frontier areas, the borders of these empires were zones rather than lines. The breakdown of the Roman Empire and the evolution of the feudal system strongly influenced the concept of a boundary during the Middle Ages. The links binding vassals to their lords were more personal than territorial. The mosaic of fiefs, of which there were over 350 in the Holy Roman Empire alone at the end of the Middle Ages, implied discontinuities, enclaves, and ruptures of authority. Indeed, the very multiplicity of frontiers undermined the efficacity of borders. However, the progressive triumph of the hereditary principle of governmental authority increased the importance of territorial boundaries. The rise of the nation-state and the revolution in cartographic techniques during the Renaissance reinforced the significance of territorial limits based on ancient hereditary and historic rights. When the latter were challenged at the time of the French Revolution, a new concept of geographic boundaries emerged. This theory of natural borders was closely associated with the idea that people have a right to self-determination. But developed without nuances and used without discernment, the linking of the notions of a nation or a national consciousness with that of a natural boundary easily provides a rationale for annexation and even oppression.[2] The principle of Manifest Destiny, which played a major role in the U.S. conquest of half of Mexico's territory and thereby led to the establishment of the present U.S.-Mexican border, was a direct descendent of the natural borders theory.

During the nineteenth century, German scholars in particular developed the principle that national borders should coincide with linguistic and cultural boundaries. The ethnographic basis of this nationalist approach differed from the French conception that borders should be defined in keeping with a consciousness of fatherland (*patrie*). The linguistic-cultural principle of nationalities was clearly triumphant at the end of the First World War, particularly in the division of the Austro-Hungarian Empire. This effort to make nationalities coincide with states tended to invest borders with the sacred character attributed to them in the distant past. Yet all of the European countries that have been created during the past 150 years still have border region problems arising from the demands of minorities seeking to realize their "national" values within the framework of an organized state.[3] Moreover, such demands are found today among minorities within long-established nation-states; significant separatist movements exist, for example, among the Basques, Catalonians, Bretons, Corsicans, and Scots.[4]

The exaltation of nationalities in the late nineteenth and early twentieth centuries readily degenerated into an imperialist conception of borders that ignored the existence and the interests of the groups concerned in favor of the alleged needs of an aggressively expansionist state. Nazi Germany, which adopted the doctrine that the German *Volk* required more territory (*Lebensraum*), viewed European borders as mere milestones marking successive stages of military expansion, until the fortunes of war turned against the Third Reich.[5]

The principle of a contractual or negotiated border stands at the opposite pole from the imperialist principle in the sense that the delimitation process is based on bilateral discussions without resort to the threat of force. In other words, the process is one of democratic negotiation at the international level. Examples of borders established in this manner are few because some degree of force or pressure has usually been present. If the borders of the United States were modified in a genuinely contractual manner when Florida, the Louisiana Territory, and Alaska were acquired, the negotiations establishing the boundaries with Canada and Mexico were not always marked on the U.S. side by the contractual spirit reflected in our own Constitution and Declaration of Independence. Although the stability of these borders is now a long-accomplished fact, the proximity of the United States has remained a source of concern to both of our neighbors.

Having briefly sketched the history of various concepts of a border, it is now necessary to consider the economic consequences of a border for those regions that lie on the margins of different economic, social, and political systems. International trade theory, location theory, and the growth pole literature will be examined in turn.

International Trade Theory

It might be supposed that classical and neoclassical international trade theory would be able to give significant guidance with respect to border region problems. In fact, such theory is not well adapted for this purpose because it is largely oriented to the notion of equilibrium. It postulates that both trading partners gain from the exchange and that any disequilibrium will be corrected by re-equilibrating forces. It was never elaborated to deal systematically with economic inequalities, so it cannot explain the existence of underdevelopment or the process of development. Even in its modern versions, international trade theory has as its ideal the generalization of free trade in order to promote world well-being. But the notion of homogeneous markets bears little resemblance to the realities of most border regions. The latter are profoundly influenced by particular local geographical, political, and economic conditions. It has been argued that present tendencies in the evolution of the European Economic Community are forcing recognition of this fact. In this view, phenomena neglected in trade theory (as well as location theory) are in fact the key elements in any serious consideration of the problems of border regions. Thus trade theory "ignores economies of scale, external economies, the effects of domination, and the cumulative processes of economic decline or development; in brief, it does not take account of development theory and particularly its spatial implications."[6]

Location Theory

Border Region Disadvantages   Neither of the great pioneers of twentieth-century location theory—Walter Christaller and August Lösch—developed a systematic theory of border regions. Nevertheless, both tended to regard them as disadvantaged areas because of barriers to international trade and the threat of military invasion.

It is beyond the scope of this chapter to give even a complete outline of Christaller's general theory. However, it may be noted that he employed the term "central place" to denote all urban agglomerations and pointed out that there is a mutual interdependence between any central place and its complementary region. He constructed now-familiar geometric models to demonstrate the possible hierarchical relations among central places in an economic landscape. If the objective is to supply all parts of a region with all conceivable central goods from the minimum possible number of functioning central places, then the market principle should be the determining factor in spatial organization. But if the objective is to satisfy as many demands for transportation as possible with a minimum cost, then as many important central places as possible should lie on traffic routes; relatively more central places would then be needed in comparison with spatial organization according to the market principle.[7]

It is especially relevant in the context of border regions that Christaller also recognized a third system of spatial organization based on the "sociopolitical separation principle."[8] This system arises when there are strong notions of community and defense and protection. The determination of its exact laws lies in the domain of theoretical political geography, but Christaller held that the separation principle "has neither the authority nor the rationality of the economic principles, but it has the authority of stately and sovereign might."[9]

Border regions may be fragile in Christaller's scheme because national frontiers artificially fragment complementary regions. Christaller further maintained that capital costs have great importance in the development of central places because they primarily determine the lower range limit of central goods, and particularly those with a high proportion of capital costs to total costs.[10] In unstable border areas capital costs would contain a high risk premium, and consequently goods would have to be sold at higher prices. This in turn would lead to a transfer of consumption to other central places. Central places on unstable borders will thus have relatively small complementary areas and limited development. Of course, cities may grow on national borders for defensive purposes, but they may have only fractional hinterlands. Or cities that once had a large complementary region (e.g., Vienna before the First World War) may lose most of their market areas when drastic political boundary revisions take place (e.g., Vienna after the First World War). Although Christaller illustrated a possible system of central places according to the separation principle,[11] the only general conclusion to be drawn when this principle is operative is that many more central places will be required to supply a region with central goods than would have been the case if the economic principles had been followed.

Lösch derived theoretical economic regions as functions of distance, mass production, and competition, but he was quite aware of complicating factors in the real world. He argued that border regions may encounter special problems because of conflicts between political and economic goals. The goals of economic landscapes are, in order of priority: prosperity, *Kultur*, power, and continuance. However, the political goals of the nation-state have exactly the reverse order.[12]

Lösch argued that it is characteristic of national frontiers to hamper the crossing of boundaries by market areas, to create new gaps in a market network where none existed, and to discourage industries from settling near a boundary, where they often would have a market in one direction only. This also explains why after a shifting of political frontiers the new border regions frequently become depressed areas. When a boundary creates market gaps and when no multiplication of the interior market can be achieved by regrouping—which is also relatively uneconomic—the result is greater profits but almost certainly a poorer supply for the consumer. Political boundaries have this effect because of specific secondary phenomena usually associated with them. First, tariffs separate economically complementary market areas; second, differences in language, customs, and national character have the same effect as customs duties; third, public contracts and "official traffic" do not cross the border; and fourth, border areas are the most threatened in military terms.[13]

In contrast to Christaller and Lösch, Herbert Giersch developed a spatial model for the explicit purpose of examining the locational consequences of political boundaries.[14] His model assumes a large plain in which transportation costs are proportional to distance. The plain is a circle surrounded by a desert, which Giersch regarded as the strongest possible substitute for a national frontier and a barrier to international trade and factor movements. Natural resources, population, and production units are assumed to be equally distributed over the entire area. In some respects what Giersch proposed is a von Thünen–type model of economic union; the principal difference is that Giersch introduced capital growth as a dynamic element.

Giersch argued that the lower the costs of transportation of a product and the greater the internal economies of large-scale production, the larger will be the market areas and the fewer the firms that will emerge. What is particularly significant is that the larger the market areas, the fewer will be the entrepreneurs who choose a location near the frontier. There is a network of markets for every commodity, but the whole system of networks tends to become denser in the center than at the extremities. When capital growth, internal and external economies (due to indivisibilities), and rent-lag are introduced into the model, the advantages of the favored location cumulate, an agglomeration center necessarily appears, and the spatial distribution of economic activities can be described by a density function shaped like an inverted cone. Thus, in Europe, for example, political boundaries and national agglomeration have produced a form of international deglomeration. The European distribution of industries is broader than that of the United States, with its unitary market, but the resulting pattern has been unfavorable for European border regions.

Edgar Hoover, in his influential study of the economics of location, pointed out that tariffs and other restraints on international trade increase transportation costs, distort market areas and supply networks, and increase the costs of producers located near borders.[15] Consequently, "producers are likely to shun the territory near a trade barrier which would curtail their market or supply area"[16] and locate in an area that is more central relative to domestic markets.

The clear implication of much of the location theory literature is that border regions will be weakly developed because they are unattractive for many economic activities. However, despite this unfavorable picture, location theorists have also recognized that border regions may have some advantages.

Border Region Advantages Christaller noted that central places on stable political boundaries may benefit from the development of trading activity at the border, the storage of goods, and earnings derived from the collection of duties, even though they may have no— or almost no—complementary region. For some central goods, for example, concerts and dining, the border may not be an impediment, in which case the complementary region has the ideal form of a circle that may extend far into the neighboring country.[17]

Lösch pointed out that border regions may benefit from transfrontier investments made in order to avoid customs duties. Thus, Swiss entrepreneurs had long established branches in German border regions for this reason, although lower wages may also have been a motive. Headquarters were maintained in Switzerland to save on taxes, but branches could readily be managed from the home office, Swiss key personnel employed, and contact with Swiss financial backers maintained. Similarly, Lösch argued that many branch plants of U.S. firms would never have been established in Canadian border areas in the absence of a political frontier.[18]

In terms of Giersch's analysis, international economic integration would weaken the international deglomeration effects of national agglomeration. Within a European Common Market, for example, particular regions would tend to gain economically because of their location near the industrial center. However, it is somewhat difficult to speak of border region advantages here because the areas in question would in fact no longer be border regions. Furthermore, Bertil Ohlin has noted that a movement of industries toward the center of a country would take place only under certain circumstances and only when industries producing for the domestic market are involved.[19] Export-oriented industries tend to locate near borders (or at other points where international transfers can be facilitated) in order to reduce transportation costs.[20] In addition, the location of export activities in border regions will attract labor, capital, and related economic sectors to these regions.[21] The conclusion that may be drawn from this position is that the existence of tariffs does not necessarily cause a diminution of economic activities in border regions. The extent to which tariffs and other barriers to exchange will repel economic activities and result in economic stagnation in border regions depends on the market characteristics of the affected industries. This is an important point, and one that was overlooked by both Giersch and Lösch.

Hoover maintained that if the location of economic activities in regions on one side of a tariff wall is likely to be unattractive to entrepreneurs, regions on the other side are likely to be desirable locations for the same activities.[22] This would be especially true to the extent that new activities are created by the implementation of tariffs. If a country decides to import raw materials to produce a commodity that it had previously imported, then

> the location of minimum transfer costs for the new protected industry is at the port of entry for the materials, *i.e.*, as close to the material supply as it is possible to be while still remaining within the protected market area. Even if the protected industry is not definitely material-oriented, ports of entry may be ideal locations because they are transshipment and junction points and also usually the centers of important local markets.[23]

And to the extent that ports of entry are located in border regions, these areas may well become centers of industrial activity.

Border Regions as Incomplete Growth Poles

Growth pole theory emphasizes that international and interregional inequalities are an inevitable part of the development process. A great deal of attention is given to the importance of economies of scale and to larger considerations of external economies of agglomeration. In the past two decades, a large theoretical literature has evolved around these notions and growth pole policies (usually intended to induce growth in lagging regions) have been adopted by planning authorities all over the world, although the extent to which they have been influenced by growth pole theory has varied considerably. Detailed examination of the history, nature, and significance of growth pole theory and practice is beyond the scope of this chapter, but such studies are available elsewhere.[24] Suffice it to say here that the theory has been criticized for being poorly articulated and less general than the theory of innovation diffusion; and growth center policies have not been notably successful in generating regional development.

Nevertheless, an influential French literature has continued to maintain that the growth pole approach could be particularly useful in studying border regions. For example, Gendarme argued that the main consequence of a political frontier is to check the spread effects (effets de diffusion) of a development pole[25]—they will not have the same strength in inducing other activities that they would have had inside a national space. He called particular attention to situations where zones of underdevelopment on one side of a border coexist with zones of "overdevelopment" on the other. This phenomenon, which he described as an "incomplete development pole," is a result of such factors as customs barriers, failure to take advantage of complementary natural resources, a tendency for transportation routes to run parallel with borders rather than across them, and supply and demand problems with respect to labor market integration.

Gendarme recognized that investments are made across a border in order to penetrate a foreign market and still maintain control of operations from a position of proximity in the country of origin. However, he regarded such investments as exceptional in the total scheme of things; more significant is the tendency of countries to react negatively, for narrowly nationalist reasons, to foreign investments.

Moreover, within nations capital mobility has worsened the economic situation in border regions. A "fortress mentality" has led to stagnation because industrialists refuse to invest in threatened areas, with the exception of activities related to national defense or when essential resources (iron ore, coal) are found there. For such reasons Alsace could be regarded as already having experienced World War II in 1933. Similarly, Lorraine's lack of investments in manufacturing activities related to the steel produced there can be attributed to the region's proximity to Germany. In fact, in the 1930s some plants originally located between the Maginot Line and the Siegfried Line were dismantled and reassembled in central France. Thus, given a lack of investment from abroad and of reinvestment by local firms in other activities, it is not astonishing that border regions have economies that are vulnerable or depressed.

In contrast to capital mobility, Gendarme asserted that nation-states have always taken a more permissive attitude toward international labor mobility, even to the extent of helping to organize it. Labor mobility across political boundaries has represented a kind of safety valve helping to maintain a favorable level of equilibrium in the labor markets of border regions. Alsace again provides a case in point. German and Swiss border regions exert an important influence on the Alsatian labor market. Each working day thousands of Alsatians cross a border to work in Basel or in Baden, where wages are higher than in Alsace. The German city of Karlsruhe is a veritable pole of attraction for the entire area around Wissembourg, in northern Alsace.[26] This fluidity is not without its problems. For example, early in 1966 wages on the German side of the border were 21 percent higher than on the French side; many Alsatian firms felt that as a result they were losing needed skilled workers to German firms. In contrast, during the 1966–67 German recession, many Alsatian workers were affected by layoffs.

To the extent, then, that Gendarme's arguments with respect to factor mobility are correct, it would follow that border regions are characterized by a relative immobility of capital but some mobility of labor, the extent of which will depend on the economic situation in the neighboring country.

Jacques Boudeville, the leading French proponent of the growth pole approach to regional development issues, similarly rejected classical economic analysis of border regions because of its static quality and its neglect of institutional factors. However, at the time of his recent death he had not really developed more than a sketch of how growth pole theory might be specifically adapted to the study of border regions. Boudeville held that international solidarity could be realized within the framework of geographical and technical external economies of agglomeration. In this regard he referred to integration poles which would put into communication regional economic systems that hitherto had been essentially isolated.[27] An integration pole is "a multi-focal development pole, connecting two urban systems which remained separate from each other, thus creating propulsive circuits and feedbacks in each of them. It gives birth to new propulsive nodes and to new evolutionary possibilities."[28] The strength of the integration pole is due to three factors: first, the addition of a new activity creating technical accessibility between two regions; second, the creation of new elements in the transport network between neighboring towns resulting in improved geographic accessibility; and third, the elaboration of common urban development planning which improves social accessibility. According to Boudeville the most general type of polarized integration is triangular. French examples include Orléans-Blois-Tours, Pau-Lourdes-Tarbes, Caen-Rouen-LeHavre, Reims-Epernay-Châlons, and Belfort-Montbéliard-Mulhouse, the last being built in order to balance Basel's "dangerous polarisation at the junction of the Rhine and the Swiss plateau."[29]

The growth pole literature offers numerous examples of zones whose development has been impeded by more or less arbitrarily fixed frontiers which divide natural economic regions into two or three parts, but it remains to be seen if it will provide any truly new insights into border region problems and their resolution. A major shortcoming in Gendarme's analysis is its emphasis on the military vulnerability of border regions. Clearly not all border regions live under threat of attack. Even though this was the case in Western Europe's past, today and in the foreseeable future it is highly unlikely that one Western European nation would attack another. Rather, the real issue of present concern is economic integration. However, neither Gendarme nor Boudeville nor any other growth pole theorist really develops a systematic theory relating border regions to the growth pole literature.[30] Many of the examples cited of the consequences of an incomplete development pole were already recognized, at least implicitly, in classical location theory, and it is difficult to see what is to be gained by adopting the jargon of growth pole theory.

Moreover, the identification of an incomplete development pole with the absence of spread effects from core urban centers to their adjacent hinterland areas or to neighboring urban centers might at first appear to be a useful point of departure for the analysis of border regions. But this is precisely the point where growth pole policies have most frequently failed to measure up to expectations. Even where growth has been induced in selected centers, spread effects usually have been either nonexistent or much less than anticipated. The principal reason is that economic linkages tend to be very diffused spatially; they are not primarily a matter of a center and its hinterland or even an orderly filtering process from higher-order to lower-order centers within an urban hierarchy.[31] Thus the reduction of border region problems to the issue of spread effects appears to be too simplistic.

To this point it has been argued that neither international trade theory, nor location theory, nor the growth pole approach to spatial development provides an adequate basis for analyzing the economics of border regions. This lack of understanding of border regions and their problems may be in part both an effect and a cause of persistent nationalism in the face of attempts to achieve greater economic integration among countries.

Theory, Evidence, and the U.S.-Mexican Borderlands

The classic works in twentieth-century location theory were written in Germany between the two world wars. In the context of the time it is not surprising that both Lösch and Christaller emphasized the negative aspects of political boundaries and the threatened status of border regions. The French growth pole literature—the major source of border region theory since the Second World War—grew out of the seminal works of François Perroux. A key element in his general effort to provide a dynamic interpretation of economic activity is the concept of dominance, which "consists of an irreversible or partially reversible influence exercised by one unit upon another. An economic unit exercises this effect by reason of its dimension, its negotiating strength, the nature of its activity, or because it belongs to a zone of dominant activity."[32] In addition, "as soon as any inequality appears among firms, the breach is opened by which the cumulative effect of domination insinuates itself."[33] This effect, according to Perroux, has both economic dimensions (among sectors) and geographic dimensions (among regions). Firms that are dominant and propulsive in economic terms make the regions in which they locate dominant and propulsive in spatial terms.[34] Other French growth pole theorists have seized upon these notions to argue that one side of a border area will tend to dominate the other side. More specifically, they have maintained that France's eastern border regions are threatened with domination from neighboring German and Swiss border regions.

All of these concepts and attitudes have their counterparts in discussions of the U.S.-Mexican borderlands. It will be argued here that for the most part they are no more helpful in clarifying basic issues in the U.S.-Mexican borderlands context than they have been in Europe. Indeed, in both cases they are frequently erroneous and have done more to hinder understanding than to promote it.

A major study of the U.S.-Mexican borderlands claims that border regions are always disadvantaged.

Boundaries between nations are obstacles to development. This is true all over the world, and the boundary between the United States and Mexico is no exception. . . . It may be taken as a general principle that regions along international boundaries grow less rapidly than comparable regions in the interior, or those which have access to the sea. If we look at the U.S.-Canadian boundary, the only concentrations of population are, in effect, seaports along the Great Lakes. Along the 49th parallel the cities of any importance are 50 to 150 miles from the boundary. This same pattern seems to be repeated in Europe and elsewhere. No significant development takes place along boundary lines, except where cities are placed near the border by boundary changes, where an unusually good harbor exists, or where an area is heavily subsidized.[35]

In his recent history of Ciudad Juárez, Oscar Martínez states his "conviction that a case study of this type not only adds to our overall understanding of the economy of the Mexican northern border but also provides insights into the general workings of international boundaries."[36] He also argues that "regions situated at or near borders generally develop at a slower rate than comparable interior areas"[37] and that "normally no significant development occurs along boundary lines."[38]

In the past there was some justification for the argument that border region development was sometimes inhibited by the threat of military invasion. This was true not only in Europe but also in Mexico. Following the war with the United States, Mexico deliberately neglected its northern border regions. "The philosophy that reigned was to create a desert between both countries, thereby affording the interior and the capital some protection from the clutches of the American manifest destiny."[39] But this attitude has long since changed. Today the Mexican government actively promotes the growth of northern border cities, several of which are among the world's most rapidly growing urban areas. Compared to most interior regions, the northern border regions have relatively high levels of per capita income; and though many critics bemoan their dependence on the United States, they continue to attract migrants because they offer them improved economic opportunities.

Because so much attention has been given to the dependency relationship of Mexico's border regions vis-à-vis the United States, it is instructive to return briefly to the similar theme of domination in the French growth pole literature. In this context, it also would be appropriate to give more general consideration to the evidence concerning Europe's allegedly disfavored border regions.

When France's twenty-one planning regions are ranked in order of their gross regional product per capita, nine of the twelve highest-ranking are border regions. The four regions bordering Germany and Switzerland—the "threatened" regions—may not be quite as prosperous as their foreign neighbors, but in relation to the rest of France they are relatively strong in economic terms. Their respective gross regional product per capita rankings are fourth (Lorraine), fifth (Rhone-Alps), seventh (Alsace), and ninth (Franche-Comté).[40]

Other European evidence also contradicts the allegation that border regions are disadvantaged. Since the mid-1960s, West Germany's border regions (with the exception of those on the tightly controlled boundaries with East Germany and Czechoslovakia) have had higher rates of growth in population, nonagricultural employment, and per capita gross regional product than nonborder regions.[41]

Domestic politics in Spain is strongly conditioned by the fact that the wealthier Basque and Catalonian regions—both border regions—feel that they are being exploited by the nation's relatively poor regions. (The Basque and Catalonian ethnic and cultural communities spill over into France at the western and eastern ends of the Pyrenees, respectively.) Vizcaya, in the strongly separatist Basque region, has the highest level of per capita income of all Spain's fifty provinces. The four Basque provinces are among the eight highest-ranking provinces in this regard. Similarly, the four Catalonian provinces are among the twelve highest-ranking provinces.[42]

Finally, small countries such as the Benelux nations, Switzerland, and Austria are among the most prosperous in the world. In a very real sense their territories are entirely border regions, yet they have managed to deal quite well with their obvious international dependencies.[43]

If the central issues raised with respect to Mexico's northern border regions usually concern high unemployment and low per capita incomes in relation to corresponding U.S. levels and the dependency of these regions on the United States, those usually raised with respect to the southwest borderlands emphasize high rates of unemployment and poverty and low per capita income levels in relation to the United States as a whole, as well as commuting and migration pressures from Mexico, which allegedly make it nearly impossible to close the economic gap between the borderlands and the rest of the nation.

Recent United States policy initiatives pertaining to the borderlands reflect a number of inherited notions about border regions in general. These preconceptions are particularly evident in the application, already referred to in chapter 1, that the four border-state governors submitted to the U.S. Department of Commerce requesting the creation of the Southwest Border Regional Commission. The three major border region themes encountered in the relevant theoretical literature—uniqueness, fragility, and homogeneity—are clearly echoed in the opening sentence of the covering letter to the Secretary of Commerce, signed by the governors: "We believe that our states share a series of unique and very serious problems, problems directly resulting from our position along the border of Mexico."[44] The same themes are restated in the preface. "In 1975, Congress explicitly recognized the uniqueness and severity of a wide spectrum of socioeconomic problems"[45] in the borderlands. "The economic health of the region is, and has been on the decline and constitutes a pernicious drain on the overall economies"[46] of the four border states. "The region's problems are of common economic and social characteristics and extend across jurisdictional boundaries."[47] Later, in a "chapter" that in fact is less than half a page, it is stated that "there is no question of homogeneity in the proposed region; it clearly exists by all standards, and hence lays the foundation for the creation of a regional commission."[48]

In subsequent chapters it will be argued in some detail that the southwest borderlands area is not homogeneous and that there is little economic interaction among the area's subregions. Moreover, the economic fragility of the borderlands—to the extent that it exists—needs to be qualified in an international context. As for the uniqueness of the southwest borderlands, it is true that, in the words of the document just cited, "Nowhere within the community of nations does a boundary separate two countries with a greater economic disparity than that between Mexico and the United States";[49] and that "Any economic development models considered for application to problems of the border *must* be modified to account for the regional culture."[50] This regional culture reflects the close symbiotic relationship between the Mexican and U.S. sides of the border.

Some critics maintain that economic conditions in the southwest borderlands would be improved if stricter measures were taken to make the U.S.-Mexican boundary a line that divides the two sides and insulates them from one another. For example, a prominent student of the border economy urged that the existence of the political boundary should be the starting point for economic analyses of the borderlands. Thus, "borders not only have social, cultural, and political importance, but they are of considerable economic consequence. For it is largely within the confines of these boundaries that most of the crucial government policies that affect the quality of life for the citizens of each nation are made. Nominally there may be a world community, but the welfare of most people is dependent upon the decisions of their own government."[51] This view clearly coincides with the nineteenth-century nationalist view of borders. Apart from the international tensions and aggressions that it has produced in the past, it poses a special problem in the case of the U.S.-Mexican border.

When the present boundary was fixed in the middle of the last century, few people lived in the border regions. The border in effect became a line that attracted people. Especially in the present century, large numbers of Mexicans have migrated to the U.S. borderlands, and many have become U.S. citizens, while still retaining ties with relatives and acquaintances in Mexico. Along the U.S. borderlands, per capita income is closely and inversely related to the proportion of the total population accounted for by Mexican Americans (see chapter 7). These are the people who allegedly would be most benefited economically by a relatively closed border. Yet for the most part they have not favored restrictive border policies. To gain an adequate perspective on these issues it is necessary to understand the history of the participation of Mexican workers in the economy of the U.S. borderlands.

The next chapter gives brief general descriptions of subregions of the southwest borderlands, with the caveat that the areas discussed are not intended to be a definitive set; they simply are intended to illustrate the variety of local situations to be found along the border. Other subregional delineations could be justified, depending on the specific issue or issues being considered. Then chapter 4 discusses recent economic development patterns along the border in terms of employment and earnings. Here too it will be seen that the borderlands are not a homogeneous region. The remaining chapters critically examine the nature and significance of Mexican and Mexican American participation in the economy of the southwest borderlands.

3. Subregions of the Southwest Borderlands

The San Diego Metropolitan Area

Gaspár de Portolá, the first governor of California, founded the San Diego presidio in 1769. The site was chosen because of its proximity to Mexico and the excellence of the nearby harbor. At the same time, Father Junípero Serra dedicated San Diego mission, the first of the California missions; the missionaries introduced native Indians to agriculture, which was to remain the mainstay of the local economy for many years. After its successful revolt against Spain, Mexico took control of the presidio in 1822. Local Indian tribes were finally pacified in 1834; inhabitants of the presidio then descended to the flatlands to build what was to become known as Old Town. By 1840 there were still only 140 persons living in San Diego. The U.S. conquest brought few changes; San Diego remained essentially a Mexican village, and the surrounding area, like the rest of southern California, consisted primarily of large cattle ranches. The first major promoter of San Diego's growth was Alonzo Horton, who arrived in 1867 and proceeded at once to buy up and develop the area around the wharf. The arrival of the transcontinental railroad in 1885 produced a major population and real estate boom. By 1887 San Diego's population had risen to 40,000 inhabitants, and most of the towns in San Diego County were founded during this period. With the exception of the depression of the early 1890s, San Diego's growth has been continuous and rapid since then.[1]

During the First World War, San Diego became a major naval base. However, until 1920 the city was primarily a fashionable resort and a center for agriculture-related activities. In the 1920s, the aircraft industry grew rapidly, largely because of San Diego's favorable climate. With two of its basic activities geared to defense operations, the city's economy burgeoned during the Second World War. After the war all segments of San Diego's economy continued to record steady gains, and the Korean War further accelerated growth.

San Diego's population increased by over 85 percent during the 1950s. Between 1961 and 1965, when employment related to the production of aircraft and missiles dropped sharply, total employment nevertheless rose by 7,500. Since then employment opportunities have become increasingly diversified, so that present growth—as well as that anticipated for the foreseeable future—is broadly based on tourism, government, education, aerospace and nonaerospace manufacturing, and technical and research activities.[2]

The factors that have contributed to San Diego's remarkable growth—the San Diego SMSA accounts for over half of total employment in the entire Southwest Border Regional Commission area—are basically independent of its proximity to Mexico in the sense that growth was well under way when the neighboring Mexican state of Baja California was virtually empty space, and no doubt would have continued in the absence of border urbanization in Mexico. Nevertheless, rapid expansion of population on the Mexican side of the border since 1920—which has been stimulated by the growth of southern California—has had growth-inducing feedbacks on the U.S. side.

Mexicali, which had a population of only 462 inhabitants in 1910, grew rapidly as a result of irrigation projects—largely financed by U.S. capital—utilizing water from the Colorado River.[3] Tijuana's population, which stood at only 1,028 persons in 1920,[4] rose dramatically for other reasons. In addition to strong demand for Mexican workers in the U.S. southwest (encouraged in part by the introduction of strict controls on immigration from the Orient), urbanization in Mexico's northern border area was induced by what a French scholar has termed the "tourism of vice."

> California prohibited horse racing in 1915 and prostitution and dance halls in 1917; the eighteenth amendment to the U.S. Constitution (prohibition of alcoholic beverages) took effect in 1920. American promoters and consumers rushed to the Mexican side of the border, where the distractions of the tertiary sector became the economic driving force in such cities as Tijuana and Ciudad Juárez.[5]

In more recent times, enterprising Mexican growers and suppliers have responded to the persistent if illegal U.S. demand for marijuana, but the image of Mexican border towns as vice centers is now outdated. In fact, "illegal commerce directly touches the lives of very few Mexicans and for decades now the border cities have increasingly become industrial and commercial centers."[6]

Tijuana's population grew from 165,690 in 1960 to 340,583 in 1970; it is estimated that it will reach 709,340 by 1980. Mexicali, Tijuana, Ensenada, and Tecate—the four major cities in northern Baja California—had a combined growth rate of 284 percent between 1950 and 1970; the corresponding rate for the present decade is expected to be 70 percent, which would give them a total population of 1,477,000 in 1980. If present trends continue, by 1995 Tijuana alone will have a larger population than San Diego and its adjacent suburbs.[7]

Between 1973 and 1977, the number of U.S. citizens crossing at the San Diego–Tijuana border station ranged between 14.0 million and 14.6 million persons per year.[8] Most Americans go to Tijuana to enjoy normal tourist activities in a foreign city, but increasing numbers also travel farther south to find good beaches, solitude, or trails for exploring the countryside in offroad vehicles.

The counterstream of aliens entering the United States rose from 26.2 million in 1972 to 38.9 million in 1977.[9] It is noteworthy that there was even an increase between 1976 and 1977, despite the devaluation of the peso in 1976. Mexicans shop on the U.S. side for goods that are either difficult to find at home or considered to be of better quality in the United States; and they have dollars because U.S. currency is accepted on both sides of the border. In 1976, Mexican citizens who legally crossed the border spent approximately $200 million in San Diego. A substantial part of this sum was a repatriation of dollars spent by U.S. tourists in Mexico. Moreover, the San Diego Human Resources Agency has estimated that some 60,000 undocumented Mexican aliens were employed in the San Diego area in 1976. This figure represented about 10 percent of the total local civilian labor force. Assuming that undocumented workers earned, on average, an hourly wage of $2.00 and that they worked 1,000 hours per year, their total earnings would have amounted to $120 million. If half this amount was spent in San Diego, total direct purchases by Mexicans in San Diego totaled $260 million.[10] And, as pointed out in chapter 1, undocumented workers do not constitute a net burden on local social services.

In 1976, the value of all exports passing through the San Diego Customs District was $614.9 million; the corresponding value for imports was $610.1 million. Mexico was clearly San Diego's principal trade partner, accounting for 91 percent of total exports and 84 percent of total imports.[11]

If San Diego's interdependence with Baja California has been a positive factor in many respects, it also has produced problems related to water, smog, sewage, flood control, transportation, and uncontrolled border crossings. Resolution of these difficulties will require understanding and cooperation on both sides. Nevertheless, San Diego is not a "typical" border community; its border-related problems may be similar in kind to those of other U.S. border cities, but, owing to the diversity of its economy, they are not the same in degree.

It is increasingly recognized that the favorable geography and climate of the San Diego region may be a mixed blessing, largely because the rate of inmigration tends to outstrip the rate of job creation. Retirees generate greater demand for public services, and many who also seek supplemental income contribute to local unemployment. Dependents of military personnel have increased the female labor force participation rate; and chronically unemployed persons have been attracted to the region by good weather and relatively low living costs.[12] In view of these considerations, the San Diego Region Overall Economic Development Program points out that:

> the region must continue to create as many new jobs as possible, yet be consistent with growth management policies, maintaining a clean environment and fiscally sound private and government sectors. The key to this regional growth is diversification of the existing industries. This is essential to minimize the impact of cyclical variations in the economy and oscillating federal and state policies.[13]

The Imperial Valley

The Imperial Valley of California is separated from San Diego and the Pacific coastal plain by the peninsular mountain ranges of eastern San Diego and western Imperial County. It is entirely below sea level and extends about 50 miles from just south of the U.S.-Mexican border to the southern end of the Salton Sea. Average rainfall in the area is only about 3.5 inches.

Before 1900 the Imperial Valley was virtually uninhabited wasteland. The Imperial Canal, which was opened in 1901, marked the first attempt to divert Colorado River water to the valley's deep, rich soils. In 1905 and 1906 floodwaters destroyed diversion controls and the waters of the Colorado ran into the Salton sink, creating the Salton Sea. The Southern Pacific railway, fearing that its route would be blocked by the inundation of the entire Imperial Valley, financed a line of protective levees. Nevertheless, fear of possible new breaks caused the area to languish. The threat of flooding was finally removed by the completion of the Hoover Dam in 1935. In 1940 the All-American Canal was opened, and the valley became independent of the old Imperial Canal. The transformation of the desert to green fields was now assured. In 1974, Imperial County had 513,000 acres under cultivation. The products include truck crops, alfalfa, cotton, sugar beets, and livestock. The principal commercial centers in the valley are Brawley, Calexico, and El Centro in California and Mexicali in Mexico.

The cultivated acreage in Imperial County is not particularly large by California standards, nor is the number of farms. But this is a land of large farms organized by corporate agribusiness. In 1974, the proportion of Imperial County farms with sales over $40,000 was 67.3 percent, the highest for any California county. The total value of farm products sold in 1974 by farms with sales of $2,500 or more was $574 million in Imperial County, which placed it second only to Fresno County.[14]

While the production and value of crops produced in Imperial County have been generally rising, there has been a substantial drop in the size of the agricultural labor force because of mechanization. Before 1960, agriculture was responsible for about 15,000 jobs, but between 1960 and 1974 agricultural employment in Imperial County declined by 48 percent, and further declines are anticipated. The labor market impact of this phenomenon affects Mexico at least as much as the United States. As many as 25,000 residents of Mexicali hold green cards permitting them to work in the United States. As of 1975, approximately 14,000 green card holders were crossing daily at Calexico, California.[15] Although not all were agricultural workers, many were.

The Arizona Borderlands

Four counties—Yuma, Pima, Santa Cruz, and Cochise—comprise the Arizona borderlands. The southwestern part of Arizona is an arid region that forms part of the Sonoran Desert. Much of the land is owned by the federal government, and certain large sections that have been devoted to military uses and to wildlife protection are off limits to the general public. Population settlement in Yuma County is as sparse as the rainfall; the density in 1975 was only seven persons per square mile. The city of Yuma, on the border with California, accounted for 30,018 of Yuma County's total population of 66,020 in 1975.[16] Yuma City was established as an offshoot of the California gold rush of 1849. Difficulties associated with crossing the Colorado River led to the original settlement, whose growth was further encouraged by knowledge that there was gold to be found in the general vicinity. Today, Yuma is a major distribution point for citrus fruits, cantaloupes, cotton, and other crops grown on land irrigated by waters from the Colorado River. One of the largest open-pit copper mines in the United States is located in the desertlands of western Pima County. A smelter to handle the ore is also located here, near Ajo. Copper has turned out to be more valuable than gold in the economic development of Arizona, which produces about 10 percent of the total world supply.[17]

Southeastern Arizona was the scene of numerous real-life events that helped to create the popular image of the Wild West. Tombstone, which was founded in 1879, became one of the largest silver camps in the west. In the 1880s it had a population of between 10,000 and 15,000 persons, making it the largest city between San Antonio and San Francisco.

Tucson, which has roots going back to the Spanish, once went through a growth period because of its proximity to Tombstone.[18] But today the latter is a small town (albeit an official national historic landmark) of some 1,250 people, whereas Tucson for some time has been one of the nation's most rapidly growing cities. Today the Tucson SMSA accounts for three-fourths of the entire population of the Arizona borderlands. Tucson, like other lands south of the Gila River, became a part of the United States as a consequence of the Gadsden Purchase of 1853. By 1882, the east-west transcontinental rail route through Tucson was completed. Soon the city became a major mining, agricultural, and commercial center for southern Arizona. In 1891, the University of Arizona was established at Tucson. It has since become an important part of the local economy; enrollment now exceeds 30,000 students, and employment at the university exceeds 10,000 persons. With the exception of wartime operations, the first large manufacturing facility in Tucson was that built by the Hughes Aircraft Company in 1951. It formed the nucleus for what has since become an industrial zone near the airport; other employers in this area include Burr-Brown, Gates–Lear Jet, and IBM. Between 1950 and 1977, the population growth rate of the Tucson SMSA was exceeded by the growth rates of per capita retail sales, savings deposits, vehicle registrations, motor fuel consumption, and total employment. Between 1950 and 1970, employment grew more rapidly than did the civilian labor force. Since 1970 the converse has been the case, primarily because of a continuing high rate of inmigration and increasing labor force participation rates. In addition, over 4,750 copper miners were laid off in 1977, and the recovery of this locally important sector has been sluggish.[19]

Water scarcity, an increasing problem throughout the southwest, is a major potential constraint on the future growth of the Tucson SMSA. Tucson and eastern Pima County residents have been wholly dependent on groundwater; but the water table has been declining because consumption has been running at three to five times the amount of natural recharge. Conservation measures and price increases have reduced per capita water consumption in recent years, but Tucson water rates—which apply to the surrounding region served by Tucson—still "are competitive with other southwestern states."[20] Critics argue that the price of water does not yet reflect its true scarcity. Indeed, federal water programs have generally encouraged profligate use of water in the southwest. The Colorado River has been the focus of controversy in this regard because:

it helps slake the thirst of 11 million people from Denver to San Diego. Diverted into canals and ditches, it waters 3.4 million acres producing crops worth well over $1 billion yearly. Forced through turbines, it sends electricity leaping out of canyon power plants to more than 200 utilities, rural electric co-ops and others. The only substantial source of surface water in the Southwest, it is relied upon as few rivers are anywhere.[21]

Unfortunately, the quality of Colorado River water has been deteriorating, and total legal claims exceed the average flow. Under the terms of the 1922 Colorado River Interstate Compact, the Upper Basin states of Utah, Wyoming, New Mexico, and Colorado agreed that half of the then average water flow—15 million acre-feet— would be guaranteed to the Lower Basin states of Arizona, California, and Nevada. In 1944, Mexico, by treaty with the United States, received an annual entitlement of 1.5 million acre-feet, bringing the total amount of legal claims to 16.5 million acre-feet. But the division of Colorado River water was based on a brief and unusually high rate of flow; since 1922 the actual flow has averaged only 13.5 million acre-feet. Moreover, California has been "borrowing" more than its share, which has prompted the Upper Basin states to push for the completion of water resource projects in their area so that the Lower Basin will not continue to overdraw its allotment. A further complication involves the water rights of Indian reservations, which were completely ignored when the 1922 compact was drawn up. Recent Supreme Court decisions have guaranteed water supplies to reservations for irrigation, and the Navajos in particular could conceivably absorb a substantial share of all Colorado River water. So far the Navajos have not pressed a lawsuit, but they have made a survey of irrigable land, the results of which have not been released.

One of the biggest drains on Colorado River water will be the Central Arizona Project, which will deliver 1.2 million acre-feet to Tucson and Phoenix by the mid-1980s. Congress has authorized an initial outlay of $1.6 billion for this massive undertaking, and tunnels already are being bored through the Buckskin Mountains to construct the first link of a 300-mile aqueduct. As has been the case with other Colorado River projects, the users of the water will no doubt pay only a fraction of the true costs of supplying it, which in turn provides little incentive for conservation.[22]

In 1979, controversy concerning whether Mexico should pay for damage to Texas beaches that resulted from a massive oil spill from a Mexican-leased rig in the Gulf of Mexico became linked to a dispute between the United States and Mexico over Colorado River water. Mexican President López Portillo said that Mexico would not pay for oil spill damage because the United States had not paid for damage to the Mexicali Valley caused by salty water coming from the Arizona side of the border.

The history of this issue goes back to 1961. Before then Mexico received more Colorado River water than the 1.5 million acre-feet guaranteed in the 1944 treaty. This excess flow served to dilute saline irrigation return flows from the United States to the point that the quality of the water going to Mexico was about that of water used in Arizona. In 1961, however, the Wellton-Mohawk Project of the Bureau of Reclamation began operating a system of drainage wells that discharged saline water into the Colorado River below the last U.S. diversion point. At the same time, the United States began storing water in Lake Powell, the reservoir for the nearly completed Glen Canyon Dam, and the average flow to Mexico dropped to 1.5 million acre-feet. In consequence, for a period in 1962 the salinity of water delivered to Mexico was one and a half times higher than it had been in 1960. Mexican farmers reacted vigorously to the adverse effects on crop yields and the Mexican government lodged formal protests to the United States.[23]

During a 1972 visit to Washington, Mexican President Echeverría termed the Colorado River salinity problem "the most delicate bilateral problem" between the two countries.[24] This set the stage for a 1973 agreement by which the United States set out steps to reduce the Colorado's salinity and agreed to "provide nonreimbursable assistance for those aspects of the Mexicali rehabilitation program that related to salinity."[25] No amount of damages was specified in the agreement, and Mexico has never officially estimated the costs, though it still could produce a claim. Meanwhile, interim measures have been taken to solve the salinity problem. Residual irrigation drainage water is now moved west in a channel and discharged directly into the Gulf of California; water removed from the Colorado River for irrigation is currently replaced with clear water from the Hoover Dam. By 1983 or 1984, a desalinization plant will be in operation so that water used in irrigation can be returned in pure form to the river. The cost of these efforts is estimated at $350 million and mounting because of inflation. None of this benefits U.S. users directly, though additional salt control projects are underway upstream for them.[26]

There are, however, some indirect benefits to be gained for the U.S. side by promoting—or at least not destroying—the productivity of agriculture in the Mexicali Valley. A great deal of the income earned in the latter is spent in the United States. Between April 1977 and March 1978, Mexicans made an estimated 3.8 million visits to Yuma alone and spent $93.5 million. Among Arizona cities these figures were exceeded only by Nogales, which had 5.1 million visits and Mexican expenditures of $137.4 million. Because Tucson is located 65 miles from the border it accounted for only 2.6 percent of total Mexican visits to Arizona, but it accounted for 12.4 percent of total expenditures by Mexicans. For the one-year period in question, Mexicans made a total of 11.5 million visits to Arizona and spent $315.3 million.[27]

The El Paso BEA Economic Region

The El Paso BEA economic region includes eight counties in southern New Mexico and six counties at the far western end of Texas. All five of the New Mexico counties in the Southwest Border Regional Commission are in the El Paso economic region; as the data in table 1.1 indicate, the commission counties in New Mexico are the only ones that are entirely nonmetropolitan. It has been remarked that "New Mexico has no significant impact on border dynamics. Very few Mexicans migrate to New Mexico, and there are no major border-crossing points between New Mexico and Mexico. The Spanish-speaking people who do live in New Mexico are primarily descendents of the early Spanish settlers, so that in 1960 over 96 percent of them were born in the United States."[28]

El Paso's proximity to both Mexico and New Mexico and its location on the major north-south transportation and population axis of New Mexico serve to make it the latter's link to Mexico.

Grant, Luna, and Hidalgo counties, in southwest New Mexico, have a combined population of fewer than 50,000 persons. Copper mining provides the principal economic base for this area, whose population growth has been steady due to an influx of retired persons, particularly to Deming.[29] Dona Ana and Otero counties, which both border El Paso County, Texas, had a combined population of 122,320 in 1975. Dona Ana County's population grew by 30 percent between 1960 and 1974, largely because of increases in government research activities—the White Sands Missile Range is located here— and in enrollment and employment at New Mexico State University in Las Cruces. Although Las Cruces is the largest urban center in southern New Mexico, it still depends on El Paso for television, newspapers, and many higher-order goods and services.[30]

El Paso's development has long been subject to hispanic influences. In the sixteenth century a number of Spanish expeditions used the mountain pass at this site. In 1659 a mission was founded at the present location of Ciudad Juárez, Mexico. Americans began visiting the region in the early nineteenth century; present-day El Paso was first settled in 1827. According to the terms that ended the war with Mexico, the middle of the Rio Grande became the boundary between the United States and Mexico. The colony north of the river at the pass was originally called Franklin, but it became known as El Paso during the 1850s. In 1888, the south-bank city of Paso del Norte was renamed Ciudad Juárez in honor of Benito Juárez, the Indian intellectual, reformer, and president who symbolized self-determination for Mexico. In 1880 El Paso was a dusty adobe village with 736 inhabitants, but the arrival of four railroads in the early 1880s guaranteed the rapid and continuous growth of the city. "Capital flowed immediately into El Paso, and the area's agriculture, trade, and industry received significant impetus. The city quickly acquired a dominant position not only in its own region on the U.S. side, but also in relation to northern Mexico."[31] Today it has more than 400 manufacturing plants, including oil refineries, a copper smelter and a copper refinery, cement plants, cotton and food processing plants, and clothing manufacturers. El Paso also is a military, educational, and tourism center. The major component in the relatively large government sector is the Fort Bliss military complex; once the largest cavalry post in the nation, it is now the headquarters of the U.S. Army Air Defense Center, as well as a training center for the U.S. Army and the West German Air Force. The University of Texas at El Paso, with over 16,000 students, is a major regional center of higher education.

Hispanics account for well over half of El Paso's total population, and the economies of El Paso and Juárez are so interrelated that it is difficult to discuss one without considering the other. Although per capita income in El Paso is low by U.S. standards, "Juárez and El Paso vividly illustrate two styles of life and starkly define two disparate standards of living. Perhaps the most telling dissimilarity is the low income of the population residing south of the boundary compared to the relative affluence of residents on the U.S. side, a disparity which is closely related to the existence of the demarcation line."[32] Yet proximity to the United States has given residents of Juárez economic opportunities not available in most of Mexico. The *maquiladora* program, which is discussed in chapter 5, tourism, expanding commercial activity, and commuting to work on the U.S. side—about one-third of all Mexican trans-border commuters work in El Paso[33]—have all contributed to the explosive growth of Juárez. In 1960, the population of Juárez was 276,995; it was estimated to be 650,000 in 1977.[34]

While El Paso and Juárez benefit in many respects from their symbiotic relationship, it also gives rise to numerous problems. For example, El Paso's large and growing hispanic population is particularly affected by high unemployment rates and poor social and economic conditions. El Paso has one of the highest local tax rates in the nation, but disadvantaged persons do not share much of the tax burden to support community services. El Paso is in a sense an "impacted area" whose problems are not altogether under its own control or influence because of its proximity not only to Juárez, but also to New Mexico. It has been argued that:

> The major obstacles to economic growth and independence are external regulations imposed by federal and state statutes and agencies relating to El Paso's border location—to another state and another nation—and restrictive procedures against sharing services or spending monies which in any way benefit that foreign nation's citizens or those of the neighboring state. It is the very isolationist policies of "helping only our own" which prevent local solutions with neighboring states and foreign country urban areas. Thus, it seems that either state laws or federal mandates must be relaxed to allow bi-national and bi-state agreements to handle local problems such as mosquito control, rabies, venereal disease, pollution, and transportation facilities, or else compensatory subsidies must be supplied to compensate for these contrived obstacles to economic self-sufficiency.[35]

The issue, then, is one of finding appropriate mechanisms for dealing with problems in the spatial context in which they actually occur, rather than in the confines of geographic units that are artificially fragmented in terms of day-to-day realities. The need for such mechanisms exists all along the border, but nowhere is it more evident than in the El Paso–Juárez area.

The five nonmetropolitan Texas counties in the El Paso BEA economic region consist primarily of high plateaus crossed by canyons and ravines as well as by a number of mountain ranges, the highest of which rises to 8,751 feet. Ranching, agriculture, and tourism are the principal economic activities in this thinly populated area. The Guadalupe Mountains and Big Bend national parks attract numerous visitors from outside the region. Because they are off the beaten track, their natural state has remained well preserved. Recreation visits represent a promising development opportunity for the region so long as the growth of tourism does not degrade the quality of its fragile environment.[36]

The Middle Rio Grande Region of Texas

Pecos and Terrell counties represent a transition zone from the Trans-Pecos area of west Texas to the Middle Rio Grande border area, which includes Val Verde, Edwards, Real, Kinney, Uvalde, Maverick, Zavala, and Dimmit counties. The southwestern portion of the Edwards Plateau includes Terrell, Edwards, and Real counties, as well as parts of Pecos, Val Verde, Kinney, and Uvalde counties. The Rio Grande Plain, which commences near Del Rio, includes part of Val Verde, Kinney, and Uvalde counties, as well as the remaining border counties in Texas.

Rainfall on the Edwards Plateau is generally adequate for range grasses but marginal for dry farming. Nearly all the land is devoted to cattle, sheep, and goat ranching. The small proportion of cropland is primarily used for growing livestock fodder. Nearly all the land in the plains portion of the Middle Rio Grande region is in farms and ranches; about 80 percent is devoted to beef cattle ranches. Irrigated farmland, mainly along the Rio Grande and Nueces rivers, accounts for another 10 percent of the area. Irrigated farm products include cotton, corn, vegetables, fruits, and melons. The remaining, unirrigated farmlands are used to produce cotton, grain, sorghum, flax, and hay. Groundwater is adequate for present uses in the northern part of the plain; the Amistad Reservoir in particular has produced a major recharge of groundwater in its immediate vicinity. However, in the southern portion of the plain heavy pumping for irrigation has lowered water levels to the critical point in some zones, and especially those that have been the most desirable for truck farming. In many of these zones a shift is already under way in favor of crops that require less frequent irrigation.[37]

Agricultural workers in the Middle Rio Grande area have traditionally been paid less than workers in other sectors. However, because of recently enacted minimum wage legislation, many labor-intensive agricultural activities are being terminated in favor of mechanized farming. Increasing U.S. reliance on Mexican fresh agricultural produce should increase the importance of Del Rio and Eagle Pass as trans-shipment centers. The packaging and redistribution of imported produce may become a major source of employment for workers displaced from the local agricultural sector.[38]

Manufacturing, which accounts for less than 10 percent of total area employment, continues to experience locational and labor force limitations. The internal market for locally produced goods is very restricted—in 1975 the nine relevant counties had a combined population of just over 100,000—and San Antonio, the nearest metropolitan area, is approximately 150 miles away from local population centers. The region has no airline freight service. In addition to transportation cost disadvantages, much of the local labor force does not have the education or training required by many industrial firms.[39]

The South Texas Region

The South Texas border area consists of Jim Hogg, Starr, Webb, and Zapata counties, which together comprise the South Texas Development Council. The area's 1977 population was estimated to be 116,700. The Laredo SMSA (Webb County) accounted for nearly three-fourths of this total, and Starr County accounted for about 19 percent.[40] The local economy is based primarily on ranching, oil and gas, tourism, and international trade. Laredo, the oldest continuously settled site in Texas, is the largest inland port of entry into the United States. It is strategically located on the most direct route from most of the United States to Mexico. More than 100 freight forwarders and brokers are located in Laredo; over 5 million automobiles and other vehicles cross the border from Mexico to Laredo annually. A daily average of 151 railroad freight cars entered Laredo from Mexico in 1978. Per capita retail sales are the highest in the nation, largely because of purchases made by Mexican citizens.[41] In 1979, Laredo's wholesale and retail trade sectors accounted for 35.6 percent of total SMSA employment and the service sector accounted for another 13.5 percent. In contrast, manufacturing made up only 7.9 percent of total employment.[42] The labor force lacks diversification and the great majority of workers are unskilled. Over

85 percent of the population and over 95 percent of the labor force are Mexican Americans. In addition, many residents of Mexico commute to work in Laredo. It has been estimated that migrant farm workers and their families—who seasonally fan out to many states in the west and middle west—represent between 17 and 20 percent of the population of the South Texas area. Nearly all of these migrants are Mexican Americans.[43]

The Laredo SMSA is the only SMSA on the entire border with Mexico that is part of a BEA functional economic region having its major metropolitan core located away from the border. As pointed out earlier, the Laredo SMSA is part of the San Antonio BEA region even though it is 150 miles away from San Antonio. When BEA regions were first delineated in 1969, Laredo was considered to be part of the Corpus Christi BEA region; the Corpus Christi and San Antonio BEA regions both had an erroneously pronounced east-west orientation, extending from the Gulf of Mexico in the east to the Mexican border in the west. In fact, the major spatial economic interactions in the southern part of Texas run north and south.[44] The BEA regions as revised in 1977 correctly reflect this phenomenon. The north-south linkages also connect San Antonio and Mexico. In addition to the fact that Mexican Americans account for half of San Antonio's total population, its trade and tourism relationships with Mexico "are quite strong and offer both economies important growth potentials. The 1973 estimates from the Greater San Antonio Chamber of Commerce suggest that retail trade with Mexican citizens accounts for 25 to 30 percent of the city's total income in this sector."[45]

The Lower Rio Grande Valley

In Texas, when someone mentions the "Valley" it is generally understood that the area concerned is the Lower Rio Grande Valley. Although Starr and Willacy counties often are regarded as part of the region, the Valley essentially consists of a sprawling metropolitan area with multiple urban centers. For the sake of simplicity, the two contiguous SMSAs in the Valley are referred to in this study as McAllen (Hidalgo County) and Brownsville (Cameron County). However, their official names as defined by the U.S. Bureau of the Census—McAllen–Pharr–Edinburg and Brownsville–Harlingen–San Benito—give a more accurate sense of the dispersed nature of urbanization in the Valley. The three most populous cities—Brownsville, McAllen, and Harlingen—together account for only about 40 percent of the total population of the two counties, which was estimated to be 408,800 in 1977. Between 1970 and 1977 the population growth rates of the McAllen and Brownsville SMSAs were among the highest in the country; that for McAllen was 28.0 percent while that for Brownsville was 25.7 percent.[46] On the Mexican side of the Valley the principal cities are Matamoros and Reynosa, each of which had a population of about 138,000 in 1970. Because growth along the border has been more rapid than in the interior of Mexico in recent years, the total population on the Mexican side of the Valley probably exceeds 500,000 at the present time.[47] Thus, the combined population of the Valley's international community is rapidly approaching 1 million persons.

In the nineteenth century, from the time of the Texas Republic, conflict and violence characterized much of the contact between Anglos and Mexicans in the Valley. Boundary disputes, frictions between Anglo ranchers and Mexican land grantees, and systematic Anglo economic dominance and control of the local political system created a legacy of distrust that has influenced inter-ethnic relations even down to the present time. Nevertheless, during the U.S. Civil War both Mexicans and U.S. citizens briefly realized substantial commercial gains from border interdependency. For a time Brownsville was the only Confederate port not effectively blockaded by the Union; Matamoros' population jumped to 40,000 while that of Brownsville rapidly rose to 25,000, only to drop back to 3,000 following the war.[48]

Sustained growth of the Valley population and economy began in the early twentieth century, when ranches were divided into irrigated farmlands and national railroads reached the area. With the principal exception of Brownsville, the Valley's urban centers were initially developed at this time.

"Home-seekers" from the north bought the land after first being enticed by attractive brochures and free visits sponsored by land developers; many of these land developers soon became the nucleus in structuring the local banking and financial system. Mexicans served as the labor force for the agricultural infrastructure—irrigation canals, railroad lines and cleared lands which made agricultural development possible. From the beginning the availability of a cheap source of potential farm labor was advertised by land developers as a major attraction to farmers. Initial capital to develop the land could be offset by minimal investment in machinery or farm labor.[49]

One does not need to embrace the full Marxist point of view to acknowledge that:

No real Mexican-American middle class developed in the small agricultural towns until after World War Two, and even then it possessed few class interests in its struggle over limited resources. A large Mexican-American and Mexican underclass came to populate the *barrios* of Brownsville; Brownsville served then (as it does now) both as a "receptacle" and a "springboard" for Mexican immigrants.[50]

With the exception of the decade of the 1960s, the Valley has experienced steady growth throughout this century; even during the 1960s the Mexican American population rose by 10 percent while the Anglo population fell by 35 percent.[51] Today Mexican Americans account for approximately 80 percent of the Valley's total population. Over half the population lives below the poverty level, and 90 percent of all families in this category are Mexican American.[52] Many of the latter cannot afford the costs of meeting city health and safety ordinances, so they band together in rural "colonias." These squatter settlements often have inadequate water and sewer facilities, unsafe drinking water, poor health conditions, and poor housing. In 1975, about 10 percent of the Valley's population lived in 65 colonias, most of which were in Hidalgo County. A high proportion of workers living in colonias are farm laborers.[53] The number of migrant and nonmigrant seasonal farm workers in the Valley has never been carefully measured; however, estimates have placed the number of migrants at between 96,000 and 116,000 persons, and the number of seasonal farm workers at about 20,000 persons.[54]

Agriculture continues to be the mainstay of the Valley economy. Principal crops include citrus fruit, cotton, vegetables, grain sorghum, and sugarcane. In addition, Brownsville has the nation's most important shrimping industry. Food processing was the first major manufacturing activity in the Valley and remains the most important. Apparel manufacturing is the second largest industry.

Durable goods manufacturing is concentrated in the Brownsville SMSA, whereas the McAllen SMSA has a much higher concentration in agriculture. Both areas have a relatively low level of federal government employment and a relatively high level of transfer payments. Wholesale and retail trade provide a larger share of personal income in the Valley than in Texas as a whole. In the McAllen SMSA, nearly 40 percent of all trade employment involves wholesale trade, over half of which is concentrated in the wholesaling of fruits and vegetables. The Brownsville SMSA is more oriented toward retail trade; Mexicans account for most retail purchases in the central business district. The primary deterrent to industrial location in the Valley is the distance to major markets. However, the industrial potential of the area should be enhanced by a new natural gas pipeline from the interior of Mexico to the Valley.[55]

The Valley's warm climate and access to Mexico and to the Gulf of Mexico have been highly conducive to the development of tourism and related activities. "Winter Texans," most of whom come from the upper midwest, add upwards of 30,000 persons to the Valley's winter population. South Padre Island has been experiencing a major boom (partly with Mexican capital) in the construction of vacation hotels and second-home condominiums. During the 1980s it could develop into a tourism and recreational area comparable to Miami Beach.[56]

Conclusion

This brief survey has indicated that although there are similarities among the subregions of the southwest borderlands, there also are many differences in kind and in degree. The one attribute that they clearly have in common is location on the border with Mexico, but this proximity has had varying subregional consequences. For example, San Diego would probably have experienced a similar pattern of rapid growth even if Baja California had remained virtually unpopulated (though the same cannot be said of Tijuana if southern California were unpopulated). In contrast, the development of such cities as El Paso and Ciudad Juárez or "los dos Laredos" can only be understood in terms of close symbiotic relationships. Thus, varying local circumstances need to be kept in mind when considering recent changes in employment and earnings along the border.

4. Regional Development: Structure and Change of Employment and Earnings

This chapter analyzes the structure and change of employment and earnings in the southwest borderlands. Primary attention is given to Southwest Border Regional Commission counties, but summary results also are presented for borderlands Bureau of Economic Analysis (BEA) functional economic areas. The rationale for investigating both of these areas was given in chapter 1. The data sources are the BEA employment series and the one percent Continuous Work History Sample (CWHS). The nature and limitations of these sources are discussed in appendixes C and D, respectively. The principal advantage of the BEA series is its more comprehensive employment coverage. The main advantage of the CWHS is that it provides a unique basis for longitudinal investigations; for such areas as the borderlands, it is the only detailed information source available on the same workers over time.[1]

Employment Structure and Change in Southwest Border Regional Commission Counties: The BEA Employment Series

Total employment and government employment in the Southwest Border Regional Commission counties, in the rest of the counties of the border states, and in the United States are presented in table 4.1.[2] Government employment includes all federal civilian, state, and local government employees plus military personnel. It is given particular attention because it accounts for a large share of total employment, particularly in the borderlands.

Employment in the border states has been growing at a much more rapid rate than that in the nation as a whole; and the employment growth rate in the borderlands counties exceeds that for the rest of the border-state counties. Between 1969 and 1976, total employment in the borderlands rose from 1,251,528 to 1,495,642, an

Table 4.1. Total Employment and Government Employment in Southwest Border Regional Commission Counties, Remainder of Border States, and United States, 1969 and 1976

	California border		Rest of California	
	1969	1976	1969	1976
Total employment	728,931	846,183	7,133,918	8,119,363
Government employment	298,298	298,542	1,544,687	1,696,644
Government as % of total employment	40.9	35.3	21.7	20.9
	Arizona border		Rest of Arizona	
	1969	1976	1969	1976
Total employment	171,477	223,087	452,763	605,682
Government employment	57,397	75,627	93,648	138,262
Government as % of total employment	33.5	33.9	20.7	22.8
	New Mexico border		Rest of New Mexico	
	1969	1976	1969	1976
Total employment	54,872	62,282	283,426	368,241
Government employment	24,996	27,355	87,276	105,425
Government as % of total employment	45.6	43.9	30.8	28.6
	Texas border		Rest of Texas	
	1969	1976	1969	1976
Total employment	296,248	364,090	3,884,926	4,740,185
Government employment	94,970	97,864	799,238	949,425
Government as % of total employment	32.1	26.9	20.6	20.0
	Total border		Total rest of border states	
	1969	1976	1969	1976
Total employment	1,251,528	1,495,642	11,755,033	13,833,471
Government employment	475,661	499,388	2,524,849	2,889,756
Government as % of total employment	38.0	33.4	21.5	20.9
	Total U.S.			
	1969	1976		
Total employment	78,247,265	85,884,900		
Government employment	15,882,583	17,690,000		
Government as % of total employment	20.3	20.6		

increase of 19.5 percent. This was about twice the corresponding national rate of 9.8 percent. Employment in the rest of the border states grew by 17.7 percent. The employment growth rate in the borderlands of every border state exceeded that for the nation; the highest borderlands rate was that for Arizona (30.1 percent), followed by Texas (22.9 percent), California (16.1 percent), and New Mexico (13.5 percent). Although California's share of total borderlands employment declined between 1969 and 1976, it still accounted for 56.6 percent of the total in 1976; Texas accounted for 24.3 percent of the 1976 total, while Arizona had 14.9 percent and New Mexico 4.2 percent.

The borderlands have a relatively high, though declining, dependence on government employment. In both 1969 and 1976, government employment was about one-fifth of total employment in the United States as well as in the nonborder portions of the border states (with the exception of New Mexico). In contrast, the government sector's share of total borderlands employment was 38.0 percent in 1969 and 33.4 percent in 1976. Between 1969 and 1976, government employment in the United States increased by 11.4 percent, while in the borderlands it increased only by 5.0 percent. There was virtually no increase in government employment in the California borderlands, and in the Texas borderlands the growth rate for this sector was only 3.0 percent. Arizona accounted for 76.8 percent of the total growth of government employment in the borderlands.

The data in table 4.2 show the proportion of nongovernment employment in 1969 and in 1976 accounted for by three key activities: wholesale and retail trade, services, and manufacturing. Data are given for the borderlands, by state; for the remaining portions of the border states; and for the United States. More detailed information concerning employment by sector in the borderlands and in the United States is contained in appendix C.

In comparison with the United States as a whole, the border states are relatively overrepresented in terms of employment in trade activities. Moreover, the borderlands are overrepresented in trade employment in relation to the nonborder portions of the border states. In 1976, 26.2 percent of U.S. nongovernment employment was in trade; the corresponding borderlands proportions ranged from 28.9 percent in California to 33.1 percent in Texas. With the exception of New Mexico, which has only a small share of total borderlands employment, the proportion of employment in trade was

Table 4.2. Percent of Nongovernment Employment in Trade, Services, and Manufacturing in Southwest Border Regional Commission Counties, Remainder of Border States, and United States, 1969 and 1976

Area	Trade		Services		Manufacturing	
	1969	1976	1969	1976	1969	1976
Border						
California	27.0	28.9	26.2	27.2	21.1	17.2
Arizona	28.0	30.6	26.8	29.2	9.6	11.0
New Mexico	23.9	29.3	26.8	23.8	9.8	10.1
Texas	31.0	33.1	21.4	20.3	17.2	19.7
Total	28.0	30.3	25.3	25.5	18.0	16.8
Rest of border states						
California	25.2	26.8	23.4	25.3	28.3	24.3
Arizona	26.1	29.7	23.3	24.7	23.3	18.8
New Mexico	27.6	30.5	28.9	27.1	8.9	10.2
Texas	26.5	28.5	22.8	22.9	23.5	21.2
Total	25.7	27.6	23.3	24.5	26.1	22.6
United States	24.0	26.2	21.3	23.8	32.5	27.9

higher in the border counties of each state than in the remainder of the state.

The situation is much the same with respect to service employment, which in 1976 accounted for 25.5 percent of total nongovernment borderlands employment, compared with 24.5 percent in the rest of the border states and 23.8 percent for the United States. The proportion of service employment is particularly high in the borderlands of California and Arizona.

In contrast to trade and services, the border states are relatively underrepresented in terms of employment in manufacturing; and the borderlands are underrepresented in manufacturing employment in relation to other portions of the border states. Nationally, manufacturing employment declined from 20.3 million in 1969 to 19.0 million in 1976. This was a drop of 6.1 percent. During this period each of the borderlands areas experienced growth in manufacturing employment. The growth rate in Texas was 51.0 percent; in Arizona, 49.0 percent; in New Mexico, 19.4 percent; and in California, 4.5 percent. For the borderlands as a whole, the increase was

19.8 percent. The proportion of nongovernment employment accounted for by manufacturing increased in the borderlands of Arizona, New Mexico, and Texas, but declined in California. Because of the relatively great weight of California in the borderlands total, the share of manufacturing employment in the borderlands as a whole declined from 18.0 percent in 1969 to 16.8 percent in 1976. This was substantially below the corresponding proportions of 22.6 percent in the other parts of the border states and 27.9 percent for the United States as a whole.

The relative employment patterns shown in table 4.2 are in part a reflection of conditions related to the borderlands' proximity to Mexico. Trade and service activities cater not only to the population of the U.S. borderlands, but also to hundreds of thousands of Mexicans on a regular basis (see chapter 5). In contrast, manufacturing employment in the borderlands historically has been relatively low because of the area's remoteness from major U.S. markets. However, decentralization of manufacturing from the old industrial heartland of the northeast and Great Lakes areas has been accompanied by the growth of manufacturing employment in the borderlands. Proximity to Mexico has influenced the nature and magnitude of manufacturing employment in the borderlands, but contrary forces have been at work in this regard. To the extent that U.S. firms in search of cheap labor locate production facilities on the Mexican side of the border, the U.S. borderlands may lose actual or potential employment. On the other hand, complementary activities on the U.S. side of the border may owe their existence to the advantages of location in Mexico, especially if the alternative to location in Mexico was location somewhere else abroad, which would remove the basis for related activities in the borderlands (see chapter 5).

Finally, it should be noted that the relatively rapid growth of the borderlands is reflected in contract construction employment. In 1976, this sector accounted for 4.2 percent of total employment nationally. The corresponding proportion was about the same in the California borderlands (4.1 percent) but greater for the borderlands areas of Arizona (5.1 percent), New Mexico (5.3 percent), and Texas (4.3 percent). Contract construction employment as a proportion of total nongovernment employment in 1976 was greater in each of the borderlands areas than in the United States. The U.S. proportion was 5.3 percent; for the borderlands of California it was 6.2 percent; for Arizona, 7.7 percent; for New Mexico, 9.4 percent; and for Texas, 5.9 percent.

Structure and Change of Employment and Earnings in Southwest Border Regional Commission Counties: The One Percent CWHS

The Data Base   The one percent Continuous Work History Sample (CWHS) data used in this section were specially processed by the BEA. The nature and limitations of these data have been discussed in considerable detail;[3] a summary presentation is given in appendix D. One difficulty that should be mentioned here is incomplete coverage of the work force. For the borderlands this is especially evident with respect to the government sector.

Comparable data for borderlands counties in California, Arizona, New Mexico, and Texas are presented in tables 4.3 to 4.6, respectively. In each case, the total work force is shown for 1968, 1972, and 1976, along with the estimated average annual wage earnings for each year. For both the 1968–1972 and 1972–1976 periods, the change in the work force is broken down into a number of components. For example, the 1968–1972 portion of table 4.3 shows 85,800 inmigrants. Inmigrants are workers whose Social Security numbers were reported in counties *other than* California borderlands counties in 1968 but were reported in workplaces *within* California borderlands counties in 1972. The 64,100 outmigrants were workers whose Social Security numbers were reported in workplaces *within* California borderlands counties in 1968 but were reported in workplaces in counties *elsewhere* in 1972. The 196,300 nonmigrants were reported as working in the California borderlands in both 1968 and 1972. The "military and other" category includes 18,700 persons in the 1972 California borderlands work force whose 1968 status was not specified. The 160,500 workers in the category "entered covered work force" had no reported Social Security number in 1968 but were reported as working in California borderlands counties in 1972. The 108,000 workers in the category "left covered work force" were reported as working in California borderlands counties in 1968, but their Social Security numbers were not reported anywhere in 1972. As a result of these various additions to and subtractions from the initial 1968 covered work force of 372,400 workers, the final 1972 covered work force amounted to 465,300 workers. Similar data are presented for the 1972–1976 period.

The inmigration total is further broken down to show, in the example of table 4.3, inmigration from Texas, New Mexico, and Arizona borderlands counties, respectively; and from the rest of the states of Texas, New Mexico, Arizona, and California, respectively. Finally, inmigration from the rest of the United States is listed. Corresponding data are presented in table 4.3 for outmigration from California borderlands counties.

CWHS and BEA Employment Data Compared CWHS and BEA employment estimates are compared in table 4.7. As already pointed out, the CWHS has very limited coverage of government employment in the borderlands. Therefore the CWHS estimates of total employment are compared with BEA estimates of nongovernment employment. For the borderlands as a whole in 1976, the BEA estimate is higher than the CWHS estimate, but the difference is less than 1 percent. The largest discrepancy is in Arizona; the smallest is in New Mexico.

When CWHS estimates for 1968 are compared with BEA estimates for 1969, the correspondence between them is closer than the correspondence between the 1976 estimates with respect to the proportion of borderlands employment accounted for by each state area. The Texas proportion is the same in both 1968 and 1969, 25.9 percent. The discrepancy in Arizona is 1.2 percentage points, and it is less than 1 percentage point in both California and New Mexico. However, the BEA estimate is higher than the CWHS estimate in each state. For the borderlands as a whole, the BEA estimate is 14.3 percent higher. The explanation apparently is that in the late 1960s the CWHS series did not cover as many workers as it did in 1976, when the CWHS and BEA estimates were similar. This means that the CWHS series overestimates employment increases between 1968 and 1976, because part of the "growth" consists of new coverage of already-employed workers. On the other hand, the additional coverage is spread fairly uniformly among areas, so that although growth rates are exaggerated, it is still valid to make comparisons of growth rates among areas.

It should be pointed out that the one percent CWHS shows fairly steady employment growth in the borderlands of California, New Mexico, and Texas for the 1968–1972 and 1972–1976 periods. In contrast, the Arizona borderlands registered a small decline in employment between 1968 and 1972, but then employment in the area went from 105,600 in 1972 to 165,200 in 1976, an increase of 56.4 percent. It seems likely that the one percent CWHS overesti-

Table 4.3. Structure of Employment in California Borderlands Based on SSA-CWHS (One Percent Sample), 1968–1972 and 1972–1976

| | 1968–1972 | | | | | | 1972–1976 | | | | | |
	Thousands Workers	% Total	1968 Wages	1972 Wages	% Change Wages		Thousands Workers	% Total	1972 Wages	1976 Wages	% Change Wages	
Initial covered work force	372.4	100.0	5,674				465.3	100.0	6,947			
Immigrants	85.8	23.0	5,675	7,744	36.5		87.5	18.8	6,298	8,903	41.4	
Outmigrants	64.1	17.2	5,225	7,353	40.7		76.3	16.4	6,357	9,420	48.2	
Net migration	21.7	5.8					11.2	2.4				
Nonmigrants	196.3	52.7	6,671	9,080	36.1		217.3	46.7	7,860	10,976	39.7	
Net military and other	18.7	5.0					−7.4	−1.6				
Entered covered work force	160.5	43.1		3,920			211.7	45.5		4,659		
Left covered work force	108.0	29.0	4,266				149.6	32.2	5,551			
Final covered work force	465.3	124.9		6,947			531.2	114.2		8,035		
Immigrants from:												
Texas border	.4	.5	2,935	3,930	33.9		.2	.2	4,020	8,325	107.1	
New Mexico border	.3	.3	8,347	9,553	14.5		.1	.1	110	5,710	5090.9	
Arizona border	1.0	1.2	5,256	8,703	65.6		1.1	1.3	6,951	6,130	−11.8	
Rest of Texas	2.2	2.6	5,281	9,437	78.7		2.9	3.3	5,830	9,310	59.7	
Rest of New Mexico	.2	.2	1,850	8,285	347.8		.2	.2	3,765	4,545	20.7	
Rest of Arizona	1.1	1.3	4,636	7,985	72.2		1.6	1.8	6,451	7,942	23.1	
Rest of California	47.2	55.0	6,017	7,967	32.4		52.2	59.7	6,499	9,049	39.2	
Rest of U.S.A.	33.4	38.9	5,295	7,307	38.0		29.2	33.4	6,006	8,803	46.6	
Military and other	22.7	.0	3,182	6,892	116.6		14.7	.0	5,876	8,013	36.4	
Outmigrants to:												
Texas border	.0	.0					.4	.5	5,060	8,880	75.5	
New Mexico border	.2	.3	85	1,340	1476.5		.4	.5	1,168	2,403	105.8	
Arizona border	.9	1.4	4,692	6,828	45.5		.9	1.2	5,067	7,536	48.7	
Rest of Texas	2.1	3.3	5,193	6,466	24.5		3.3	4.3	7,517	8,479	12.8	
Rest of New Mexico	.2	.3	2,960	2,275	−23.1		.5	.7	8,090	11,348	40.3	
Rest of Arizona	1.7	2.7	5,762	7,408	28.6		2.1	2.8	6,833	11,663	70.7	
Rest of California	34.6	54.0	5,430	7,862	44.8		41.3	54.1	6,630	9,899	49.3	
Rest of U.S.A.	24.4	38.1	4,981	6,814	36.8		27.4	35.9	5,875	8,776	49.4	
Military and other	4.0	.0	1,937	4,258	119.8		22.1	.0	9,465	11,319	19.6	

Table 4.4. Structure of Employment in Arizona Borderlands Based on SSA-CWHS (One Percent Sample), 1968–1972 and 1972–1976

	1968–1972					1972–1976				
	Thousands Workers	% Total	1968 Wages	1972 Wages	% Change Wages	Thousands Workers	% Total	1972 Wages	1976 Wages	% Change Wages
Initial covered work force	107.9	100.0	5,244			105.6	100.0	7,446		
Inmigrants	15.7	14.6	5,239	7,819	49.2	28.5	27.0	6,099	8,501	39.4
Outmigrants	16.9	15.7	4,499	7,756	72.4	12.5	11.8	7,864	10,629	35.2
Net migration	−1.2	−1.1				16.0	15.2			
Nonmigrants	59.1	54.8	5,969	8,701	45.8	73.6	69.7	7,435	10,288	38.4
Net military and other	1.1	1.0				−.5	−.5			
Entered covered work force	27.5	25.5		4,602		60.0	56.8		4,702	
Left covered work force	29.7	27.5	4,424			15.9	15.1	6,726		
Final covered work force	105.6	97.9		7,446		165.2	156.4		7,894	
Inmigrants from:										
Texas border	.6	3.8	4,290	9,095	112.0	.3	1.1	2,107	5,323	152.7
New Mexico border	.1	.6	2,970	3,230	8.8	.2	.7	5,355	10,615	98.2
California border	.9	5.7	4,692	6,828	45.5	.9	3.2	5,067	7,536	48.7
Rest of Texas	.0	.0				.8	2.8	5,069	7,950	56.8
Rest of New Mexico	.2	1.3	3,250	8,215	152.8	.5	1.8	7,444	10,246	37.7
Rest of Arizona	6.3	40.1	4,788	8,100	69.2	7.6	26.7	6,694	9,114	36.2
Rest of California	1.8	11.5	4,853	6,533	34.6	3.3	11.6	5,657	8,445	49.3
Rest of U.S.A.	5.8	36.9	6,141	8,000	30.3	14.9	52.3	6,056	8,266	36.5
Military and other	3.3	.0	2,805	6,902	146.1	3.1	.0	5,287	7,277	37.6
Outmigrants to:										
Texas border	.0	.0				.2	1.6	3,010	5,145	70.9
New Mexico border	.1	.6	7,510	11,100	47.8	.3	2.4	9,137	14,503	58.7
California border	1.0	5.9	5,256	8,703	65.6	1.1	8.8	6,951	6,130	−11.8
Rest of Texas	.6	3.6	4,413	6,990	58.4	.2	1.6	6,065	8,330	37.3
Rest of New Mexico	.1	.6	5,520	9,010	63.2	.1	.8	21,780	20,490	−5.9
Rest of Arizona	7.0	41.4	4,378	8,231	88.0	7.5	60.0	7,387	11,481	55.4
Rest of California	2.2	13.0	3,638	7,492	106.0	.8	6.4	10,931	6,503	−40.5
Rest of U.S.A.	5.9	34.9	4,777	7,131	49.3	2.3	18.4	8,598	11,179	30.0
Military and other	2.2	.0	2,545	4,543	78.5	3.6	.0	9,409	11,191	18.9

Table 4.5. Structure of Employment in New Mexico Borderlands Based on SSA-CWHS (One Percent Sample), 1968–1972 and 1972–1976

| | | | 1968–1972 | | | | | | 1972–1976 | | | | |
	Thousands Workers	% Total	1968 Wages	1972 Wages	% Change Wages		Thousands Workers	% Total	1972 Wages	1976 Wages	% Change Wages
Initial covered work force	22.6	100.0	4,236				29.1	100.0	5,499		
Inmigrants	5.5	24.3	5,918	7,543	27.5		7.6	26.1	6,253	9,059	44.9
Outmigrants	5.7	25.2	3,789	6,741	77.9		5.2	17.9	4,424	9,846	122.6
Net migration	−.2	−.9					2.4	8.2			
Nonmigrants	9.2	40.7	5,171	7,177	38.8		12.6	43.3	6,899	10,155	47.2
Net military and other	.6	2.7					−.7	−2.4			
Entered covered work force	13.4	59.3		3,557			14.0	48.1		4,512	
Left covered work force	7.3	32.3	3,590				9.6	33.0	4,312		
Final covered work force	29.1	128.8		5,499			35.2	121.0		7,558	
Inmigrants from:											
Texas border	.6	10.9	5,047	5,363	6.3		1.2	15.8	6,599	8,678	31.5
Arizona border	.1	1.8	7,510	11,100	47.8		.3	3.9	9,137	14,503	58.7
California border	.2	3.6	85	1,340	1476.5		.4	5.3	1,168	2,403	105.8
Rest of Texas	.5	9.1	5,420	8,020	48.0		.4	5.3	2,663	9,055	240.1
Rest of New Mexico	1.2	21.8	5,593	6,672	19.3		1.8	23.7	5,152	7,345	42.6
Rest of Arizona	.1	1.8	7,260	13,400	84.6		.1	1.3	10,290	10,920	6.1
Rest of California	.8	14.5	6,426	7,450	15.9		.7	9.2	3,747	6,141	63.9
Rest of U.S.A.	2.0	36.4	6,732	8,787	30.5		2.7	35.5	8,297	11,440	37.9
Military and other	1.0	.0	3,187	4,845	52.0		1.0	.0	4,399	6,068	37.9
Outmigrants to:											
Texas border	.4	7.0	2,433	4,775	96.3		.9	17.3	2,199	5,334	142.6
Arizona border	.1	1.8	2,970	3,230	8.8		.2	3.8	5,355	10,615	98.2
California border	.3	5.3	8,347	9,553	14.5		.1	1.9	110	5,710	5090.9
Rest of Texas	.7	12.3	3,534	6,043	71.0		.9	17.3	3,503	12,423	254.6
Rest of New Mexico	2.2	38.6	3,375	5,903	74.9		1.4	26.9	5,355	9,804	83.1
Rest of Arizona	.5	8.8	3,118	6,764	116.9		.1	1.9	960	2,880	200.0
Rest of California	.3	5.3	2,793	4,020	43.9		.6	11.5	7,058	15,075	113.6
Rest of U.S.A.	1.2	21.1	4,608	9,599	108.3		1.0	19.2	4,961	9,464	90.8
Military and other	.4	.0	880	4,438	404.3		1.7	.0	5,116	8,840	72.8

Table 4.6. Structure of Employment in Texas Borderlands Based on SSA-CWHS (One Percent Sample), 1968–1972 and 1972–1976

	1968–1972						1972–1976					
	Thousands Workers	% Total	1968 Wages	1972 Wages	% Change Wages		Thousands Workers	% Total	1972 Wages	1976 Wages	% Change Wages
Initial covered work force	176.2	100.0	3,768				216.8	100.0	4,720		
Inmigrants	27.5	15.6	4,843	6,183	27.7		35.4	16.3	5,149	8,050	56.4
Outmigrants	28.5	16.2	3,786	6,204	63.9		32.0	14.8	4,602	8,741	90.0
Net migration	−1.0	−.6					3.4	1.6			
Nonmigrants	99.9	56.7	4,291	5,809	35.4		113.3	52.3	5,506	8,321	51.1
Net military and other	4.9	2.8					−2.1	−1.0			
Entered covered work force	82.7	46.9		2,864			103.0	47.5		4,013	
Left covered work force	46.0	26.1	2,718				64.9	29.9	3,527		
Final covered work force	216.8	123.0		4,720			256.2	118.2		6,531	
Inmigrants from:											
New Mexico border	.4	1.5	2,433	4,775	96.3		.9	2.5	2,199	5,334	142.6
Arizona border	.0	.0					.2	.6	3,010	5,145	70.9
California border	.0	.0					.4	1.1	5,060	8,880	75.5
Rest of Texas	12.7	46.2	4,512	5,915	31.1		16.7	47.2	4,596	7,963	73.3
Rest of New Mexico	1.4	5.1	3,353	4,784	42.7		2.6	7.3	6,554	9,287	41.7
Rest of Arizona	.4	1.5	3,660	3,963	8.3		.7	2.0	9,181	13,503	47.1
Rest of California	2.7	9.8	4,916	4,802	−2.3		2.4	6.8	5,018	5,525	10.1
Rest of U.S.A.	9.9	36.0	5,603	7,246	29.3		11.5	32.5	5,687	8,326	46.4
Military and other	6.7	.0	2,917	5,367	84.0		4.5	.0	5,714	7,185	25.7
Outmigrants to:											
New Mexico border	.6	2.1	5,047	5,363	6.3		1.2	3.8	6,599	8,678	31.5
Arizona border	.6	2.1	4,290	9,095	112.0		.3	.9	2,107	5,323	152.7
California border	.4	1.4	2,935	3,930	33.9		.2	.6	4,020	8,325	107.1
Rest of Texas	15.1	53.0	3,690	5,846	58.4		15.1	47.2	4,069	7,944	95.2
Rest of New Mexico	1.0	3.5	5,486	8,207	49.6		1.5	4.7	4,215	9,547	126.5
Rest of Arizona	.6	2.1	6,925	7,302	5.4		.5	1.6	6,208	11,464	84.7
Rest of California	3.0	10.5	3,270	5,162	57.9		2.6	8.1	5,654	10,403	84.0
Rest of U.S.A.	7.2	25.3	3,604	6,976	93.6		10.6	33.1	4,937	9,339	89.2
Military and other	1.8	.0	1,304	4,330	232.1		6.6	.0	3,529	6,679	89.3

mates 1976 employment in the Arizona borderlands because the relevant BEA estimate is 147,500—and BEA estimates generally (with the additional minor exception of New Mexico in 1976) are higher than corresponding CWHS estimates for borderlands areas.

Average Annual Wage Earnings   There is a marked tendency for average annual wage earnings to decrease from west to east (table 4.8). The one exception occurs in 1972, when California's $6,947 was second to Arizona's $7,446. The Arizona case is curious in that between 1968 and 1972 employment decline was accompanied by a relatively sharp increase in per worker earnings; then relatively rapid employment growth between 1972 and 1976 was accompanied by only relatively small growth in per worker earnings.

Although Texas and, to a lesser extent, New Mexico have lagged well behind California and Arizona in terms of average wage earnings, there was a convergence over the 1968–1976 period. Between these years, average wage earnings in California increased by 41.6 percent; in Arizona, by 50.5 percent; in New Mexico, by 78.4 percent; and in Texas, by 73.3 percent. In 1968, per worker wage earnings in Texas were only 66.4 percent of the corresponding California value; in 1972 this value increased slightly to 67.9 percent; however, by 1976 it had risen to 81.3 percent. Moreover, whereas the absolute gap between California and Texas widened from $1,906 in 1968 to $2,227 in 1972, it declined in 1976 to $1,504. The coefficient of variation for the four borderlands areas was about the same in 1968 and 1972, but it declined markedly between 1972 and 1976.

Table 4.7. Comparison of One Percent CWHS and BEA Nongovernment Employment Estimates for Southwest Border Regional Commission Counties, by State

	CWHS (1968)		BEA (1969)	
	Employment (thousands)	% of Borderlands	Employment (thousands)	% of Borderlands
California	372.4	54.8	430.6	55.5
Arizona	107.9	15.9	114.1	14.7
New Mexico	22.6	3.3	29.9	3.9
Texas	176.2	25.9	201.3	25.9
Total	679.1	100.0	775.9	100.0

Worker Migration Flows   The data in tables 4.3 to 4.6 indicate that net changes in the covered work force mask large gross in- and out-migration flows as well as large gross flows of workers who enter and leave the work force. In the California borderlands counties, the 85,800 inmigrants during the 1968–1972 period accounted for 18.4 percent of the 1972 work force, although the net migration figure of 21,700 workers represented only 4.7 percent of the 1972 total. Similarly, the 160,500 new entrants to the work force accounted for another 34.5 percent of the 1972 California total, even though the balance between entrants and exits represented only 11.3 percent of the total. Inmigrants and new entrants together made up 52.9 percent of the 1972 California work force; for the 1972–1976 period these groups accounted for 56.3 percent of the 1976 California work force. The corresponding proportions for Arizona were 40.9 percent in 1972 and 53.6 percent in 1976; for New Mexico, 64.9 percent in 1972 and 61.4 percent in 1976; and for Texas, 50.8 percent in 1972 and 54.0 percent in 1976.

During the 1968–1972 period, the California borderlands counties experienced net inmigration of 21,700 workers. However, the borderlands counties in each of the other three states had net outmigration, though the total was only 2,400 workers. In every border state the 1972 average wage earnings of inmigrants was well above the 1972 average for the total covered work force. In California and Arizona the 1972 average wage earnings of inmigrants was less than the 1972 average for nonmigrants; however, in New Mexico and Texas the opposite situation prevailed. The 1972 average earnings

CWHS (1976)		BEA (1976)	
Employment (thousands)	% of Borderlands	Employment (thousands)	% of Borderlands
531.2	53.8	547.6	55.0
165.2	16.7	147.5	14.8
35.2	3.6	34.9	3.5
256.2	25.9	266.2	26.7
987.8	100.0	996.3	100.0

Table 4.8. Estimated Average Annual Wage Earnings in Southwest Border Regional Commission Counties, by State, 1968, 1972, and 1976

	1968	1972	1976
California	$5,674	$6,947	$8,035
Arizona	5,244	7,446	7,894
New Mexico	4,236	5,499	7,558
Texas	3,768	4,720	6,531
Unweighted mean	4,730	6,153	7,505
Standard deviation	762	1,094	588
Coefficient of variation	.161	.178	.078

per worker of inmigrants and outmigrants were not greatly different, but for each state's borderlands the outmigrants had a greater percentage increase in earnings than did inmigrants.

The borderlands in each state experienced net inmigration between 1972 and 1976, although the California balance declined from 21,700 workers in 1968–1972 to 11,200 workers in 1972–1976. Arizona, which had net outmigration of 1,200 workers in 1968–1972, had the greatest inmigration between 1972 and 1976, 16,000 workers. New Mexico and Texas had net inmigration of 2,400 and 3,400 workers, respectively, between 1972 and 1976. In keeping with the previous period, the 1976 average annual earnings of inmigrants was considerably greater than that of the total covered work force in each state. However, in each state the 1976 average earnings of inmigrants was less than the corresponding figure for nonmigrants. The difference ranged from $2,073 in California to $271 in Texas. Outmigrants consistently had higher 1976 earnings than did inmigrants and, with the exception of New Mexico, their percentage increase between 1972 and 1976 was also greater than that for inmigrants.

The origin and destination data for migrants shown in tables 4.3 to 4.6 indicate that there is very little interaction among the borderlands of the respective states. For example, California accounted for 63.8 percent of total borderlands inmigration for the 1968–1972 period. However, only 2.0 percent of all inmigrants to the California borderlands came from borderlands in the other three states. Similarly, California accounted for 55.6 percent of all borderlands outmigration, but only 1.7 percent of all borderlands California outmigrants went to the borderlands of the other three states. This pattern also characterized the 1972–1976 period. Inmigration to and outmigration from the California borderlands primarily involves the rest of California, and most of the remaining flows involve nonborder states. In the other borderlands areas, migration flows are also predominantly intrastate or with nonborder states. In the late eighteenth century efforts were made to locate and mark trails between New Spain's northern provinces, yet Texans, New Mexicans, Californians, and residents of Pimería Alta (southern Arizona) had virtually no contact with each other.[4] Lack of mobility along the border appears to be a persistent phenomenon despite the changes of the past 200 years.

Entries to and Exits from the Work Force As might be expected, new entrants to the work force consistently had much lower average earnings than the total covered work force. The data in table 4.9 indicate that new entrants are in fact relatively young. More unexpected is the finding that exits, workers who left the covered work force, also had relatively low average earnings. It might be assumed that exits would tend to be older workers. In general they were older than entrants, outmigrants, and inmigrants. However, they tended to be younger than nonmigrants. Only in the cases of New Mexico for the 1968–1972 period and Arizona for the 1972–1976 period were exits older than nonmigrants. For the 1968–1972 period, exits in each state had the lowest 1968 earnings of any category of workers. For the 1972–1976 period, with the exception of Arizona, exits had the lowest 1972 earnings.

In view of its pattern of low earnings the exit category warrants closer examination. California will be considered in detail because it accounted for slightly over half of the total borderlands exits for the 1968–1972 period and for 62 percent of the total for the 1972–1976 period. Moreover, the California case is typical of the borderlands as a whole with respect to the nature of workers who left the covered work force. Nearly half (48.6 percent) of the exits who were in the 1968 work force were female. Their average annual earnings were only $2,861 compared to $5,594 for males. Of the exits who were in the 1972 work force, 45.3 percent were female; their average earnings were only $3,625 compared to $7,144 for males. In the

1968 work force, 29 percent of the exits were under 30 years old and 38.8 percent were under 35 years. Of the total exits in the 1972 work force, 30.2 percent were under 30 years old and 42.0 percent were under 35 years. Exits from the 1968 work force under 30 years old had average earnings of $2,416 compared to $4,266 for all exits from the 1968 work force. Exits from the 1972 work force under 30 years old had average earnings of $3,201 compared to $5,551 for all exits from the 1972 work force. Of the total exits from the 1968 work force, 59.2 percent were employed in the trade and services sectors. Exits from the trade sector had relatively low average earnings of $3,064, and exits from the services sector had relatively low average earnings of $3,457. Of the total exits from the 1972 work force, 57.4 percent were employed in the trade and services sectors. Their earnings also were relatively low; $4,143 in the case of workers in trade and $4,589 for services employees. Although no breakdown is available for younger women employed in the trade and services sectors, the evidence nevertheless suggests that the low average earnings of exits from the work force is explained in part by this category of workers. It is likely that many of these young women dropped out of the work force when they married or when they had children.

It is noteworthy that 53.3 percent of the entrants to the 1972 California work force and 54.9 percent of the entrants to the 1976 work force were female. In both years over half of the entrants were under 25 years old. Of the total entrants to the 1972 work force, 66.2 percent were employed in the trade and services sectors; the corre-

Table 4.9. Median Age[a] of Workers in Southwest Border Regional Commission Counties, by Category and by State, 1972 and 1976

	Nonmigrants		Outmigrants		Inmigrants	
	1972	1976	1972	1976	1972	1976
California	44.7	42.3	34.5	32.9	34.9	32.4
Arizona	45.2	41.7	35.8	35.0	36.1	31.1
New Mexico	43.2	43.6	32.9	29.3	36.0	34.4
Texas	41.8	40.1	32.2	32.9	35.7	32.2

[a]In relation to tables 4.3 to 4.6, the median age of workers listed for the 1968–1972 period is given here for 1972. The median age of workers listed for the 1972–1976 period is given here for 1976.

sponding figure for entrants to the 1976 work force was 70.2 percent. Here again the California case is typical of the borderlands as a whole. There is a great deal of turnover in the work force, but on balance a relatively large number of younger women have entered or re-entered the work force, and the trade and services sectors have had relatively rapid growth in terms of net exits and entrants. This phenomenon is probably associated with increasing labor force participation rates among Mexican American women. Between 1975 and 1978 alone, the proportion of Mexican American women 16 years old and over in the labor force increased from 42.1 percent to 47.0 percent.[5]

Trade Services and Manufacturing Table 4.10 contains one percent CWHS data on 1976 employment in trade, services, and manufacturing in the borderlands. The proportion of borderlands employment accounted for by each of these sectors, as shown here, is in fairly close agreement with the 1976 BEA estimates shown in table 4.2. The trade estimates are similar for all borderlands areas, and the services and manufacturing estimates are similar for California and Texas. The greatest discrepancies are in the services and manufacturing estimates for Arizona and New Mexico; in both cases the CWHS estimates are higher for services but lower for manufacturing.

Comparable national CWHS data are not available for 1976, but structural data from the 1972 one percent CWHS have been tabu-

Exits		Entrants	
1972	1976	1972	1976
41.3	39.5	23.9	22.3
43.4	53.9	23.0	23.8
47.5	37.0	23.3	25.3
39.0	38.2	22.8	21.4

Table 4.10. Employment in Trade, Services, and Manufacturing in Southwest Border Regional Commission Counties, by State, 1976

	Borderlands	California	Arizona	New Mexico	Texas
Trade					
Number	313,600	169,900	46,000	9,800	87,900
Percent of					
work force	31.7	32.0	27.8	27.8	34.3
Services					
Number	245,900	129,300	59,800	10,900	45,900
Percent of					
work force	24.9	24.3	36.2	35.2	17.9
Manufacturing					
Number	141,500	86,200	7,300	2,600	45,400
Percent of					
work force	14.3	16.2	4.4	7.4	17.7

lated for the nation as a whole.[6] The 1972 data indicate that 22.9 percent of the covered U.S. work force were in the trade sector, 21.8 percent were in services, and 27.4 percent were in manufacturing. In terms of these figures, the borderlands areas in every state are overrepresented with respect to employment in the trade sector; this is especially the case in California and in Texas. Services are also overrepresented in each state except Texas, and especially in Arizona and New Mexico. In contrast, the proportion of employment accounted for by manufacturing in the borderlands is only about half that in the United States.

The covered work force in Texas increased by 40,600 workers between 1968 and 1972; manufacturing jobs increased by 7,800. For the 1972–1976 period, Texas added 39,400 covered workers, of which 2,200 were in manufacturing. New Mexico had a decline of 200 manufacturing workers between 1968 and 1972 and a small increase of 1,200 manufacturing workers between 1972 and 1976. Arizona's manufacturing employment declined by 3,100 between 1968 and 1972 and grew by 1,600 workers during the 1972–1976 period. Between 1968 and 1972, California added 92,900 jobs but only 1,100 manufacturing jobs; the corresponding figures for the 1972–1976 period were 65,900 and 5,100. While the growth in total borderlands manufacturing employment between 1972 and 1976 may appear modest, it was greater than that for the 1968–1972 period. Moreover, national manufacturing employment actually declined from 1972 to 1976 because of a major recession within this period.

Summary The data presented in this section indicate that average annual wage earnings of the work force decrease from west to east along the borderlands. This is consistent with other findings that welfare indicators' values decline as one moves from the California borderlands across to Brownsville, on the Texas Gulf Coast.[7] However, during the 1968–1976 study period there was a convergence of average wage earnings along the border. In this interval the increase in average earnings in California was only 41.6 percent, compared to 50.5 percent in Arizona, 78.4 percent in New Mexico, and 73.3 percent in Texas. The absolute average earnings gap between California and Texas decreased from $1,906 in 1968 to $1,504 in 1976; the Texas average in relation to the California average rose from 66.4 percent to 81.3 percent.

There also was convergence along the border in terms of net migration. The California borderlands had a net inmigration of 21,700 workers between 1968 and 1972; in contrast, the other three borderlands areas had net outmigration. However, between 1972 and 1976 net inmigration to California declined to 11,200 workers and net migration became positive in the other borderlands areas. Arizona in fact had the greatest net inmigration, 16,000 workers.

Detailed breakdowns of the origins and destinations of migrants show that there is very little interaction among the borderlands of the respective border states.

In comparison with the United States as a whole, the borderlands areas in each border state are overrepresented in terms of employment in the trade sector; and each state except Texas is overrepresented in terms of employment in the services sector. The proportion of borderlands employment accounted for by manufacturing is only about half that for the United States, but manufacturing employment in the borderlands increased between 1972 and 1976, a period when employment in this sector was declining nationally.[8]

Average annual earnings in the large and relatively rapidly growing trade and services sectors are relatively low. The evidence suggests that this is associated with high turnover in the female work force. It appears that many young women exit from the trade and services sectors, but there has been an even larger influx of young women entering or re-entering them.

Employment and Earnings in Borderlands BEA Regions

In chapter 1 it was pointed out that, in addition to examining Southwest Border Regional Commission counties, it is instructive to consider the borderlands in terms of Bureau of Economic Analysis (BEA) functional economic regions. The borderlands area covered by BEA regions is more extensive than that made up of regional commission counties; the major difference is the addition of numerous Texas counties in the San Antonio BEA region.

One Percent CWHS Data   One percent CWHS data were used to analyze the five borderlands BEA regions—San Diego, Tucson, El Paso, San Antonio, and Brownsville—in a manner that paralleled the analysis of the regional commission counties.[9] The results are not given here in detail because they are so similar to those just presented for the commission counties. For example, in 1968, earnings per worker consistently declined from west to east. Average earnings in the Brownsville BEA region were only 58 percent of those in the San Diego BEA region. By 1976, the tendency for average earnings to decline from west to east was still in evidence, but between 1972 and 1976 there was a pronounced reduction in regional earnings disparities. Brownsville's level of earnings per worker in 1976 was 77 percent of the San Diego level and 76 percent of that in Tucson, which had replaced San Diego as the region with the highest average earnings. The coefficient of variation in per worker earnings declined from .190 in 1968 to .104 in 1976.

There also was convergence along the border in terms of net migration. The San Diego BEA region had net inmigration of 15,100 workers during the 1968–1972 period while all of the other regions had net outmigration. However, during the 1972–1976 period net inmigration to the San Diego region declined to 10,800 workers; and net migration became positive in the other regions with the exception of San Antonio, where net outmigration declined to only 500 workers.

Detailed breakdowns of the origins and destinations of migrants indicate that there is very little interregional movement within the borderlands.

In comparison with the United States as a whole, each borderlands BEA region is overrepresented in terms of employment in the trade sector; and each region except Brownsville is overrepresented in terms of employment in the services sector. The proportion of borderlands employment accounted for by manufacturing is only about half that for the United States, but manufacturing employment has been increasing. For example, between 1968 and 1972 the San Antonio BEA region added 1,600 manufacturing jobs; the corresponding gain for the 1972–1976 period was 3,500. Finally, average annual earnings in the large and relatively rapidly growing trade and services sectors are relatively low; the evidence also suggests that there has been a high degree of turnover of female workers in these sectors.

Shift-Share Analysis of Employment Change A shift-share analysis of 1972 to 1977 employment change by sector in the respective borderlands BEA regions was carried out using data in the BEA employment series.[10] Shift-share analysis is essentially a descriptive method that breaks down regional employment change into components that reflect national employment change patterns, the regional distribution of employment among sectors, and the degree to which regional sectors grow more rapidly or slowly than their national counterparts. Because it is relatively technical, details of the analysis are discussed in appendix E. However, the general results are incorporated into the following summary and conclusions section.

Summary and Conclusions

The data series used in this chapter do not in themselves provide any direct evidence of the Mexican connection. Unfortunately, no comparable data exist for the employment and earnings of Mexican nationals who, on either an undocumented or legally authorized basis, reside in the United States or commute to work across the border. The limited available data concerning Mexican Americans are presented in chapter 7. Despite these constraints, it is possible to make reasonable inferences about the role of the Mexican connection in the regional development of the southwest borderlands.

The rate of growth of employment in the borderlands exceeds that of the United States and the nonborder portions of the four border states. The BEA employment series indicates that between 1969 and 1976, borderlands employment growth amounted to 30 percent in Arizona, 23 percent in Texas, 16 percent in California, and 14 percent in New Mexico. The corresponding national rate was about 10 percent.

The borderlands area has a high, though declining, dependence on government employment. In both 1969 and 1976, government employment accounted for about 20 percent of total national employment. The government's share of total borderlands employment went from 38 percent in 1969 to 33 percent in 1976. During this period, the rate of growth of borderlands government employment was less than half the national rate of 11 percent. The shift-share analysis of borderlands BEA region employment changes between 1972 and 1977 indicates that in 1972 every region except Brownsville had a high proportion of military employment in relation to the United States as a whole. National cutbacks in military employment between 1972 and 1977 adversely affected the Tucson, Brownsville, and, especially, San Antonio regions. However, because of positively competitive regional conditions, military employment remained about the same in the San Diego region and even increased substantially in the El Paso region. Overall gains in government employment in the borderlands were largely a result of increases in the state and local sectors. Problems arising from relatively poor social and economic conditions along the border have generated substantial state and local employment growth in agencies whose objective is to alleviate such conditions; much of this expansion has in fact been supported by some form of federal revenue sharing. Many of the issues with which these growing bureaucracies deal are related to undocumented migration from Mexico and to long-standing disadvantages experienced by Mexican Americans, topics that will be considered in detail in subsequent chapters.

Manufacturing has traditionally been relatively unimportant in the borderlands economy, but there are indications that this is changing. The BEA and CWHS data series both reveal manufacturing gains during a time when manufacturing employment has been stagnating nationally. The shift-share results show that the border area has regional advantages with respect to manufacturing even though it has yet to exploit them fully (a negative allocation effect). San Diego and Tucson have amenities conducive to the location of new, diversified production activities, but more general regional advantages in the borderlands are related to proximity to Mexico, as well as to the pronounced tendency for manufacturing to decentralize from the old industrial heartland of the northeast and north-central states. Relatively cheap labor and possibilities for twin plant linkages with assembly plants (*maquiladoras*) on the Mexican side of the border have been viewed with particular favor by increasing numbers of manufacturing firms. It may be noted here that the whole issue of the location of U.S. firms on both sides of the border needs to be considered in the context of the new international division of labor, which is examined in the next chapter.

In relation to the rest of the United States, the borderlands area has a high proportion of its total employment in the trade and services sectors. This is especially the case for retail trade because the large and rapidly growing Mexican border population makes many of its purchases in U.S. stores. For example, as pointed out in chapter 3, Mexican purchases in San Diego probably amounted to about $260 million in 1976 alone; between April 1977 and March 1978, Mexicans made a total of 11.5 million visits to Arizona and spent $315 million; per capita retail sales in Laredo are the highest in the nation, largely because of Mexican purchases; and 1973 estimates suggest that in 1973 over a quarter of San Antonio's retail trade income was accounted for by sales to Mexican citizens. (Further evidence in this regard is provided in the following chapter.) Finally, evidence suggests that the expanding trade sector is employing ever greater numbers of Mexican American females, whose labor force participation rate has increased sharply in recent years.

Although the border area is widely regarded as relatively poor, per capita income and per worker earnings in the California end are higher than the corresponding national figures. However, most welfare indicators—including those related to income—decline from west to east along the border. As will be shown in chapter 7, there is a high degree of negative correlation between the proportion of the total population accounted for by Hispanics and per capita local income. Thus, Texas border cities, which are largely Mexican American, have the poorest economic conditions. Despite the economic disparities along the border, there has been little migration of workers among borderlands subregions. Nevertheless, in recent years total net inmigration to San Diego has declined, whereas along the rest of the border net migration has shifted from negative to positive; and relatively rapid income growth in the Texas border area has produced a convergence in per capita income and per worker earnings along the border. These phenomena will be examined in chapters 7 and 8, but first attention must be turned to the historical role of Mexicans in the southwest labor force, and to the nature and significance of continuing undocumented Mexican immigration to the United States.

5. The Role of Mexican Labor in Southwestern Economic Development

Introduction

This chapter attempts to trace the contributions that Mexican labor has made to the development of the U.S. southwest, and particularly the southwest borderlands. Consideration also is given to the nature and significance of various problems associated with this phenomenon. Three types of Mexican workers have had a pronounced impact on the southwest's economy: (1) Mexican citizens who have resided and worked in the United States, whether legally or on an undocumented basis; (2) residents of Mexican border cities who have commuted to workplaces on the U.S. side of the border; and (3) employees of plants located in Mexico's border cities in response to Mexico's *maquiladora* program. In the last case, employment is dependent on U.S. firms and a significant proportion of workers' earnings is spent in the United States, reinforcing the symbiotic nature of the transnational border economy. In addition, it is difficult to gain an adequate perspective on the large and growing impact of Mexican Americans in the southwest economy without reference to the historic role of Mexican labor in the United States. This issue has in fact been raised with increasing frequency by Chicano activists, among others.

A Historical Overview

Revisionist views of the origins of Mexican American society maintain that the first Mexican Americans and their descendents should not be regarded as immigrants but rather as foreigners in their native land because the United States thrust itself upon them.[1] In this context, Mexican Americans are a charter minority in their own land, "a creation of the imperial conquest of one nation by another through military force."[2] As an outcome of the Mexican–United

States War (1846–48), Mexico did lose half of its national territory to an aggressively imperialistic United States. And there can be no doubt that Mexicans and Mexican Americans in the southwest have often been regarded and treated as less than the equals of "Anglos." This prejudiced perspective is reflected in the works of the eminent historian Walter Prescott Webb, who himself "saw Mexicans as bootleggers and smugglers, and felt that any Mexican on the United States side of the border who couldn't explain why he was there was probably up to no good. The fact that he neither spoke nor read Spanish must have hampered his efforts at understanding."[3] Yet whatever the intellectual arrogance of Anglo scholars or the physical brutality of the Texas Rangers, the notion that the Mexican Americans are a conquered people bears more resemblance to myth—acknowledging that myths may have political and social utility—than to reality.

Mexico had never successfully populated the territories ceded to the United States in 1848, largely because they were separated from historic Mexico by hundreds of miles of wasteland. Shortly before Mexico achieved independence from Spain, the latter had granted Anglo colonists the right to enter Texas; there was hope that assimilated colonists would provide a buffer against their compatriots. In 1824, the Mexican government confirmed the Austin grant, which permitted the settlement of Anglo immigrants in east Texas. Three hundred families were settled at the outset, and soon thousands more poured in. It might have been possible to assimilate Anglo immigrants had they come into a truly Mexican country, but there were only a few thousand hispanic inhabitants in Texas. Moreover, the latter were located primarily in the old mission area along the San Antonio River and along the lower Rio Grande River from Laredo south, so they were not in contact with the Anglos in east Texas. Involved as they were with coups and counter-coups, successive Mexican regimes paid little attention to Texas. There were no Mexican schools where the Anglos settled, and there was no pressure to learn Mexican ways or the Spanish language. Anglo colonists had to promise to become Roman Catholics, but in fact Mexican officials ignored this requirement. Mexican citizens were offered colonization opportunities on better terms than the Anglos received, but the elite was not interested in the remote northern hinterlands and the poor could not move because of circumstance. Mexico had no equivalent to the Anglo colonists, nearly all of whom had some education and most of whom had tools, equipment, and black slaves. In any case, if the Anglo colonists were not assimilating, they were not causing trouble. This was to change as a result of increasing Mexican arrogance and fear of the United States and of the spirit of Manifest Destiny that did indeed come to prevail in the latter.

In what is today the U.S. southwest, Texas was the only area where Anglos greatly outnumbered Mexicans even before Mexico lost control of the territory. Even so, at the time of the U.S. takeover there were only some 7,500 Mexicans in all of California and fewer than 2,000 in what is today Arizona. The most successful Spanish and Mexican settlements were in the upper Rio Grande basin, concentrated around Santa Fe and Taos but extending into present-day southern Colorado. In 1850, some 60,000 Hispanics inhabited New Mexico. Not until a hundred years later did Anglos outnumber Hispanics there.[4] Even today, hispanic culture retains a strong place in the state's pluralistic and tolerant environment. The northern New Mexicans who accounted for about 80 percent of the total hispanic population of the United States just after the war with Mexico can hardly be regarded as a conquered people.

After the war, life for the relatively few Mexican Americans near the border went on much as before. The Treaty of Guadalupe Hidalgo guaranteed former Mexican citizens the right to unrestricted travel across the border. Although crossings were supposed to be made at official checkpoints, little attention was paid to this requirement. The inhabitants of northern Mexico continued to view the U.S. side of the border as part of their own territory, and people generally crossed the border as though no barrier existed.[5]

Unofficial crossings also disregarded immigration laws. Children born on one side of the river would be baptized on the other side, and thus appear on church registers as citizens of the other country. This bothered no one since people on both sides of the river thought of themselves as *mexicanos*, but United States officials were concerned about it. People would come across to visit relatives and stay long periods of time, and perhaps move inland in search of work. After 1890, the movement in search of work was preponderantly from Mexico deep into Texas and beyond.[6]

It is difficult to know how many Mexicans immigrated into the United States during the last half of the nineteenth century because control and estimates of the movement did not begin until the 1920s. Briggs estimates that fewer than 30,000 Mexicans immigrated into the southwest during this period,[7] but this figure appears to be too low in view of the fact that the census of 1900 reported 103,393 Mexican-born persons in the U.S. population. Nearly 70 percent of this total was accounted for by Texas. Because census takers counted Mexican Americans as Caucasians it is difficult to know the actual number of Hispanics in the 1900 U.S. population. Corwin puts the total between 335,000 and 350,000,[8] whereas Martínez maintains that there were no fewer than 381,000 and perhaps as many as 552,000.[9] None of these estimates allows for the possible effects of seasonal migration between Mexico and the United States. In any case, even though it appears that a significant migratory drift from Mexico to the U.S. border states was underway before 1900, it is generally agreed that mass migration from Mexico did not occur until the present century.

If their numbers were still relatively modest in the nineteenth century, Mexicans still made important contributions to the economic development of the southwest. They introduced techniques for mining gold, silver, copper, and quartz, as well as the use of the pan for washing gold. The sheep-raising industry received its main impetus from the skills of Mexicans; and the techniques and trappings of the Anglo cowboy were virtually all borrowed from the Mexican *vaquero*. Irrigation techniques developed on the basis of Indian and Spanish-Mexican experiences were utilized to create prosperity for Anglo farmers. Mexicans planted and cultivated cotton fields, vegetable gardens, and fruit orchards from Texas to California. After 1880, Mexicans comprised some two-thirds of the section gangs on the principal western railroads. Yet, despite these contributions, Mexican workers in nearly all branches of economic activity received wages substantially below those paid to Anglos for similar work.[10]

After 1900, the continued expansion of western railroads—as well as those in Mexico, which permitted the mass movement of persons from central Mexico across the vast northern deserts—brought an accelerated flow of Mexicans to the southwest. The railroads, in addition to using large numbers of these immigrants themselves, also opened vast markets for southwestern mining and agricultural outputs, which created still more demand for workers from south of the border. Mexicans were hired with federal funds to harness the waters of the lower Colorado River, the Salt River in Arizona, and the Rio Grande in New Mexico. These projects greatly expanded the scope and nature of southwestern agriculture; former deserts now produced an abundance of labor-intensive crops, worked for the most part by low-paid, mobile Mexican labor. During the second decade of this century, domestic labor shortages caused by the First World War intensified the demand for Mexican labor; at the same time, civil strife within Mexico added a push factor to the migration process. Following a brief reversal caused by depressed conditions in U.S. agriculture and Mexican repatriation efforts, the expanding U.S. economy of the 1920s again welcomed Mexican workers, who by now had begun to fan out from the southwest. Many traveled long distances as migrant farm workers, but others entered industrial occupations in such places as Chicago and Pennsylvania. While the general mood of the country favored curbs on mass immigration into the United States, Mexicans were deliberately excluded from the restrictive provisions of the National Origins Act of 1924.

The development of the southwest provided a strong stimulus to the growth of northern Mexico, where U.S. capital and entrepreneurship were strongly represented in the mining, irrigated agriculture, petroleum, and tourist sectors. During the 1920s, Mexico's border cities catered to the demands of Prohibition-era Americans in search of worldly pleasures; and the booming breweries, racetracks, and casinos were mostly owned and operated by U.S. citizens.[11] Between 1900 and 1930, Nuevo Laredo tripled in population to 21, 636. During the same period, the population of Ciudad Juárez went from 8,218 to 39,669, and that of Tijuana went from only 242 to 8,364. Mexicali, which was virtually nonexistent in 1900, had a population of 14,842 in 1930.[12]

The advent of the Great Depression and rising unemployment during the 1930s brought a reversal of policy toward Mexican workers in the United States. The Mexicans were considered to be largely redundant in view of the availability of large numbers of American workers, who poured into the borderlands agricultural labor market from the "dust bowl" areas of Texas and Oklahoma. The first large-scale effort to apprehend undocumented aliens was undertaken in the 1930s. Over 200,000 persons in this category were deported; most were Mexican. In addition, several hundred thousand Mexicans were forcibly repatriated to Mexico. Some of these persons had married U.S. citizens or had children born in the United States;

some were eligible for citizenship but had not formally completed the immigration process.[13] No matter—political expediency dictated that they had to go.

The *Bracero* Program

Labor shortages resulting from the Second World War caused yet another reversal of U.S. policy toward Mexican workers, who were needed especially in agriculture but also by railroads. Because of the ruthless treatment of Mexicans during the 1930s and the even longer history of discrimination against Mexicans and Mexican Americans in the United States, the Mexican government balked at initial requests to supply workers to the U.S. economy. However, in 1942 the two governments agreed to implement the Mexican Labor Program, which came to be better known as the *bracero* program.

The railroad component of the *bracero* agreement was ended in 1946, but the farm program lasted until 1964. It has been estimated that some 4 million *braceros* found temporary work in the United States between 1942 and 1960. However, the prospect of employment drew so many Mexicans northward that the number of undocumented immigrants probably surpassed the number of *braceros*. An estimated 4.7 million Mexicans were returned to Mexico between 1942 and 1960 for having entered the United States illegally.[14]

The controversy surrounding the *bracero* program reveals the complexity of the issues and contending interests involved in the employment of Mexican workers in the United States. The terms of the initial agreement stipulated that *braceros* were to be given legal protections with respect to housing, transportation, food, medical needs, and wage rates, but they were not permitted to work outside the agricultural sector (with the exception of railroads during the war years). The program proved to be a particular boon for U.S. agribusiness because the southwestern agricultural labor market was removed from competition with other sectors. Although the *braceros* were not supposed to depress wage rates, the program had that effect. Initially the program was administered by the Farm Security Administration, which acted according to the letter of the law. In 1943, supervision was shifted to the grower-dominated War Food Administration. This agency—with the tacit cooperation of the Immigration and Naturalization Service, the U.S. Employment Service, and the Border Patrol—no longer enforced the guarantees that had been made to the *braceros*.

Maltreatment of Mexicans became so flagrant in Texas that in 1943 the Mexican government banned *braceros* from working there. However, the relevant U.S. agencies tolerated a virtually open border and, in addition, pressured the Mexican government into allowing the creation of border recruitment centers that would attract thousands of Mexican farm workers to the border. The *bracero* vacuum in Texas was rapidly filled by undocumented entrants, who were not provided even nominal legal protections. The provision that no Mexican laborer could be employed unless it was proven that a domestic labor shortage existed was also subverted by agribusiness interests and the U.S. Employment Service. President Truman's Commission on Migratory Labor charged that the USES masked its failure to recruit U.S. workers by proclaiming that Mexican workers were needed to maintain adequate farm production. U.S. unions insisted that the domestic labor supply was adequate and that any apparent "shortages" could be attributed to below-subsistence wages and poor working conditions that would not and should not be tolerated by U.S. workers.[15]

In 1948, a new labor agreement between the United States and Mexico prohibited the entry of "wetbacks" into the United States. Although both nations pledged to enforce strict border controls, in fact such measures were never effectively implemented. This arrangement had a certain appeal to U.S. agribusiness, since undocumented noncontract Mexican labor was not subject to internationally guaranteed work conditions. Protesting workers could simply be repatriated. In 1954, the United States even instituted a system for the recruitment of Mexican labor without the consent of the Mexican government. Between 1954 and 1959, 2½ million Mexican workers contracted to work in the United States. The 1956 total alone—445,197 workers—was greater than the combined total of both the farm and railroad labor programs from 1942 to 1947.[16] The number of undocumented Mexican aliens apprehended fell from over 1 million in 1954 to 58,792 in 1956; between 1957 and 1965, the annual number of such apprehensions ranged from 39,750 to 48,948.[17]

The Kennedy administration was responsible for the termination of the *bracero* program in 1964. It was felt that the program had adversely affected the wages, working conditions, and employment opportunities of U.S. citizens. Nevertheless, it was recognized that many Mexicans would enter the United States on an undocumented basis because of the relative lack of economic opportunity in Mexico.[18] In fact, the number of deportable Mexican aliens apprehended in the United States has steadily increased since 1964. The 1961–70 total amounted to 756,000 persons; the total for the two years 1972 and 1973 was 934,000; the total for the single year 1977 was 921,000;[19] and since then apprehensions have exceeded 1 million annually.

Undocumented Immigration

In keeping with historical precedent, the relatively high rate of unemployment in the United States in recent years has been accompanied by a great deal of alarmist journalism and political rhetoric alleging that the country is in danger of being overrun by hordes of undocumented immigrants from south of the border. In fact, no one knows how many undocumented Mexicans are working in the United States, though a widely publicized estimate of over 5 million has been shown to be grossly exaggerated.[20]

Undocumented Mexican workers have long been functionally integrated into the economy of the southwest borderlands. Their presence has been supported by social and cultural institutions and has received the tacit cooperation of legal authorities.[21] Increasingly, however, undocumented Mexicans are fanning out to other parts of the United States.

> Today what is being called the "new wetback invasion" is better described as an infiltration of new-style migrants. This migration is virtually invisible to the general public. The new "wets" are not the ragged peons or "stoop labor" of yesteryear, who in rubber-tired *huaraches* plodded over the back trails or rambled down the highways in broken-down trucks with women and little *chamacos*, looking for farm and ranch work. Today's *mojados* exemplify the increasing modernization of Mexico. . . . Now more than ever illegals head for better wages and easier work in cities, towns, farms, and ranches far from the border regions.[22]

The nature and significance of undocumented migration from Mexico are examined in more detail in chapter 6, where it is argued that there are no simple solutions to problems related to this movement. However, it may be better to have no clear formal policy in this regard—which is the case at present—than to have a policy that could not be implemented effectively or could create even greater problems. Moreover, the present informal system may not be as perverse as some critics charge.

Mexican Americans in the U.S. Population

It was pointed out previously that very few Mexican citizens lived in what is now the southwestern United States at the time of the U.S. takeover in 1848. Most were concentrated in north-central New Mexico. Even allowing for U.S. census undercounting, there probably were no more than 25,000 Mexicans in states other than New Mexico. Between 1869 and 1973, 1,755,000 Mexicans legally immigrated to the United States, but in no single year before 1904 were there as many as 1,000 legal Mexican immigrants.[23] According to the most recent Bureau of the Census estimates, there were 6,670,000 "persons of Spanish origin" living in the southwest in 1977.[24] Texas (2,366,000) and California (3,344,000) accounted for 86 percent of the total. Most of the rest resided in New Mexico. Arizona, New Mexico, and Colorado were reported as a single unit and their combined Spanish-origin population was 960,000. In a separate breakdown, not reported by state, persons of Spanish origin in the southwest were divided into Mexicans (5,695,000), Puerto Ricans (60,000), and "other Spanish" (914,000).[25] It is probably correct to assume that the last group corresponds closely with the New Mexico (and southern Colorado) hispanic population, whose members often refer to themselves as Spanish Americans (descended from Europeans) rather than Mexican Americans.

Thus, although the United States certainly conquered a great deal of Mexican territory, it did not conquer many Mexicans, or at least not many persons who considered themselves Mexicans. (Persons not identifying themselves as Mexicans no doubt included a high proportion of the southwest Indian population as well as the "Spanish" population.) Today the Mexican American population is overwhelmingly composed of persons who voluntarily moved to the United States or who are the recent descendents of voluntary immigrants.

Marxist Interpretations: A Critique

Why have so many Mexicans come to the United States? It has become somewhat fashionable to treat this issue in Marxist terms: the United States not only conquered the Mexican American people but also has gone on to exploit a reserve army of Mexican workers. Thus, Rivas finds that the northward migration of Mexicans is essentially an economic phenomenon, "the logical result of an increased demand for workers in one country and a reserve of workers in the other."[26] If one combines the push effects of poor living conditions, low wages, and high unemployment rates in Mexico "with the opening up of greater transportation links between the two countries and growing U.S. economic power, we can understand the essence of migration patterns."[27] This appears to me to be a straightforward, nondoctrinaire, and correct view. One might even infer that the United States has created opportunities for Mexicans. But the Marxist literature draws other conclusions concerning U.S. economic power. Fernandez, for example, maintains that:

> Economically, the unity that is characteristic of the border region is based upon the uneven development of the areas north and south of the border and as such is ultimately a reflection of the uneven development of the United States and Mexico. The problem of uneven development, or, more correctly, the problem of imperialism, is specific to the twentieth century. . . .
>
> The separation of the world into poor nations and rich nations is not a natural sort of phenomenon. The explanation for it lies in the development and growth of monopolistic forms of capitalism in the more economically advanced nations, the ability of these monopoly enterprises to affect the economic life of the less advanced nations and, consequently, the persistence of poverty and backwardness and at best the appearance of warped development possibilities in the poor areas of the world.[28]

In other words, the remarkable economic growth of the United States has been a kind of unnatural perversion. The literary critic V. S. Pritchett has remarked that "Marxists do not allow the posing of the question: they state the answer first and then create the question."[29] In the present case, it seems to me that it would be more fruitful to explore the possibilities for generating more rapid economic development in Mexico than to blame the United States for attaining a high level of development. Would Mexico be better off today if per capita income in the United States were to have remained at a level equivalent to that in Mexico? Fernandez notes that in the late nineteenth century, U.S. companies "made large-scale attempts at irrigation [in the southwest], and their success resulted in large profits, particularly after the railroads opened up eastern markets."[30] He adds that at that time "only large companies could farm profitably. The growth of agribusiness had begun."[31] Would Mexicans have been better off if the irrigated southwestern deserts had been left barren?

Southwest agribusiness and the railroads were the first large-scale U.S. employers of Mexican workers, and these sectors did exploit the ready availability of cheap labor. More generally, U.S. corporations have exploited cheap foreign labor in many instances and have at times meddled in the internal affairs of other countries in order to maintain at least some degree of dominance. This has been especially evident in Latin America. But it does not necessarily follow that the growth of multinational corporations is based essentially on the imperialistic exploitation of cheap labor in developing countries. Cost accountants may relish cheap labor, but marketing departments seek out sources of large effective demand. Thus, most U.S. direct investment abroad goes to Canada and Europe. In the five years from 1973 to 1977, for example, the annual proportion of U.S. direct foreign investment accounted for by all of the developing countries ranged from 18 percent to only 23 percent.[32] Moreover, today pressures in favor of relaxed border controls come mainly from the activist Chicano movement—on the grounds that border controls are a form of ethnic discrimination and that Mexicans deserve special exemptions because the southwest once belonged to Mexico. "Agribusiness, railroads, and other corporate groups are not at the moment pressing hard for an open border or a contract-labor program. Mechanization, union protests (including the Huelga movement), the diminishing influence of the farm bloc in Congress, and access by giant agribusiness and certain industrial groups to cheap labor in Mexico itself are some factors that explain the current relaxing of pressure."[33]

Before examining more closely the issue of access to cheap labor in Mexico, attention should be given to another point frequently raised in the Marxist literature, namely, the distinction between legal and undocumented immigrants.

The most important separation is between legal and illegal migrants. It is the latter type that most perfectly fits the "job description" of the agricultural (or industrial) hand. The illegal entrant is available in large numbers whenever and wherever he is needed and is completely at the mercy of immigration authorities when he is not wanted. The illegal migrant does not require education, training, or sustenance (except for the portion of the year during which he works), the costs of his rearing are borne by his home country; and because of his legal status—the fact that he can be deported at a moment's notice—he is likely to be a "loyal," if not an especially hard-working, laborer.[34]

It is not necessary to embrace the full Marxist version of U.S.-Mexican relations to acknowledge that so long as U.S. business interests wanted undocumented migrants they were tacitly welcomed, but when they were no longer needed the U.S. government enforced the letter of the law. From the viewpoint of the United States, this system was superior to the type used in postwar Europe, where foreign workers were legally and actively recruited and given the same nonwage benefits as citizen workers. As discussed in chapter 6, Europeans failed to anticipate the permanent settlement of aliens, whom they had regarded as "guest workers."

However, the Marxist case is damaged by evidence from interviews with Mexican migrants which indicates that migrants usually prefer to seek out their own opportunities in the United States rather than to work under contract to specific employers, as under the *bracero* program. While migrants have done better economically as undocumented aliens than they did as *braceros*, they would prefer to enter the United States legally for specific periods of employment, which would reduce the dangers associated with undocumented immigration and, incidentally, encourage temporary stays.

But once in the United States, "what they seek is free market competition among U.S. employers seeking their services."[35]

The Urbanization of Northern Mexico

Northern Mexico has experienced very rapid urbanization in this century. In 1900, the population living in Mexican municipalities on the U.S. border was only about 36,000.[36] According to the 1970 census, the total population of Mexico's border states was nearly 8 million, with 2.33 million persons living in border municipalities. Juárez, Mexicali, and Tijuana accounted for about half of the 1970 border population; migrants made up 23 percent, 34 percent, and 47 percent of their respective populations.[37]

Urbanization on Mexico's northern border has been strongly conditioned by the proximity of the United States, and it has been both a cause and an effect of migration from the interior. The movement of undocumented migrants to the United States has been facilitated by large urban centers that serve as bases of operations. The border has also drawn many persons who live in Mexico but cross the border regularly to work. These commuters are *de facto* as much a part of the U.S. labor force as the Mexicans who reside and work in the United States. Commuters and other Mexican border residents also do much of their shopping on the U.S. side. U.S. residents in turn flock into the Mexican cities for tourism, entertainment, and bargain hunting. Indeed, on balance border transactions have traditionally been favorable to Mexico. All along the border, twin cities exist in a highly symbiotic relationship.

A recent study of internal migration in Mexico indicates that "While greater regional employment growth encourages in-migration and discourages out-migration, in-migration in turn hastens employment growth whereas out-migration depresses such growth, especially in the agricultural sector. Moreover, in-migration encourages greater rates of earnings growth."[38] Minimum wage rates in Mexico vary by state and by economic subregions within states. The subregions on the border have relatively high rates; Baja California has the highest in all Mexico,[39] as well as the highest median monthly earnings.[40] Even so, wage rates on the Mexican side of the border are considerably lower than those on the U.S. side, which in turn are low in relation to the United States as a whole. Thus, the growth of Mexico's border cities has been partly a result of opportunities to work across the border.

Mexican Commuters

Mexicans may gain entry to the United States by procuring a "green card," which was originally intended for permanent resident aliens. The legality of permitting green card holders to work in the United States even though they reside in Mexico has been upheld by the Supreme Court. Precise data are not available, but it has been estimated that there are some 50,000 green card commuters.[41]

Most undocumented Mexicans who work in the U.S. border area enter legally by using a border crossing card, which is a visa allowing any number of visits of up to seventy-two hours within a distance of twenty-five miles from the border—but not permitting employment. Even so, U.S. homes and businesses regularly hire thousands of "white card" holders to work as maids, salesclerks, gardeners, busboys, janitors, and day laborers. "The long lines of 'shoppers' entering the U.S. early Monday morning and returning Friday night and Saturday morning are mute evidence of this institutionalized abuse of the temporary visitor/shopping card. Some live-in maids return to Mexico only once or twice a year unless they are discovered or reported."[42] More than a million currently valid border crossing cards have been issued to Mexicans, and the backlog of applications runs into the hundreds of thousands. There is no consistent control on the return of white card holders to Mexico or on the temporary permits that are issued for visits beyond the border area. The border crossing card can be revoked if it is abused, but once in the United States the undocumented resident or worker frequently sends it to friends or relatives in Mexico for safekeeping. If apprehended, an undocumented alien may claim, under a pseudonym, that he or she crossed the border unseen, in which case the person is classified as an EWI (entered without inspection). Under the nonpenalty voluntary departure agreement the person is then deported to Mexico, and from there the white card can be used again to re-enter the United States.[43]

In addition to pushing for stricter measures against undocumented Mexican aliens, U.S. labor unions have led the fight against the employment of Mexican green card commuters. Union leaders argue that commuters depress wages and increase unemployment among U.S. citizens and that they make it difficult to organize and maintain unions. Mexican workers fear management reprisal against union membership, and when not on the job the commuters are hard to contact. For the most part, union influence is weak in border counties unless a unionized national industry or a substantial federal government construction project exists. Unionization of commuters has been most successful in San Diego because of a cooperative program between the San Diego Labor Council and the Mexican Confederation of Workers of Baja California. California also has a state minimum wage law. Most commuters work in Texas, which is more susceptible to commuter employment because of a right-to-work law and the absence of a state minimum wage statute.[44] In 1973, one-third of all green card commuters lived in Juárez and worked in El Paso. They represented 9 percent of El Paso's labor force and accounted for an estimated 20 percent of Juárez's employed work force.[45]

Proponents of the green card commuting system maintain that commuters attract industry to the border and hold jobs that U.S. citizens frequently will not take, and that it would greatly aggravate social problems on the U.S. side if commuters and their families were forced to move across the border. Moreover, commuters spend much of their earnings in the United States.

Gathering complete and accurate data on Mexican-U.S. border transactions has proven to be a nearly impossible task. So much activity goes on in the economically integrated border areas that measuring it is nearly as difficult as measuring the transactions among the boroughs of New York City. Nevertheless, there is some survey evidence concerning purchases made by Mexican residents on the U.S. side of the border. For example, workers in U.S.-operated plants in Agua Prieta, Sonora, spent 52 percent of their earnings in Douglas, Arizona, and other U.S. towns.[46] Fully 84 percent of Mexicali families did their routine shopping in the United States, a third of them on a daily basis.[47] Perhaps 40 percent of the income of residents of Juárez comes from employment in El Paso, but between 50 and 85 percent of this money is spent on the U.S. side.[48] Meanwhile, Mexican urban centers on the border have failed to develop as complete central places supplying goods and services to their own inhabitants or to those of their hinterlands.[49]

In addition to Mexicans who reside and work in the United

States and those who commute to work there, there is another category of Mexican workers that needs to be considered in the present context: persons employed in U.S. plants that locate just across the border to take advantage of relatively cheap Mexican labor. While these persons technically do not work in the United States, in reality they are dependent on U.S. employers and they participate in the transnational border economy in virtually the same way as green card commuters. In order to gain an adequate perspective on this phenomenon, it is first necessary to examine the broader issue of the nature and significance of manufacturing decentralization in the United States, and indeed in the world.

The New International Division of Labor

The data in table 5.1 indicate that manufacturing employment in the United States dropped by 2.8 percent between 1970 and 1977. However, the aggregate picture masks substantial differences both among and within regions. Essentially, manufacturing activity has been shifting from the northeast and north-central regions of the country to the south and west, and from large metropolitan areas to smaller cities and rural areas. Metropolitan areas in the combined

Table 5.1. Absolute and Percentage Change in U.S. Manufacturing Employment by Region[a] and Metropolitan-Nonmetropolitan Status,[b] 1970–1977

	Metropolitan		Nonmetropolitan		Total	
	Change (in thousands)	%	Change (in thousands)	%	Change (in thousands)	%
U.S.	−1055	− 7.1	487	9.4	−568	− 2.8
Northeast	−878	−17.8	− 48	− 5.3	−926	−15.9
North-central	−359	− 7.4	60	3.6	−299	− 4.6
South	85	2.9	377	16.6	462	8.8
West	96	4.6	100	30.2	196	8.1

SOURCE: Computed from Bureau of Labor Statistics and Employment Service data by Claude Haren, Economics, Statistics, and Cooperative Service, U.S. Department of Agriculture.
[a]The regions are those defined by the U.S. Bureau of the Census.
[b]Metropolitan status as of January 1, 1978.

northeast and north-central regions—roughly the traditional industrial heartland—lost 1,237,000 manufacturing jobs while the nonmetropolitan south was gaining 377,000, an increase of 16.6 percent. Manufacturing employment in the west rose by 30.2 percent, though the absolute increase of 100,000 jobs was much less than the corresponding southern increase. These trends are quite consistent with the "filtering down" theory of industrial location, which maintains that:

In national perspective, industries filter down through the system of cities, from places of greater to lesser industrial sophistication. Most often, the highest skills are needed in the difficult, early stage of mastering a new process, and skill requirements decline steadily as the production process is rationalized and routinized with experience. As the industry slides down the learning curve, the high wage rates of the more industrially sophisticated innovating areas become superfluous. The aging industry seeks out industrial backwaters where the cheaper labor is now up to the lesser demands of the simplified process.[50]

The concept of spatial-industrial filtering is closely related to the notion of a product life cycle, which may be regarded somewhat arbitrarily as having three phases: early, growth, and mature.[51] In the early phase, scientific and engineering skills are the critical human input. Because of the relatively short production runs associated with a changing technology, capital outlays are relatively low. Producers depend instead on external economies and subcontracting. In the growth phase, the capital-labor ratio is increased by the introduction of mass production techniques. Competition from other firms forces price cuts; some firms in the industry go out of business, while others may merge or vertically integrate their operations. Management skills are vital in this phase. Finally, in the mature phase there is little technological innovation; the product is manufactured in long, routine production runs. Cheap, low-skill labor becomes the key human input; but capital intensity remains relatively high because large amounts of specialized equipment are used. In order to remain competitive, corporations respond to changing input needs—corresponding to differing phases of the product cycle—by changing the geographic location of production. Thus,

The relative importance of various production factors in different phases of the product cycle (in rank order of importance)

Production Factors	Product Cycle Phase		
	early	growth	mature
Management	2	1	3
Scientific-Engineering Know-How	1	2	3
Unskilled Labor	3	2	1
External Economies	1	2	3
Capital	3	1	1

SOURCE: Rodney A. Erickson and Thomas R. Leinbach, "Characteristics of Branch Plants Attracted to Nonmetropolitan Areas," in Richard E. Lonsdale and H. L. Seyler (eds.), *Nonmetropolitan Industrialization* (New York: Halsted Press, 1979), p. 59.

corporations increasingly manufacture multiple products in multiple branch plants in multiple locations.

A study by Persky indicates that such capital-intensive industries as paper products and chemicals have played a major role in the growth of the southern economy. Moreover, his analysis of the textile industry suggests that here too southern "and particularly the South Atlantic plants have relatively high capital-labor ratios. On the other hand, southern wages in this industry are quite low. This observation is difficult to explain from any simple neoclassical position."[52] Persky indicates that the dualism between coexisting labor-intensive and capital-intensive sectors in the south is a reflection of the ability of new entrants to move to highly efficient technologies with limited possibilities for substituting labor for capital. Presumably firms in the old industrial heartland stick with older technologies from inertia or an unwillingness to make the sacrifices required by a large investment program. Persky concludes that dualism has contributed to the remarkable growth of manufacturing in the south, but he is unable "to establish the plausible grounds for this attractive outcome as opposed to the usual sins attributed to dualism in the less developed countries."[53]

It is significant that Persky attributes the growth of capital-intensive activities in the south to new entrants. In fact, a great deal of publicity has been given recently to studies that seem to demonstrate that the decentralization of manufacturing to the south (and west) has been a consequence of the birth of new firms or the expansion of existing firms; it is extremely rare for firms to relocate, especially over long distances.[54] These findings are based exclusively on Dun and Bradstreet data. Unfortunately, the relevant data records do not include the year of initial operation of branch plants. Without the start date it is impossible to know whether or not a branch was opened during any given time period. Since most branch plants were in operation at the beginning of the periods studied, all branch plants may—lacking other information—be assumed to be "old." But while this procedure results in less upward bias in measuring employment change, it clearly involves a downward bias in branch plant starts.[55] In fact, increasing empirical evidence reveals that branch plants are clearly the mechanism through which manufacturing decentralization is taking place.[56] Moreover, although Persky does not consider the product cycle and spatial filtering-down explanations, they are perfectly consistent with his findings: one expects to find high capital intensity and cheap labor associated in decentralized manufacturing.

Those branch plants closest to the main factory are not only smaller, but they typically are rather dependent, requiring constant managerial attention and often maintaining direct flows of materials with the main plant.

More distant branch plants are not only larger, but also are more self-contained in management capability and functionally independent from the main plant and corporate headquarters, manufacturing standardized products whose specifications and technology have reached a stage where they need little change.[57]

Similarly, evidence from France indicates that manufacturing decentralization primarily involves capital-intensive branch plants employing unskilled or low-skilled labor. Production processes are becoming more heterogeneous and specialized, but within individual plants the work performed by individuals is becoming more homogeneous. Manufacturing activities have greatly decentralized from the Paris region in recent years, in keeping with government policy and incentive measures. But a 1975 survey showed that of 788 decentralization operations in question, only 30 were influenced by government subsidies. Nonaided areas have attracted most of the plants, and workers in these plants nearly always come from "the privileged reservoir of unskilled labor: women, rural residents, immigrants, and young people."[58]

In the early 1970s, while speculating on where industrial decentralization might next spread in the United States, I suggested that:

> Yet another possibility—maybe the most likely—is that industrial filtering will spread to foreign countries rather than major lagging regions of the United States. In this event the United States would tend to become an international center of tertiary activities, with secondary activities being increasingly relegated to countries with low wages. Of course, whatever the economic rationality or feasibility, constraints of a political and military nature would no doubt eventually be placed on such a process.[59]

As shown previously, manufacturing decentralization within the United States has been continuing, largely in favor of the non-metropolitan south. But while manufacturing employment in the United States has been declining, an increasing number of persons employed abroad by U.S. companies are producing goods for sale in U.S. markets. In the past, Third World countries typically were regarded as markets for Western-produced goods as well as sources of raw materials for Western factories. Today, a new international division of labor is evolving. It is basically a major geographical extension of locational factors that have already been at work within the United States and other Western countries: the decomposition of complex production processes, better transportation technology, improved telecommunications systems, and cheap labor. But if U.S. corporations can profitably establish plants in such distant places as Hong Kong, South Korea, and Taiwan, why not locate in Mexico? And within Mexico, why not locate on our own doorstep, in the border cities? In fact, this process has been taking place with the blessing of both the Mexican and U.S. governments.

The *Maquiladora* Program

The major vehicle for manufacturing expansion in Mexico's borderlands has been the *maquiladora* (assembly plant) program, which was established by the Mexican government in 1965. This program takes advantage of U.S. tariff code provisions allowing foreign-based subsidiaries of U.S. firms to assemble products whose parts were originally made in the United States and then export the products to the United States—with duties being imposed only on the value added. The advantages for U.S. firms are the low cost of Mexican labor, the fact that duties essentially are only paid on labor inputs, and the proximity of Mexican border cities. Although wages in Mexico are not as low as in the Far East, the difference is often more than offset by lower transportation costs of shipping machinery and materials to foreign plants and of importing finished products. The advantages Mexico has expected to gain are greater employment, more foreign exchange, and an expanded industrial base for border cities.

Initially most assembly plants were small, utilizing converted old buildings and little capital. In the past decade there has been a steadily increasing trend in favor of greater capital intensity and the use of large new plants in modern industrial parks. Complete and accurate data on employment in *maquiladoras* have been difficult to obtain. Prior to the 1975 recession it was variously estimated to have reached 53,680,[60] 70,738,[61] or 80,000.[62] The recession and concomitant minimum wage increases in Mexico brought about the closure of some thirty plants, while many others cut back their employment. In all, an estimated 35,000 workers were laid off.[63] With general economic recovery and the devaluation of the peso in 1976, *maquiladora* employment rebounded rapidly; at present it is estimated to be over 110,000.[64] Moreover, the recession being experienced in the United States at this writing does not appear to be affecting *maquiladora* employment adversely.

Critics of the *maquiladora* program argue that it is just one more device to increase Mexico's dependence on the United States. As originally conceived, it was supposed to provide jobs for unemployed males, the former *braceros*, but in fact over four-fifths of the workers are women. Training programs are supposed to develop Mexico's human resources, but skill levels remain minimal because of the nature of fragmented assembly work. (The electronic equipment and textile sectors account for four-fifths of total *maquiladora* employment.) Critics also maintain that whatever the employment gains attributable to the program, it has stimulated so much migration from the interior of Mexico that it may actually have aggravated unemployment problems along the border. The spread effects of the *maquiladoras* within Mexico are minimal; they use U.S. equipment and their outputs are all delivered to the United States. Moreover, a high proportion of the incomes of *maquiladora* workers is spent across the border. In view of such considerations, the program has been described as the "institutionalization of uneven technological development between the United States and Mexico."[65] On the other hand, unions, which oppose the program on the ground that it takes jobs from U.S. workers, have exerted pressure on Congress to remove the tariff advantages enjoyed by U.S. corporations operating abroad.

On the positive side, recent data from a survey of *maquiladora* workers indicate that not more than 5 percent came to the border in search of *maquiladora* employment, though the number of such migrants may be increasing.[66] In any case, increases in *maquiladora* employment clearly reduce unemployment in Mexico as a whole. In addition, the multiplier effects of the outlays of *maquiladora* workers generate nonmanufacturing employment for other Mexican residents, whether they work in Mexico or commute across the border. The Mexican government would like to see more domestically owned and controlled manufacturing activity in the border cities, yet it nevertheless continues to promote the program, feeling that the gains outweigh the disadvantages. Recently the Mexican government has been attempting to encourage the establishment of *maquiladoras* in the interior, in order to lessen dependency on the United States. However, it is questionable whether U.S. firms can be induced to forego the perceived advantages of Mexican sites adjacent to the United States.

From the U.S. perspective, lower production costs in Mexico translate into lower product prices for U.S. consumers. Some of the products now assembled in *maquiladoras* would be dropped altogether if they had to be produced with higher-cost and sometimes less efficient U.S. labor.[67] Still other companies would—or so they claim—move their operations to other labor-surplus countries if the advantages of locating on the border were curtailed. In any case, the proximity of Mexico's border cities creates balance of payments and indirect employment advantages for the United States in comparison to locating in distant countries, because *maquiladoras* use U.S.

materials and machinery. As the manager of the Samsonite plant in Nogales, Mexico, put it, "If we were located in the Far East, there wouldn't be a plant in Tucson fabricating our components, nor would we be buying our materials from General Tire and other companies in the U.S."[68] Moreover, U.S. managerial personnel in the *maquiladoras* are able to reside in the United States.

Some critics maintain both their economic nationalism and their benevolence toward Hispanics by urging that the *maquiladora* program, like the presence of Mexican workers in the United States, is a threat to the United States in general and to Chicanos in particular. Curiously, few Chicano organizations have adopted this position. Perhaps this is because the U.S. borderlands area, with its relatively high proportion of Chicanos, has been a major beneficiary of the *maquiladora* program, whereas evidence is lacking that "runaway" U.S. plants would have come to the U.S. side of the border if they had not been lured to Mexico.

In addition to the employment and income generated on the U.S. side of the border by "twin plants" and other activities linked to the *maquiladoras*, workers in the latter spend as much as 75 percent of their income in U.S. border cities.[69] In 1972, the 5,800 *maquiladora* employees in Nogales, Mexico, earned approximately $8 million, of which at least 60 percent was spent in the United States, mostly in Nogales, Arizona. An input-output analysis indicated that for Nogales, Arizona, alone, the 1972 outlays of *maquiladora* workers generated 460 person-years of employment, or a 14 percent increase over the pre-program level.[70] A survey of *maquiladora* employees by an El Paso bank found that about half their earnings were spent in El Paso.[71]

The devaluation of the peso in 1976 had immediate negative effects on business in U.S. border cities. As would be expected, the greatest impacts were in communities whose retail trade is highly oriented toward Mexican clients. Merchants in Nogales, Eagle Pass, Laredo, Hidalgo, and Brownsville were especially hard hit, and local sales tax receipts suffered accordingly. In contrast, San Diego and Tucson on the whole were not greatly affected; both are located somewhat away from the border and both have relatively diversified economies. Other border cities experienced at least a moderate loss of sales to Mexicans.[72] Controlling for other factors, the unemployment rate in the Texas border area increased by 2 percentage points following devaluation.[73] At present, however, it appears that the long-run effects of devaluation were exaggerated by observers who predicted stagnation for much of the U.S. border economy. Evidence from Texas border cities suggests that the peso was overvalued during the 1973–1976 period. While this stimulated U.S. retail trade, it discouraged border tourism by U.S. residents. Sales growth in border cities has now returned to the levels existing prior to devaluation.[74] Moreover, devaluation also made the *maquiladora* program more attractive to U.S. firms.

Summary and Conclusions

Mexican labor has played a highly significant part in the economic development of the U.S. southwest. Unfortunately, American knowledge of this contribution has been obscured by lack of knowledge and, too frequently, by Anglo prejudice. During periods when U.S. labor markets have been tight, Mexican workers have been not only welcomed but also actively recruited. However, during recessions they have been perceived as a threat to unemployed American workers, and as such they have been directly or indirectly forced to return to Mexico. Undocumented migration has facilitated this process. Undocumented Mexican workers have long been functionally integrated into the economy of the U.S. borderlands. Their presence has been supported by social and cultural institutions and has received the tacit cooperation of legal authorities. Undocumented entrants have been available in large numbers whenever and wherever needed but at the mercy of immigration authorities when they have not been wanted.

In 1848, when the United States took over half of Mexico's territory, there were few Mexicans in the conquered lands. The present-day Mexican American population is overwhelmingly composed of persons who voluntarily moved to the United States or who are the recent descendents of voluntary immigrants. Large-scale migration from Mexico is largely a twentieth-century phenomenon, though the movement was clearly under way in the late nineteenth century. Despite low wages and discrimination, Mexicans have come to the United States largely because economic opportunities have been better than in Mexico, though at times civil unrest in Mexico has been a "push" factor.

Marxist critics of American uses of Mexican labor have performed a service by calling attention to many of its less than ideal features. Nevertheless, they beg the question of whether Mexicans who supplied their labor to the building of the southwestern economy would have been better off in Mexico. The people in question did not seem to think so. Moreover, little is gained by blaming the United States for growing economically at a more rapid rate than Mexico. Even from a Mexican perspective, it would appear preferable to have economic opportunities being generated in proximity to Mexico than to have the U.S. borderlands economy be a mere extension of the living conditions of the mass of workers in Mexico in the past.

Demand for Mexican labor in the southwest was greatly increased by the coming of the railroads and by the irrigation of vast tracts of land. Moreover, new railroad lines through northern Mexico facilitated the movement of Mexicans from interior population centers, and until well into the 1920s the border was virtually open in terms of controls. The Great Depression resulted in mass deportations of Mexicans from the southwest, but labor shortages during the Second World War brought a reversal of policy. A contract labor agreement, the *bracero* program, brought millions of Mexican workers to the United States between 1942 and 1964, primarily for employment in agriculture. During this period the number of undocumented immigrants from Mexico may have surpassed the number of *braceros*. In 1954 alone, over 1 million undocumented aliens were deported to Mexico. From the mid-1950s to the mid-1960s, annual deportations of Mexicans varied between 40,000 and 50,000, but since then there has been a steady increase. In 1977, with unemployment at a relatively high level in the United States, 921,000 Mexicans were apprehended, and the current annual rate of apprehensions is over 1 million.

The postwar northward surge of Mexicans has been accompanied by the rapid growth of Mexico's border cities, which provide homes for persons who commute to work across the border and which serve as staging areas for migration to the United States. In keeping with the new international division of labor, many U.S. corporations have located assembly plants just across the border in Mexico to take advantage of cheap Mexican labor. This practice is encouraged by Mexico as well as by favorable U.S. tariff provisions. The persons who work in these plants technically do not work in the United States, but they are dependent on U.S. employers, the goods they produce are all sold in the United States, and they participate in the transnational border economy in virtually the same way as Mexican commuters. In both cases, a significant proportion of the earnings derived from U.S. employers is spent on the U.S. side of the border.

The fact that minimum wage rates and incomes in Mexico's border cities are high in relation to the rest of the country will continue to encourage migration from the interior of Mexico. The fact that they are low in relation to the United States will continue to encourage commuting and migration—both legal and undocumented—to the United States. In evaluating these phenomena it should be kept in mind that:

> A border is not only a line which separates, it is also a line which unites. An implication of this is that the United States–Mexican border came first and then came the population. The population was not already there in the border cities from Brownsville to Tijuana only to be afflicted later with the problems of a frontier.[75]

Both Americans and Mexicans have apparently gained something by moving to the border area, where both sides live together in a symbiotic relationship not always appreciated or even understood in the halls of government in Mexico City or Washington.

6. Undocumented Mexican Immigration: What Are the Issues? What Are the Alternatives?

Although Mexican workers have long been functionally integrated into the economy of the southwest borderlands, the extent to which their presence is reflected in employment, earnings, and other official data cannot be determined because of the presence in the United States of a large and increasing number of undocumented Mexican workers. Some undocumented Mexicans are recorded in official data, but many are not. For example, undocumented Mexicans frequently have income taxes and Social Security contributions deducted from their pay, but the deducted amounts are not always forwarded to the government; and even if employers are scrupulously honest in this regard, the Social Security numbers used by undocumented Mexicans may be "borrowed" from other workers.[1]

Although the number of undocumented Mexicans residing in the United States is not known, estimates of 5 million or more probably are exaggerated.[2] Nevertheless, in 1976 alone 757,000 deportable Mexican aliens were apprehended in the United States, a figure exceeding that for the entire decade of the 1960s. In 1977, the number was 921,000, or 88 percent of all deportable alien apprehensions.[3] These data should be interpreted with caution. Some undocumented Mexicans were apprehended more than once in any given year; and while some may settle permanently in the United States, many others move between Mexico and the United States on a cyclical basis. On balance, however, the evidence strongly suggests that the stock of undocumented Mexicans residing in the United States has been increasing at a rapid rate in recent years.

Numerous journalists, scholars, and highly placed public officials have argued that this influx is likely to bring about a national crisis, if indeed it has not already done so.[4] For example, Tad Szulc writes that:

> the problem of illegal Mexican immigration is wholly beyond control—and federal authorities in Washington are painfully

aware of it. The best that can be done is to stabilize the rate of migration around the three million level, perhaps to reduce it somewhat, but the problem simply cannot be solved until such time as the Mexican economy is capable of providing for the country's citizens. Given the high birth rate in Mexico and the latest economic slump—ironically we export our recession and inflation to Mexico, receiving, in turn, the Mexican human exportation that swells our own unemployment rolls— there is no likelihood that the wave of Mexican labor invasions can be halted in this century.[5]

A historical review of undocumented Mexican immigration concludes that:

The present momentum, including growing discontent in Mexico, therefore suggests that the nation has entered a new era not of strict alien control but of ombudsmanship, amnesty proposals, and perennial socioeconomic accommodations, agency by agency, community by community, and politician by politician, to spring-fed Latino groups whose political muscle in the transitional social order is "just starting to be felt."[6]

Vernon M. Briggs, Jr., an economist who is an authority on Mexican immigration, similarly concludes that "It would be self-deception to believe that this situation can continue to mount at the current growth rate without eventual dire consequence to all parties concerned."[7]

Because undocumented Mexican immigration has aroused so much controversy, the issues involved require careful consideration. However, before attempting to evaluate the consequences of this complex phenomenon it is first necessary to inquire into the reasons behind it.

Reasons for Undocumented Mexican Immigration

Nowhere else do two nations with such disparate levels of economic welfare share a common border. Large-scale Mexican immigration to the United States can be attributed to the inability of the Mexican economy to provide jobs for a large proportion of its rapidly expanding labor force and to the desire of relatively poor Mexicans to better their lot by seeking out employment opportunities north of the border. In most discussions of undocumented Mexicans, these or similar propositions are advanced to "explain" the problem; they are not incorrect, but taken at face value they tend to mask more complicated realities. For example, marked economic disparities between Mexico and the United States existed prior to mass Mexican immigration. Why didn't large numbers of Mexicans move to the United States earlier? And in view of the contemporary situation, why don't even more Mexicans move to the United States? The first question was implicitly dealt with in chapter 5. Until the present century, population centers of Mexico and the United States were separated by vast wastelands that effectively inhibited communication between the two countries. The borderlands were very thinly populated until the coming of the railroads, which, on an east-west basis, linked the U.S. side to the rest of the nation and, on a north-south basis, linked the Mexican heartland to the border. Poverty and revolutionary upheaval provided push forces, but the actual employment of undocumented Mexicans has in large degree been determined by cyclically changing demand-pull circumstances in the United States. In more recent times, the *bracero* program brought large numbers of Mexicans into contact with U.S. labor markets—both formal and informal. "For many rural Mexican males, the Bracero Program was an eye opener; they learned about American jobs and American wages; many responded to their U.S. employers' interest in bypassing the federally regulated program during its existence; and many kept travelling north after the program ended, despite the fact those trips were illegal."[8]

If the termination of the *bracero* program provided an impetus to undocumented migration, it should be emphasized that the workers in question have not been the product of a stagnant Mexican economy; rather, Mexico has been experiencing a rapid industrial revolution. Well before the confirmation of massive oil reserves, technological progress was clearly in evidence in Mexico's factories and fields.[9] This dynamism was reflected in the fact that, in 1977, fully half of all commercial bank loans to developing countries were received by Mexico and Brazil.[10] Unfortunately, the "green revolution," rural mechanization, and the breakdown of the feudal patron-peon system have dislocated large numbers of uneducated and unskilled peasants who cannot yet be absorbed by the industrial sector. These persons have poured into Mexico City and northern border cities in search of work—any work—even if it does not necessarily provide higher income than they had been receiving. Moreover, general social and economic improvements in Mexico have created a revolution of expectations. Many potential emigrants live in urban areas and possess skills—often acquired in subsidiaries of U.S. companies—for which the economic rewards are greater in the United States than in Mexico. Thus, even if poverty were to be completely eliminated in Mexico, the desire for economic improvement would still create pressure for migration to the United States.

Common attributes of undocumented Mexicans—low educational attainment, lack of knowledge of English and of the social system of the United States, and vulnerability inherent in illegal alien status—mean that they typically must rely on the assistance of relatives and friends, who often come from the same area of Mexico.[11] While some undocumented Mexicans migrate directly from the interior of Mexico to the interior of the United States,[12] others reach their destinations after a series of moves in which the borderlands serve as a staging area. The latter process has five phases,[13] although given individuals do not necessarily pass through each one. The first phase entails movement from the interior of Mexico to northern border cities. The second involves employment (legal or illegal) on the U.S. side of the border but continuing residence on the Mexican side. The third is residential relocation to the U.S. borderlands. Seasonal migration—which is especially important in South Texas and the Lower Rio Grande Valley—to the north constitutes the fourth phase. The final phase consists of outmigration from the border area to other places in the United States.

It should be pointed out that the migration process just outlined implies a "linear" mobility path, but in reality there is often a high degree of circularity involved in the migration histories of undocumented Mexicans—that is, many of these persons periodically move back and forth between the United States and Mexico. Moreover, return moves to Mexico do not necessarily imply failure in the United States. Michael Piore argues that "It is absolutely essential to dispel the notion that seems to emerge in naive versions of this idea of settlement as *success* that the essential aspect of *success* is *income*. As was stressed earlier, migrants tend to be target earners, and *the effect of rising incomes, all other things being equal, is to increase the rate at which they return home.*"[14] Piore's position suggests that the view of the settlement process as either success or failure probably exaggerates the degree to which it is subject to control simply by manipulating economic variables at one or the other end of the migration stream. What Piore does not explain is why a temporary migration stream becomes permanent; yet he recognizes that "Though nobody may intend to stay, a nucleus of more or less permanent migrants seems inevitably to grow up. Although the industrial society may find this permanent settlement undesirable, it appears unable to prevent it."[15]

What makes the situation of undocumented Mexicans different from most other international migrants is the geographic contiguity of the United States and Mexico, and the close symbiotic relationship that exists between Mexicans and Mexican Americans, a relationship that also blurs distinctions between legal and illegal Mexican immigrants. As Charles Hirschman points out:

> it is clear that legal and illegal immigration cannot meaningfully be separated as pertaining to different populations. It appears that prior residence in the United States is widespread among legal Mexican immigrants and the process of immigration is not a single step phenomenon. The modal process seems to be circular flow in which knowledge, experience, and family ties are acquired in the United States which may enable some immigrants to legitimize their status in the United States. While this finding may not be surprising to many knowledgeable observers, it does represent an atypical pattern of international migration.[16]

Nowhere is institutional support for undocumented Mexicans stronger than in the borderlands, where friends and relatives assist them in obtaining and retaining jobs, teach them U.S. practices, and eventually aid them in legitimizing their presence in the United States.[17] In San Antonio, undocumented Mexicans have been an accepted part of the work force for many years. They readily blend into the Mexican American population, whose ancestors often originally came to the city as undocumented workers. Data obtained by Gilbert Cardenas from interviews with undocumented Mexicans in San Antonio indicate that most came from rural areas of northeastern and north-central Mexico, as well as from remote villages in Jalisco and Michoacán. Friends or relatives assisted them to cross the border, but then the migrants usually walked to San Antonio—a journey of up to five days. Only six percent of the interviewees had used paid smugglers; the smuggling business is probably more common among undocumented Mexicans seeking employment in northern cities.[18] In relation to the situation in the borderlands, un-documented Mexicans have had little institutional support in cities such as Chicago or Detroit,[19] but there is evidence that this is rapidly changing.[20]

Within the southwest borderlands there also is variability in the degree of implicit support for undocumented Mexicans. Such support tends to be greater in areas where Hispanics account for a relatively high proportion of the local population and where people perceive that the two sides of the border are mutually interdependent. Reactions to the "Tortilla Curtain" incident are instructive in this regard. In response to appeals from the Border Patrol, Congress authorized the reconstruction of fences in the El Paso–Ciudad Juárez and San Diego–Tijuana border areas. In 1978, publicity given to this project provoked strong reactions at the local, state, and national levels in both Mexico and the United States. In the spring of 1979, a group of militant Mexicans blockaded the Cordova Bridge between El Paso and Ciudad Juárez; a young Mexican girl was accidentally killed, and threats of greater violence mounted on both sides. The cooperation of local border mayors helped to ease the potentially explosive situation. Moreover, U.S. federal government officials agreed to make modifications in the fence, clearing the new design with Mexican officials. This display of sensitivity to Mexican sentiments was sufficient to restore calm to the border. A survey of leading citizens in Ciudad Juárez indicated that while 86 percent were opposed to the fence, none denied that the United States had the right to build the barrier. A similar survey of El Paso leaders showed that 70 percent were opposed to the fence. In contrast, several opinion polls in San Diego found that two-thirds of the population were in favor of the barrier.[21] For San Diego, which has a relatively small hispanic population and is less dependent on trade from Mexicans, "such a physical barrier, financed from funds other than local taxes, represents a greater security from the presence of illegal Mexican aliens, who are perceived as responsible for the deteriorating economic conditions in the U.S. and the rising tax rates."[22] Moreover, "San Diego residents have been erroneously convinced that undocumented Mexican workers in their midst are responsible for high welfare costs, an assertion rejected by repeated scientifically conducted studies. Thus, they do not feel a mutual dependency between their own economy and the Mexican laborers from across the border."[23] They are not alone. As pointed out at the beginning of this chapter, the notion that undocumented Mexicans represent a threat to the

United States is widespread. Some critics also maintain that the present uncontrolled Mexican immigration system is harmful to Mexico and to the migrants themselves.

The Case against Undocumented Mexican Workers

The most frequently encountered argument against undocumented Mexican immigration is its alleged tendency to depress wages and increase unemployment. In this view, already disadvantaged U.S. citizens are forced to work at low wage levels acceptable to the undocumented Mexicans or to become unemployed and possibly go on public welfare. Mexican Americans in the southwest have been most harmed, but other racial and ethnic groups increasingly are affected as undocumented Mexicans fan out to more distant cities.

Initially, undocumented Mexicans may not have represented any great burden on tax-supported social services because they did not bring their families and they tended to return to Mexico during slack employment periods. But to the extent that they bring their families or marry U.S. citizens and settle in the United States, they could be a costly drain on community services.

Undocumented migration also creates problems for the migrants. Many work-hungry Mexicans are exploited by a complex underground industry run by so-called coyotes or *polleros* (chicken handlers), who recruit customers and promise to manage border crossings, to provide hiding places across the border, and even to arrange for transportation to interior U.S. cities. The recent going rate for this package of services was around $300;[24] even if the smugglers make good on their promises, this is a very considerable sum for poor people to pay. In addition, the living conditions of undocumented Mexicans frequently are deplorable, and sometimes they are exploited by employers cognizant of their vulnerability to detection.

Mexico, too, suffers in the process. Family life is disrupted, relatively ambitious workers are lost, and hundreds of thousands of Mexican citizens are at the mercy of decisions made in a foreign land. When economic activity declines in the United States, remittances fall off and unemployed workers return home. The immigration process also raises expectations in Mexico that cannot be met by public policy makers there; thus instead of being a safety valve, it may be a generator of crisis.

Critics of the status quo usually favor concerted efforts to return undocumented workers to Mexico and to erect effective barriers against future undocumented migration. They believe the hiring of undocumented workers by U.S. employers should be made a criminal act. The critics are not anti-Mexican, but feel that such measures would benefit both the United States and Mexico. Nor are their proposals entirely negative. They maintain that U.S. financial and technical aid—channeled through international organizations— should be made available to Mexico to implement regional development programs and to promote labor-intensive processing activities in rural areas. In addition, they favor expanding free trade with Mexico because the impact of increasing imports could be widely spread throughout the American economy, in contrast to the impact of undocumented immigration that particularly harms already disadvantaged groups.

Positive Aspects of the Status Quo

Because there is widespread recognition of at least some potential merit in the arguments just presented, it is difficult to find explicit advocacy for the status quo. However, eclectic evidence indicates that undocumented immigration from Mexico may well have positive consequences for all parties concerned.

The unqualified contention that undocumented Mexicans displace U.S. citizen workers implies that one person's gain is another person's loss. This notion—known as the "lump-of-labor fallacy"— suggests that there is only a fixed total amount of work that can be performed in our society. In fact, the size of the nation's economic pie depends on the ways in which all productive factors—labor, capital, land, and entrepreneurship—interact. The addition of undocumented Mexicans to the existing land and capital assets produces a larger social pie, and the migrants gain a share of the incremental product simply because they have earned it.

Undocumented Mexicans may in effect create their own employment, or jobs may be created for them because they have special skills or because they are willing to perform tasks shunned by U.S. workers.[25] The fact that undocumented Mexicans have little difficulty in finding jobs in the United States suggests that they do not displace U.S. citizens to any large degree.[26] Allan King's numerical estimates of the national unemployment effects of undocumented Mexican immigration indicate that they are likely to be minimal.

According to his analysis, the presence of 7.5 million undocumented workers would cause less than 1 percentage point of the total U.S. unemployment rate.[27] Mexican workers, who account for an estimated 60 percent of the total number of undocumented workers in the United States, would thus cause only about one-half of 1 percentage point of the total U.S. unemployment rate in this hypothetical situation. In fact, though, adverse unemployment effects are not uniformly spread among the entire U.S. population. Workers in the secondary labor market[28] and workers in regions where undocumented Mexicans tend to concentrate bear the brunt of the unemployment effects. On both counts this implies that Mexican Americans in the borderlands are the principal victims of undocumented migration. Yet Mexican American organizations have tended to oppose legislation that would impose fines on employers of undocumented workers, fearing that such legislation would result in the harassment of all Hispanics.[29] César Chávez's United Farm Workers is a notable exception, but this organization has at varying times both favored and opposed strict measures to curtail undocumented immigration. This ambivalence appears to reflect not so much a fear of Mexican workers *per se* as opposition to the deliberate use of undocumented workers by U.S. employers in their efforts to break strikes by Mexican American workers. In any case, it might be argued that Mexican Americans who condone undocumented immigration are not acting in their own interest, perhaps because they do not recognize the economic trade-offs involved. But those who hold this view bear the burden of proof. Moreover, because of the historical community of interests that has linked Mexicans and Mexican Americans, the latter may be willing to trade off some economic gains for what they perceive to be noneconomic benefits to themselves. In any case, the problem of worker displacement should diminish in the near future. Because of the exceptionally low U.S. birthrate in recent years, there will be fewer Americans available to take low-skill, entry-level jobs. The number of teenagers in the work force is already leveling off and will begin to decline in the early 1980s. By 1985, the annual growth rate in the work force will be about 1.5 million compared to the current rate of 2.5 million.[30]

If the main impact of undocumented migration is to depress wages rather than to cause outright unemployment, then wages along the U.S.-Mexican border should particularly reflect this phenomenon. Although numerous scholars have asserted the notion of depressed border-region wages, their findings have been largely based on casual observation and deductive inference. However, a recent study did statistically estimate the magnitude of the alleged wage and income differentials between the Texas border area and Houston. After controlling for variations in the cost of living between regions, Smith and Newman found that annual real incomes in the border area are $684 less than in Houston, approximately an 8 percent differential. Thus, if migration from Mexico is having a negative impact on border-area wages, the impact is not as severe as many have contended. "In fact, this differential is of the order of magnitude that it could represent the implicit premium that individuals along the border are willing to pay for nonpecuniary advantages such as remaining close to their cultural heritage."[31]

If undocumented Mexican migration to the United States were to cease, one result might be higher prices for goods and services now produced by alien workers; and higher labor costs could cause some employment opportunities to disappear altogether if mechanization became economically feasible. The elimination of jobs now filled by aliens could also result in a loss of complementary jobs for U.S. citizens. The extent to which these difficulties would arise cannot be accurately assessed without detailed studies of specific industries, firms, and occupations, and little work has been done in these areas.

The charge that undocumented Mexicans freeload on community services has never been documented; indeed all the evidence is quite to the contrary. They must pay state and local taxes, and most have income and Social Security taxes deducted from their earnings. There are other deductions as well for unemployment and disability insurance and private pension plans, even though few undocumented Mexicans will ever receive the corresponding benefits. Field research studies generally agree that undocumented Mexicans make very little use of social services in the United States.[32] In San Diego, for example, the social services consumed by undocumented Mexicans recently amounted to $2 million per year; in contrast, these persons contributed nearly $50 million annually to the support of local services.[33]

The fear that undocumented Mexicans will become a burden as they settle permanently in the United States so far has little justification simply because the vast majority have not wanted to live there permanently and in fact have returned to Mexico within a year of leaving.[34] For example, on the basis of a three-year study in Mexican communities from which undocumented migration is common, Cornelius concludes that while some migrants manage to take up permanent residence in the United States, "they are outnumbered—probably by a margin of at least 10 to 1—by illegals who prefer to maintain a pattern of seasonal or 'shuttle' migration. Nearly three-quarters of the illegals . . . resumed their normal occupation in their home community upon returning from their most recent trip to the United States."[35]

It is possible that studies based on traditional patterns of migration from rural areas of Mexico may underestimate the degree of permanent Mexican stays in the United States, because migrants from urban areas in Mexico to larger U.S. cities may be more prone to remain. Organized smuggling, which involves considerable expense to the migrant, may also encourage more permanent residence in the United States. Moreover, there is some evidence that the longer an undocumented Mexican stays in the United States, the less likely the chance of apprehension. In San Antonio, for example, only 4 percent of the undocumented Mexicans apprehended by the immigration authorities in 1975 had been in the area for more than four years. But 36 percent of the undocumented Mexicans interviewed by Cardenas in the same year had been in San Antonio for over four years.[36] To complicate matters further, long-term residence in the United States is not always equivalent to permanent residence. Mines, for example, found that undocumented Mexicans who spent most of their time in the United States for up to ten or twelve years typically returned to Mexico to stay when they reached middle age.[37] Although the whole issue of the permanency of undocumented Mexican immigration requires considerable further study, it is nonetheless clear that alarmist reactions usually fail to take account of the fact that much of this migration is temporary. On the other hand, suggestions to give legal immigrant status to longer-term undocumented Mexican residents could encourage seasonal or short-term migrants to become permanent residents on the basis of improper documentation. Thus, "by reflecting a false view of the migration process" this approach "could have the ironic effect of establishing a larger and more permanent illegal alien population than the United States presently contains."[38]

The contention that Mexican migrants are themselves victims of the present system of undocumented immigration focuses on cases of exploitation in the United States but neglects to point out that the migrants are escaping longer hours of work, lower wages, and worse working conditions in Mexico. Moreover, the migrants tend to prefer seeking their own opportunities in the United States rather than working under contract to specific employers, as was the case under the *bracero* program. They feel that if they are free to switch employers they experience less exploitation. Whatever the abuses perpetrated by smugglers and employers, on balance undocumented migration represents a lottery with a strong probability of gain for the migrant.[39]

Although undocumented Mexicans are potentially an easily exploited group, a number of studies suggest that if there is discrimination in wages against them—that is, the payment of lower wages to undocumented workers than to legal workers with the same productivity characteristics—it is not common.[40] Piore points out that the market for undocumented workers largely respects certain standards, which serve to limit not only exploitation but also the size of the secondary labor market. What is involved here is "a network of legislative restrictions imposing minimal health and safety standards and mandating a minimum wage. By and large, that market also respects a series of other legal standards involving income, social security, and unemployment taxation. It is somewhat less effectively controlled by union organization, but it is not totally beyond that control either."[41]

It is common practice for labor union officials to tip off the Immigration and Naturalization Service (INS) concerning the presence of undocumented Mexicans who compete with U.S. union members. For example, in Austin, Texas, hiring of undocumented Mexicans for construction work is a common practice. The aliens are paid between $3 and $4 an hour, whereas union carpenters are paid $10.90 an hour. In August 1979, a group of undocumented Mexicans was arrested at a construction site after complaints were made to the immigration authorities by the business representative of the carpenters' union, who nonetheless conceded that "I'll hand it to them. They work harder than we do."[42] On the other hand, there has been a growing movement to unionize undocumented aliens in view of the fact that sending them all home is not a practical possibility. The United Farm Workers union has long ignored immigration status in its organization efforts, and recently some industrial unions in the borderlands and in some large urban centers elsewhere have been involved in similar efforts. The clothing, food and services, and light manufacturing sectors have been particularly affected, as union leaders attempt to prevent the undercutting of wage-contract levels by undocumented aliens. It has been alleged that no matter how many undocumented aliens the unions recruit, whichever side loses in collective bargaining disputes involving them calls in the INS. Yet undocumented aliens appear to be willing to join unions because the higher wages seem worth the risk of exposure. Moreover, in 1978 a U.S. appeals court decided that undocumented aliens are protected by U.S. labor laws. The court held that just as "no federal immigration statute prohibits an employer from hiring an illegal alien, it is also true that no immigration statute prohibits an illegal alien from working and voting" in a National Labor Relations Board election.[43]

The Mexican government has in practice maintained an essentially *laissez-faire* position with respect to undocumented migration, but this by no means implies disinterest. Mexicans particularly dislike references to "illegal" Mexican workers because it is not illegal to employ undocumented Mexican nationals in the United States. And in their view, the present system is primarily responsive to the needs of U.S. employers. They also recognize that undocumented migration has been given, at the convenience of the United States, broad tacit institutional support. Yet another Mexican concern involves the civil rights of undocumented workers in the United States and the exclusion of Mexicans from services that they help to finance.

Despite these difficulties, Mexico nonetheless reaps certain advantages. If this were not the case, the Mexican government would no doubt be striving to curtail undocumented migration. The most obvious benefit is that unemployed Mexicans obtain jobs in the United States. Undocumented workers also are a major source of foreign exchange to aid Mexico's balance of payments problems. Periodic remittances and savings brought back by returning migrants have been estimated to be over $3 billion per year, even though roughly two-thirds of the earnings of undocumented Mexicans remain in the United States.[44] Moreover, the shuttle migration of Mexican workers has accelerated the adoption of U.S. values in Mexico.[45] One may question whether this has been good or bad on a cultural level, but it has been conducive to economic modernization, particularly in rural areas that had been characterized by traditional, nonmechanized agricultural techniques.[46] In many instances, changing values have led to a devaluation of occupations involving traditional patterns of subordination and authority. Labor shortages may appear in the affected occupations even though other employment opportunities are lacking. But the effect is not serious if the migration also generates new activities to replace the traditional economic structure. For example, in a town in Jalisco an extensive textile industry has grown up from nothing on the basis of immigrant remittances. The local industry, which began when one returning migrant invested his savings in a single piece of machinery, competes successfully on a national scale with large mechanized factories in Mexico City and Monterrey. The major function of migration in this process was the provision of scarce capital rather than the acquisition of specific skills in the United States. The migrants came almost exclusively from among the class of peasants that does not have access to official rural credit institutions; their original motive for migration was to accumulate enough resources to purchase land. Nevertheless, their broad exposure to industrial processes and organization contributed to the success of industrial development. The new entrepreneurs have a sophisticated approach to production layout, methods of wage payment, and worker motivation and control that can be traced to their experiences as industrial workers in the United States.[47] Imported industrial techniques have also been accompanied by U.S. models of consumption. This in turn has led to extensive smuggling of U.S. durable goods, which are regarded as superior in quality to Mexican-made products.[48] Although aspirations and expectations may frequently exceed the possibilities for fulfilling them, the changing tastes and increasing incomes associated with international migration should create wider markets for better-quality goods produced in Mexico.

In sum, then, while the present system of undocumented migration has been widely condemned as being harmful to the United States, to Mexico, and to the migrants themselves, the firm empirical evidence available suggests that this is not the case. The informal mechanism currently operating has many shortcomings, but it is not clear that there are better alternatives.

The Guest Worker Alternative: Evidence from European Experience and Its Relevance to North America

The introduction of a formal "guest worker" program is increasingly discussed as an alternative to the present informal system of undocumented Mexican immigration. Among the reasons advanced for adopting this approach are recognition of the practical impossibility of keeping Mexican workers out of the United States, a perception that the United States has or soon will have a shortage of relatively unskilled labor, and a belief that a formally regulated immigration program would promote greater U.S.-Mexican political stability. Reubens, among others, suggests that a binational agreement for the temporary importation of Mexican workers would draw upon European guest worker experience.

This approach would serve to alleviate labor shortages in fields which at present do not attract enough American workers, and do attract illegal aliens; at the same time this limited-stay approach avoids committing this country to a permanent second-class labor force, and allows for an eventual upgrading of these jobs so as to attract Americans. This approach would also reduce the immediate impact on Mexico of closing off the illegal immigration. In exchange for an expanded program of legal temporary admissions, with safeguards for human rights, the Mexican government might be asked to cooperate in stronger controls over the illegal movements on both sides of the border.[49]

This section critically examines the relevant European experience, and suggests that the evidence does not support the notion that a guest worker program would be the best response to the problem of undocumented Mexican immigration.

Large-scale migration of foreign workers to northern Europe began in the early 1960s.[50] Having absorbed refugees from Eastern Europe and their own redundant farm labor, the northern countries felt that further industrial expansion was limited by labor-force bottlenecks.[51] Industry actively recruited "guest workers" from Italy and then went outside the Common Market to Spain, Portugal, Greece, and Yugoslavia; eventually even workers from Asia Minor and North Africa came into the picture. It should be emphasized, however, that international worker migration in Europe was not simply the result of formal programs. Guest worker schemes were largely reactions to situations that had come about informally, and sometimes illegally. In other words, many foreign workers were already present in northern Europe prior to the implementation of formal guest worker policies, and "guests" who were not specifically invited continued to arrive after implementation. Only about half of the guest workers in West Germany were recruited through bilateral agreements.

The foreign workers were valued as a low-cost, mobile, and highly elastic economic input. The workers themselves benefited from considerably higher wage rates than they could have hoped to earn at home as well as from social and welfare guarantees.[52] The sending countries could export their unemployment, and earnings remitted to relatives or brought back home provided welcome foreign exchange. In addition, it was expected that workers would acquire valuable industrial skills that they could apply at home later.

Estimates of the number of foreign workers legally employed in northern Europe in 1973 lie within the 7 to 8 million range.[53] West Germany and France recruited about two-thirds of all guest workers, but guest workers had their greatest labor market impact in Switzerland; in 1970 foreigners accounted for approximately one-third of the Swiss labor force.[54] In 1973 the oil crisis and the recession that ensued brought about an abrupt change in European attitudes and policies. Recruiting bans and other restrictions were placed on foreign workers;[55] West Germany and other countries even offered special inducements to encourage foreign workers to go home.[56] Suddenly a system that seemed to be mutually advantageous to all concerned became the object of numerous criticisms.

In the 1960s it was assumed that foreign workers would come without families, stay a few years, and then return home to be replaced by other foreign workers. Furthermore, the common belief was that "they would put no strain on social or health services. No school problem would arise, nor would there be much liability for unemployment compensation. The foreign workers would pay taxes and make social-security contributions, without much chance of claiming commensurate benefits."[57] The scenario did not work out this way. The arrival of families put unexpected pressure on housing, schools, and hospitals. The once welcome foreign workers increasingly became regarded as a source of unforeseen industrial costs, a heavy drain on public services, and a seemingly permanent underclass.[58] The advantages of using low-cost labor also came into question; businesspeople wondered whether accepting lower-productivity workers had not led them to neglect vital capital investments.

It also seemed less clear that the labor-exporting countries were benefiting to the degree expected. In particular, the technology transfer argument looked less than convincing. The industrial countries were attracting the exporting countries' more-skilled workers in the first place; one-third to one-half of the guest workers had some sort of skill before they left home. If the foreign workers returned to their home countries, they did little to promote agricultural modernization because they no longer wanted to go back to the villages. Nor did foreign workers aim at acquiring industrial skills for use at home; if they intended to return home, their objective typically was to accumulate enough savings to buy a house and a small business such as a shop or taxi service. Moreover, those few foreign workers who managed to advance to skilled or supervisory positions abroad showed an increasing tendency to stay on in the host countries. Transferred earnings often seemed to be the only benefit gained by the labor-exporting countries, but even these diminished as foreign workers were joined abroad by their families.[59] Thus, by the middle 1970s, Greece, Yugoslavia, and some North African countries were considering measures to discourage emigration.

Recently the international migration system has become even more complex; countries such as Italy, Portugal, Spain, and Greece, which have traditionally exported labor, have become labor-importing countries. The departure of Portuguese workers for France has left vacancies to be filled by Cape Verdians; North African workers are found in increasing numbers in Italy and Spain; and an estimated 35,000 black and Arab workers are employed in Greece.[60] Relatively high unemployment and the return of workers from northern Europe have led to efforts to expel workers belonging to this latest migration wave.

In recent years the number of foreign migrants (workers and family members) in northern Europe has stabilized at around 12 million persons. This situation is not likely to change significantly as long as general economic conditions remain relatively stagnant. Thus, what appears to have evolved in Western Europe and neighboring non-Communist areas is an extended labor market whose dynamics are largely determined by market conditions in northern Europe. However, whereas the supply of foreign workers is highly elastic during boom times, it is downwardly inelastic during recessions; that is, the supply of foreign workers does not fall during economic downturns in these areas.

The foregoing discussion provides a number of lessons for the United States and Mexico. Perhaps the clearest one is that temporary guests tend to become permanent residents, a phenomenon not anticipated by northern European countries. Even though a variety of negative and positive measures have been used to reduce the number of alien workers, the total foreign population has remained about the same because family members have joined remaining foreign workers. It is not clear that foreign workers and their families represent a net economic burden on the rest of society—an assertion heard less frequently now that the recession of the middle 1970s has passed—but there is little enthusiasm for the old, essentially *laissez-faire* system; immigration restrictions are likely to remain in force for the foreseeable future. The permanent settlement of alien workers was indirectly fostered by the fact that they were legally and actively recruited and were given the same nonwage benefits as citizen workers. But it is now widely recognized that equality in the work place is not sufficient if social problems are to be avoided. Positive policies also need to be implemented in such areas as housing, language instruction, and the education of foreign children. This effort is belatedly being made. Because so many Mexican workers are in the United States on an undocumented basis and because they have tended to return to Mexico on a regular basis, their presence has produced relatively little social confrontation. It is possible that increasing numbers of Mexican "shuttle migrants" may attempt to remain permanently in the United States and eventually bring family members. However, in the absence of the institutional inducements that prevailed in Europe, the pace of permanent settlement in the United States is likely to be relatively slow; and the United States still retains the option of stricter enforcement of the immigration laws.

Many observers of international labor migration in Europe and North America have noted that alien migrant workers are employed in the secondary labor market and that they tend to accept jobs that have been rejected by the native labor force. However, it should also be recognized that foreign workers have an important attribute that makes them especially attractive to host-country employers: they are indeed treated as members of the secondary labor market, but their behavioral characteristics tend to be those of the primary labor market. Even critics of contemporary international labor migration implicitly concede this point by arguing that the labor-exporting countries lose their most able and highly motivated workers. What keeps foreign workers in the secondary market is not their lack of motivation or unwillingness to learn but rather larger considerations involving language, culture, and racism. These issues influence the market relationship between worker and employer, but they obviously are greater in scope, involving society as a whole.

Seen in this context, income alone is not the critical analytical variable in international migration. Böhning, for example, believes that the economic distinction between primary and secondary labor markets is less relevant to European experience than the social distinction between acceptable and undesirable employment. In his view, technological progress produces an increasing number of good jobs over time, and gradually workers in socially undesirable employment obtain the skills and training needed to acquire acceptable jobs. But this leaves fewer people to do the undesirable jobs. In addition, status and other noneconomic aspects of employment become more important over time. Once a job is regarded as socially undesirable, most natives will refuse it even if they could obtain higher incomes. Foreign workers are brought in to fill the undesirable job openings, which only serves to reinforce the stigma attached to these jobs.[61] Under these circumstances, the only way to avoid foreign labor importation is to expedite labor mobility from undesirable to acceptable jobs and to export or mechanize undesirable jobs.

Piore similarly stresses the importance of the social function of the wage, but in contrast to Böhning he relates the "need" for foreign workers to the rigidity of wage hierarchies. Employers seek out foreign workers who will readily accept the low wages associated with the bottom rungs of traditionally determined wage structures. The wage paid to the lowest-status worker cannot be raised without also raising wages throughout the entire job hierarchy. For example, a restaurant owner cannot raise the wage of dishwashers without also paying the cooks and waiters more. The employer's recognition of the leverage that wage increases at the bottom impose on the entire internal wage structure and his or her unwillingness to absorb the short-run costs "could be the genesis of both the initial migration streams and evasion of the law."[62] If immigration were cut off, the upward pressure on wage structures would produce inflationary pressures in the economy as a whole, as well as a decline in living standards, slower growth, and higher native unemployment.[63]

Another aspect of the social role of the job is the process by which people develop social orientations that determine their job choices. To be sure, higher-income occupations usually carry higher social status, but the social role of the job limits the degree to which people will respond to purely economic incentives. *Temporary* international migration, however, tends to create a distinction between work and the social identity of the worker. The temporary migrant's social identity is located in the migrant's home community, whereas the work the migrant performs is asocial—that is, it is purely a means toward the end of earning income that can be taken home to enhance the worker's role within the social structure of the home community. Thus, temporary migrants often will perform tasks abroad that they never would consider doing at home.[64]

What do these socio-economic considerations imply with respect to guest worker programs? In chapter 5 it was pointed out that a new international division of labor is evolving based on the decomposition of complex industrial processes, better transportation technology, improved telecommunications, and relative labor costs. Because of severe competition in world markets, countries that do not adapt to this process are likely to experience long-run economic disadvantages. European experience indicates that the availability of guest workers promoted economic dualism, widened the gap between "good" and "bad" jobs, and made employer threats that they would go out of business without foreign workers a tautology. Thus, the presence of guest workers retarded mechanization, restructuring, and the export of low-level jobs.[65] Nevertheless, under competitive pressures European economic structures are continuing to change in favor of capital- and skill-intensive industries, labor-saving production, and skill-organized services. Many jobs formerly filled by foreign workers have already vanished and others will do so in the near future. Under these circumstances, no resumption of guest worker programs appears likely for the foreseeable future. But millions of foreigners—workers and their family members—could become a permanent lower class unless serious efforts continue to be made on their behalf in such areas as social equality, housing, general education, and job-skill training. Ironically, though, the very success of these efforts could increase social conflict, at least in the short run. The more rapidly the members of the second generation adopt the attitudes and values of the native population, the more their evaluation of jobs will also be similar—and the less likely they will be to accept employment at the lower end of the socio-economic hierarchy. If the jobs held by the original guest workers tended to complement jobs held by natives, those sought by the second generation may well lead to competitive strife. Restructuring, mechanization, and the exportation of unskilled labor activities should help to upgrade the economic status of the second and following generations, but an enhanced economic position could still be a relatively disesteemed social position if certain occupations continue to be regarded as inferior *because* they are occupied largely by minorities. For example, workers in the auto industry are well paid in Europe and the United States. Blue-collar workers in the United States have long considered employment in this sector favorably, though the Chrysler debacle may effect a change in attitude. In contrast, European workers increasingly have shunned jobs in the auto industry because it is perceived to be a domain of the guest workers.

In summary, for present purposes three principal points can be made with respect to European guest worker experience. First, guest worker programs inadvertently encouraged permanent settlement. Second, whatever the short-run economic advantages, the ready availability of guest workers hindered the restructuring and mechanization required to meet the long-run pressures of international competition. And finally, permanently settled foreign workers tend to be joined by family members; this process has resulted in unanticipated social costs that may well increase as the second generation matures.

The introduction of a formal guest worker program in the United States could be expected to induce problems similar to those that have arisen in Europe. In contrast to the European approach, the present informal system of undocumented Mexican migration serves to promote temporary residence in the United States, which is in keeping at least with the initial desires of most migrants to return home eventually. Because most undocumented Mexicans have tended to concentrate in the southwest borderlands or relatively nearby locations, social frictions have been relatively minimized in the United States. In fact, Mexican migrants have received a great deal of informal institutional support because of the many historical and cultural links between the borderlands and Mexico. Moreover, undocumented Mexicans do not appear to have retarded modernization in the U.S. economy, at least not in sectors that are subject to international competition. European guest workers were imported mainly by large enterprises, whereas the situation with respect to undocumented Mexicans in the United States has been quite different. Especially along the border many undocumented Mexicans perform household work. Others "concentrate in small businesses, often without the managerial expertise or access to capital which would permit job restructuring and/or establishment expansion."[66] For example, Cardenas found that in the San Antonio labor market most undocumented Mexicans work in small firms (fewer than twenty-five employees) in construction, wholesale and retail trade, and personal services.[67] Moreover, the way in which the "underfunded" U.S. immigration control system seems to work in practice is to concentrate enforcement activities in the borderlands and to give priority to apprehending undocumented workers in relatively high-paying, high-status jobs as opposed to those in the secondary labor market.

In general, the evidence suggests that from a U.S. perspective the informal undocumented Mexican immigration system works better than might at first seem to be the case. Migration has usually been temporary, and family formation by migrants in the United States has been low; Mexicans usually hold jobs that are regarded as complementary rather than competitive in relation to those held by native workers; and informal institutional support is available to migrants who do form more or less permanent attachments to the United States. In contrast, the introduction of a formal guest worker program could be expected to provoke problems similar to those experienced in Europe. Moreover, it is not clear who in the United States really wants such a program. Unions, and particularly farmworker organizations, are opposed on the ground that it would take jobs away from U.S. citizens. "It would be opposed by business interests afraid, as in the past, that government supervision would mean higher labor costs and smaller profits—and that it would set dangerous precedents. It would be opposed by Chicano groups, who would claim it was racist and immoral to bring in Mexicans to do work that Anglos consider too menial."[68] Indeed the Mexican American Legal Defense and Education Fund is already on record in this regard: "We oppose any kind of guest worker program in general."[69]

Even if Congress were to approve the notion of a guest worker program, many difficult questions would still have to be answered. By what test would employers be permitted to hire aliens? How long would they be permitted to stay in the United States? How would the workers be recruited and transported? Could workers change jobs or locations? Could they belong to unions? What rights would they have with respect to benefits from payments for Social Security and unemployment and disability insurance? What access would they have to nonwork social benefits? Should there be controls on remittances to Mexico? What penalties should be assessed against employers of illegal aliens? By what criteria could the program be terminated? Should the program be established unilaterally or by treaty? Should it be extended to countries other than Mexico? And who should make the decisions concerning these issues?

Some observers maintain that pressures for a large-scale guest worker program come primarily from Mexico,[70] though the Mexican government does not seem to have a clear formal policy in this regard. In any case—and without presuming to have knowledge of the various elements that would enter into the relevant Mexican decision-making process—European experience does suggest that a guest worker program might not be in Mexico's best long-term interest.

From the viewpoint of Europe's labor-sending countries, one of the major drawbacks of guest worker programs was that skilled workers had the greatest incentive to emigrate and the least incentive to return home.[71] Such countries as Greece and Yugoslavia have decided that as their own development efforts proceed it is in the national self-interest to curtail labor migration abroad. In terms of per capita gross national product, Greece, Yugoslavia, and Mexico are at about the same stages of development.[72] But Mexico's vast petroleum resources make its future development prospects potentially brighter than those of Greece or Yugoslavia. As Mexico accelerates industrialization on the basis of oil revenues, it is likely to find that in purely economic terms the Mexican people are an even more valuable asset than nonrenewable natural resources. Then guest worker programs or informal emigration should appear no more attractive than the exportation of cheap oil would be.

Conclusions

There can be little doubt that the number of undocumented Mexican workers in the United States has been increasing in recent years. Wide publicity has been given to statements by scholars, journalists, union leaders, and government officials who maintain that this influx has created a national crisis. Proposals for dealing with this presumed threat vary from strict curtailment of undocumented Mexican immigration on the one hand to the introduction of a formal guest worker program on the other. It has been argued in this chapter, on the basis of North American and European evidence, that at least for the present time neither of these approaches is warranted; indeed they might create more problems than they would solve. The informal undocumented migration system continues to function because it benefits all parties concerned, at least so long as each party looks only at its own situation and what it would be if undocumented migration were strictly curtailed. A key factor in this process is that most Mexican migrants are in the United States on a temporary basis, a phenomenon closely related to the proximity of Mexico and the United States; Mexican immigration should not be confused with the long-distance European immigration experience. As a result of the present system, Mexico gains foreign exchange and some technical skills and exports some of its unemployment. Migrants gain higher wages and, frequently, better working conditions. The United States gains cheap labor willing to perform tasks that citizen workers are reluctant to do. In addition, because for demographic reasons fewer Americans will be available to take low-wage, entry-level jobs, the issue of displacement of American workers by undocumented migrants is likely to decline in importance during the coming decade.

European experience suggests that a formal guest worker program for Mexican workers could produce disincentives for economic modernization and an increased rate of permanent settlement, with concomitant social problems. It is possible that under present conditions many Mexican "shuttle migrants" may attempt to remain permanently in the United States, but, in the absence of the institutional incentives that prevailed in Europe, the pace of permanent settlement is likely to be relatively slow. And the United States still retains the option of stricter enforcement of existing immigration laws. European experience also suggests that whatever the current benefits, in the foreseeable future Mexico may well regard international migration as a drain of valuable resources. Thus, as its industrialization proceeds, Mexico can be expected to perceive that curtailment of migration to the United States is in its own self-interest.

All things considered, there are no simple or cheap solutions to problems occasioned by the migration of labor from developing to industrialized countries, and policies that are relevant for one time period may not be for another. The United States and Mexico should be engaged in an active learning process (tempered by a little patience) in which their mutual interests are coordinated and in which there may still be something to learn from European experience.

7. Mexican Americans: The Human Connection

There is growing realization in the United States that Hispanic Americans will be the nation's largest minority before the end of this century. The national media, which virtually ignored this group in the past, now regularly put it in the spotlight. Puerto Ricans, who have largely concentrated in New York, and Cubans, who have tended to settle in Miami, are not the principal objects of this concern. They are too geographically isolated to attract sustained national attention, and together they represent only one-fifth of the hispanic population in the United States. Rather, the focus is on Mexican Americans, and for good reason. As a national newsmagazine puts it, in the inevitable prose of the genre,

> They are neither here nor there exactly—both immigrant and indigenous, tenaciously Mexican yet indisputably American. They have been part of this country as long as the Southwest that bears so much of their imprint, but they have been invisible to most of their countrymen, shrouded by their own language and culture. Now, they are growing and flexing, solving the riddle of their dual identity and marching into the American consciousness—on their own terms.[1]

The historical observations made here may be essentially correct, but the terms of the present "march" are, as will be seen, not quite so clear.

At this writing most available social science studies concerning Mexican Americans are based on ten-year-old data from the 1970 Census of Population. Moreover, it is generally acknowledged that many persons of Spanish origin were not counted at that time. The Bureau of the Census (as well as a number of other federal agencies) is making a concerted effort to improve data collection and reporting with respect to Hispanics. The results of the 1980 census will clearly be a marked improvement over the past. The Bureau asked a

Spanish-origin question on all forms; used Spanish-speaking census takers and Spanish-language questionnaires; and initiated an extensive public relations and advertising campaign, with the cooperation of community-based organizations, to generate support for the census. In addition, the Bureau has developed a more accurate method for estimating uncounted Hispanics.

Since 1973, data on the Spanish-origin population have been collected annually each March in the Current Population Survey (CPS) of the Bureau of the Census. Because of a number of changes in the CPS procedures in identifying Spanish-origin persons, these data are not strictly comparable with Spanish-origin data for years prior to 1973, including the 1970 census. In March 1978, the CPS sample of persons of Spanish origin was almost doubled, but sampling variability is still considerably greater than would be the case for a census. The 1970 census information on persons of Spanish origin was based on a sample of about one in twenty persons; the March 1978 CPS information was based on a sample of about one in eight hundred persons.[2]

Bureau of the Census publications based on CPS data frequently provide data for Spanish-origin and non-Spanish-origin populations, but data for Mexican Americans often are simply merged with those

Table 7.1. Persons of Spanish Origin in the Southwestern States, 1950, 1960, 1970, and 1978 (in Thousands)

	1950		1960	
	Number	% of Total	Number	% of Total
Southwest	2,290	10.9	3,465	11.8
California	760	7.2	1,427	9.1
Texas	1,034	13.4	1,418	14.8
New Mexico	249	36.6	269	28.3
Arizona	128	17.1	194	14.9
Colorado	118	8.9	157	9.0

SOURCES: 1950–1960, Leo Grebler, Joan W. Moore, and Ralph C. Guzman, *The Mexican American People: The Nation's Second Largest Minority,* p. 106; 1970, Vernon M. Briggs, Jr., Walter Fogel, and Fred H. Schmidt, *The Chicano Worker,* p. 7; 1978, U.S. Bureau of the Census, "Persons of Spanish Origin in the United States: March 1978," *Current Population Reports,* P-20, no. 339, table B, p. 2.

for Cuban-origin, Puerto Rican–origin, and other Spanish-origin groups, rather than reported separately. Annual CPS reports devoted to persons of Spanish origin provide the most detailed information on Mexican Americans, as well as some summary comparisons between this group and the general population. However, comparative data often are not provided, and differing reporting methods hinder data comparisons among CPS publications. Despite those difficulties, it is instructive to make at least rough data comparisons over time for the Mexican American population, as well as between Mexican Americans and other groups. The tables in this chapter use the most recent data available for the variables and geographic units shown. It will be possible to have a more adequate perspective on the social and economic evolution of the Mexican American population when the results of the 1980 census become available.

Demographic Evolution

The Mexican American demographic upsurge of recent decades is apparent from the data in table 7.1, which shows, for selected years, the Spanish-origin population resident in the four border states and

1970		1978	
Number	% of Total	Number	% of Total
4,668	12.9	7,262	17.9
2,222	11.1	3,590	16.5
1,663	14.9	2,662	20.9
324	31.9		
246	13.9	1,010	16.5
212	9.6		

Colorado; these are regarded by the Bureau of the Census as the southwestern states. As discussed in chapter 5, many members of the hispanic population in New Mexico and southern Colorado refer to themselves as Spanish American rather than Mexican American. With this exception, the vast majority of Spanish-origin people in the southwest consider themselves to be Mexican American. Since 1950, the population of the southwestern states has been growing more rapidly than that of the United States, but the region's hispanic population has been increasing still more rapidly. Between 1950 and 1978, the population of the United States rose by 43 percent; that in the southwest increased by over 94 percent; and the southwestern hispanic population grew by 217 percent. During this period, the number of southwestern Hispanics rose by nearly 5 million; Texas and California accounted for fully 90 percent of this increment. In contrast, the Spanish American population of New Mexico and Colorado has remained relatively stable, and although the rate of hispanic population growth in Arizona has been high, the absolute numbers involved are relatively low. The hispanic share of the total population in New Mexico, Colorado, and Arizona as a group actually declined from 18.0 percent in 1950 to 16.5 percent in 1978 (the Bureau of the Census did not report separate hispanic population figures for these states in 1978).

The most dramatic increase in the hispanic population has been in California. In 1950, Texas had over a quarter of a million more Hispanics than did California. By 1960, the number in California was slightly higher. Since then, the gap has widened despite considerable growth in Texas. In 1950, one in fourteen Californians was Hispanic; in 1978, the figure was one in six. In 1978, Hispanics still accounted for a greater share of the Texas population—20.9 percent—but California had by far the largest absolute number—3.6 million.

In 1978, approximately 1 million Mexican Americans lived outside the southwestern states. Growing concentrations of Mexican Americans in such cities as Chicago, Gary, Detroit, and Kansas City have served to broaden recognition that issues concerning this minority are becoming increasingly national in scope. Nevertheless, six out of seven Mexican Americans still live in the southwestern states, so data pertaining to them largely reflect southwestern conditions.

Educational Attainment

Evidence concerning socio-economic status indicates that while Mexican Americans on the whole have made considerable progress, they still lag well behind the general population in most respects. For example, the data in table 7.2 show that Mexican American educational attainment has consistently increased over time. In 1978, nearly two-thirds of the Mexican Americans in the 65 years-and-over age cohort had completed less than five years of school. The corresponding figure for the 45-to-64-years cohort drops to about one-third. Only 7.6 percent of the 25-to-29-years cohort had completed less than five years of school; however, this is still high in comparison to the 0.6 percent figure for the same non-Spanish-origin age cohort. The situation is similar with respect to the proportion of persons with four years of high school or more. Only 7.1 percent of the Mexican Americans in the 65 years-and-over cohort had this much education, compared to 38.6 percent for the non-Spanish-origin population in this cohort. In contrast, 51.3 percent of the Mexican Americans in the 25-to-29-years cohort had this much education, though this was still well under the corresponding 87.1 percent for the non-Spanish-origin population.

Occupational Distribution

Data on changes over time in the occupational distribution of Mexican American men are presented in table 7.3. The 1930–1970 data are for the southwestern states; the 1978 distribution refers to the United States as a whole because regional data are not available at this writing. However, in earlier years, when Mexican Americans were even more concentrated in the southwest than today, the southwest and United States data would be similar for this group. In general, there has been notable improvement in the occupations held by Mexican American men during the last fifty years. The biggest gains were made prior to 1950, perhaps because of labor shortages during the Second World War, and during the 1960s, when national economic growth was more rapid than during the 1970s. In the most recent period, Mexican Americans increased their proportion of employment in the managerial category and in crafts, the best paid of the manual occupations. The long-term decline of Mexican Americans in the farmer and farm laborer occupations con-

Table 7.2. Years of School Completed by Mexican American and by Non–Spanish Origin Population 25 Years Old and Over, 1978

Age	Mexican American	Non-Spanish-Origin
	Percent less than 5 years	
Total, 25 years and over	23.1	3.0
25 to 29 years	7.6	0.6
30 to 34 years	12.6	0.6
35 to 44 years	15.9	1.1
45 to 64 years	34.3	2.7
65 years and over	65.4	8.7
	Percent 4 years of high school or more	
Total, 25 years and over	34.3	67.1
25 to 29 years	51.3	87.1
30 to 34 years	44.1	84.4
35 to 44 years	37.2	76.9
45 to 64 years	21.4	62.7
65 years and over	7.1	38.6
	Percent 4 years of college or more	
Total, 25 years and over	4.3	16.4

SOURCE: U.S. Bureau of the Census, "Persons of Spanish Origin in the United States: March 1978," *Current Population Reports*, P-20, no. 339, table E, p. 6.

tinued in the 1970s. Less encouraging, however, is the fact that the proportion of Mexican Americans in white-collar occupations declined between 1970 and 1978. In relation to the total U.S. population, Mexican American men remain especially underrepresented in the professional and technical and managerial groups, and particularly overrepresented in the operative, laborer, and farm laborer categories.

Relative Income

In 1978, the median income of all U.S. families was $17,640, whereas for Mexican American families it was only $12,835 (table 7.4).

Table 7.3. Occupational Distributions of Mexican American Men, Southwest, 1930–1970, and United States, 1978

Occupation	1930	1950	1960	1970	1978 Mexican American	Total Population
Professional & technical	0.9%	2.2%	4.1%	6.4%	5.3%	15.2%
Managers	2.8	4.4	4.6	5.2	6.1	14.4
Sales	2.4 ⎱ 6.5		3.6	3.9	2.2	6.1
Clerical	1.0 ⎰		4.8	6.6	4.9	6.2
Crafts	6.8	13.1	16.7	20.8	22.6	20.6
Operatives	9.1	19.0	24.1	25.4	27.1	17.5
Service	4.0	6.3	7.5	10.5	11.5	8.9
Laborers	28.2	18.7	15.2	12.1	13.4	7.3
Farmers	9.8	5.1	2.4	0.9	0.2	2.3
Farm laborers	35.1	24.7	16.8	8.1	6.7	1.4

SOURCES: 1930–1970, Vernon M. Briggs, Jr., Walter Fogel, and Fred H. Schmidt, *The Chicano Worker*, p. 76; 1978, U.S. Bureau of the Census, "Persons of Spanish Origin in the United States: March 1978," *Current Population Reports*, P-20, no. 339, table 10, p. 26.

Table 7.4. Income of All U.S. Families and Mexican American Families, Percent by Income-Size Class, 1978

Family Income	U.S.	Mexican American
Less than $4,000	5.6	9.3
$4,000 to $6,999	8.7	11.7
$7,000 to $9,999	9.7	14.3
$10,000 to $14,999	16.6	22.9
$15,000 to $19,999	16.9	17.4
$20,000 to $24,999	14.5	10.8
$25,000 or more	27.9	13.5
Median income	$17,640	$12,835

SOURCE: U.S. Bureau of the Census, "Persons of Spanish Origin in the United States: March 1979 (Advance Report)," *Current Population Reports*, P-20, no. 347, table 5, p. 6.

Among all U.S. families, 14.3 percent had an income below $7,000 compared to 21.0 percent of all Mexican American families. At the other end of the scale, the proportion of U.S. families with an income greater than $25,000 (27.9 percent) was over twice that for Mexican American families. Nevertheless, Mexican Americans have been making relative economic progress. In 1969, the median income of Spanish-surname families in the southwest was 66 percent of the corresponding figure for Anglos.[3] In 1975, the median income of Mexican American families was $9,546, compared to $13,719 for all U.S. families.[4] Thus, between 1975 and 1978, Mexican American median family income grew by 34.5 percent, while that for all families increased by 28.6 percent. In 1975, Mexican American median family income was 69.6 percent of that for all families; in 1978, the corresponding proportion was 72.8 percent. In 1975, 9.7 percent of all U.S. families had incomes below the poverty line; 26.4 percent of the Mexican American families were in this category.[5] By 1978, the corresponding U.S. proportion was 9.1 per-

Table 7.5. Median Income of Spanish-Origin, White, and Black Families in Southwestern Border States, 1969 and 1975

	California		Arizona	
	1969	1975	1969	1975
Spanish origin	$8,430	$10,066	$7,350	$10,717
White	10,966	15,466	9,482	13,841
Black	7,482	8,374	5,716	—
All families	10,729	15,069	9,185	13,569
SO/W	.77	.65	.78	.77
SO/B	1.13	1.20	1.29	—
SO/AF	.79	.67	.80	.79

SOURCES: 1969, Vernon M. Briggs, Jr., Walter Fogel, and Fred H. Schmidt, *The Chicano Worker*, p. 47; U.S. Bureau of the Census, *County and City Data Book 1972*, table 1, p. 5; 1975, U.S. Bureau of the Census, "Money Income and Poverty Status in 1975 of Families and Persons in the United States and the West Region, by Divisions and States," *Current Population Reports*, P-60, no. 113, table 8A, p. 103, table 9A, p. 109, table 15A, p. 163; and "Money Income and Poverty Status in 1975 of Families and Persons in the United States and the South Region, by Divisions and States," *Current Population Reports*, P-60, no. 112, table 22A, p. 223, and table 22C, p. 227.

cent,[6] but that for Mexican Americans had dropped 7.5 percentage points, to 18.9 percent.[7]

The median incomes of Spanish-origin, white, and black families in the southwestern border states are shown in table 7.5 for the years 1969 and 1975. In 1969, the median family income for the Spanish-origin group decreased consistently from west to east; it was $8,430 in California and only $5,600 in Texas. By 1975, several notable changes had taken place. In that year, the highest Spanish-origin median income was in Arizona ($10,717). The difference between the California and Texas values declined from $2,830 in 1969 to $703 in 1975; the difference between the Arizona and Texas values declined from $1,750 to $1,354. Between 1969 and 1975, the standard deviation of the Spanish-origin median income values fell from $1,320 to $642; and the coefficient of variation fell from .194 to .065. This convergence of median family incomes is in keeping with the more general pattern of borderlands income convergence reported in chapter 4.

New Mexico		Texas	
1969	1975	1969	1975
$5,890	$9,396	$5,600	$9,363
8,113	12,356	8,926	13,299
5,203	—	5,330	8,791
7,845	11,798	8,486	12,672
.73	.76	.63	.70
1.13	—	1.05	1.07
.75	.80	.66	.74

In 1969, Mexican Americans had higher median family incomes than blacks in all of the border states. No comparable data are available for blacks in Arizona and New Mexico in 1975 because of inadequate sample sizes. However, in both California and Texas, the incomes of Mexican Americans increased in relation to those of blacks between 1969 and 1975.

In relation to white families and to all families, Mexican Americans made their greatest gain in Texas between 1969 and 1975. The SO/W ratio increased from .63 to .70, while the SO/AF ratio rose from .66 to .74. In sharp contrast, the SO/W ratio for California declined from .77 to .65, and its SO/AF ratio fell from .79 to .67. Thus, whereas the relative income position of Mexican Americans in California was much better than that in Texas in 1969, the situation was reversed in 1975. As discussed later in this chapter, considerations related to education and migration may account for these changes.

A number of studies agree that a substantial portion of the income differences between Mexican Americans and Anglos can be explained by differences in educational attainment, but that a considerable earnings gap remains even after educational differences are taken into account.[8] At this writing, the results of the 1970 census still represent the most recent comprehensive basis for making such comparisons.

Educational Attainment and Anglo–Mexican American Earnings Differences: Southwestern SMSAs in 1969

This section examines the role of education in explaining differences in Mexican American and Anglo earnings in southwestern SMSAs.[9] The data are taken from the one in one hundred Public Use Samples of the basic records of the 1970 census. The samples are limited here to males between the ages of 25 and 54 inclusive who were reported to be working full-time and year-round in 1969. Males alone are used to prevent the confounding of sex and race differences on earnings; males are included instead of females because they have high labor force participation rates as well as greater levels of educational attainment and earnings.

The SMSAs investigated are all located in the five-state southwestern region defined by the Bureau of the Census. However, not all southwestern SMSAs are used. Public Use Samples are not available for SMSAs with fewer than 250,000 inhabitants. In addition, a

Table 7.6. Observed and Standardized Mexican American to Anglo Earnings Ratios, in Selected Southwestern SMSAs, 1969

	Observed	Education Standardized	Opportunity Standardized
Albuquerque	.686	1.086	.814
Anaheim	.794	.936	.857
Corpus Christi	.557	.750	.747
Dallas	.697	.821	.766
Denver	.731	.865	.811
El Paso	.636	.845	.792
Houston	.642	.860	.782
Los Angeles	.679	.801	.789
Phoenix	.759	.874	.850
San Antonio	.660	.862	.818
San Bernardino	.765	.899	.852
San Diego	.699	.777	.848
San Francisco	.835	1.001	.888
San Jose	.738	.826	.786
Mean	.706	.872	.814
Standard deviation	.072	.089	.040

SOURCE: Mark Fossett, "Local Differences in Anglo–Mexican American Earnings Inequality: A Consideration of the Role of Education in the Metropolitan Southwest," Southwest Borderlands Regional Economic Development Project, Mexico–United States Border Research Program, University of Texas, Austin, 1979, p. 20A.

sample size of at least seventy-five persons was deemed necessary for both Mexican American and Anglo groups in each SMSA. The Mexican American sample size did not reach this level in eleven of the twenty-five SMSAs for which data are available. The remaining SMSAs, which are listed in table 7.6, accounted for 59 percent of the Mexican Americans in the southwest in 1970, and for 69 percent of the Mexican Americans residing in urban areas of the southwest.

Separate regression equations were computed for Mexican Americans and Anglos in each of the fourteen relevant SMSAs. In every equation the dependent variable was annual individual earnings in 1969; the independent variables were educational attainment and years of employment experience, both of which are directly related to workers' potential productivity and earnings. Component analysis and regression standardization were used to "adjust" Mexican American mean annual earnings with respect to education and to opportunity.

Column 1 of table 7.6 shows the observed ratios of Mexican American to Anglo earnings. The mean level of .706 is virtually equivalent to the Mexican American to Anglo median income ratio of .70 reported in the following section for all adult males in the United States. The observed ratios range from .557 in Corpus Christi to .835 in San Francisco, the only SMSA with a value above .800.

Column 2 of table 7.6 gives the ratios of Mexican American to Anglo earnings when Mexican American earnings are standardized to Anglo levels of educational attainment. These values reflect the change in mean Mexican American earnings that would occur if Mexican American levels of educational attainment were equal to Anglo levels, and if Mexican Americans converted their increased educational attainment into increased earnings according to the rates of return (slopes) observed in the regression equations. In relation to the observed ratios, the education standardized ratios are greater in every SMSA. Their mean value is .872—an increase of .166 over the mean of the observed ratios—and the range is from .750 to 1.086. Two SMSAs, Albuquerque and San Francisco, have education standardized ratios greater than unity. This implies that if Mexican Americans in these places had educational attainment equal to Anglos, and if they converted educational attainment into earnings as they have done in the past, they would have higher earnings levels than Anglos. Nevertheless, differences among SMSAs are no less pronounced after standardization than before; the standard deviation of .089 after standardization is slightly higher than the .072 obtained for the observed ratios. And it remains clear that, for the most part, Anglo earnings surpass those of Mexican Americans even after educational differences have been taken into account; thus, the earnings gap between the two groups cannot be uniformly attributed to educational differences.

If the SMSAs with the greatest observed inequalities in earnings have these inequalities because education differences between Anglos and Mexican Americans are greater than in other SMSAs, then it could be expected that larger shares of the difference in mean earnings would be attributable to the effects of differences in Anglo and Mexican American educational attainment. However, when the proportion of the mean earnings difference attributable to educational differences is correlated with the observed earnings ratios, the resulting coefficient of determination is positive (.21). This suggests that the portions of the Anglo to Mexican American earnings gap attributable to educational differences are greater in those SMSAs where the observed levels of inequality are relatively moderate. This point will be taken up again in the following section of this chapter.

The coefficient of determination (r^2) relating the education standardized earnings ratios in column 2 of table 7.6 to SMSA per capita income is .27; that relating these ratios to distance to the U.S.-Mexican border is .10; that relating them to percent of the SMSA population that is Mexican American is $-.09$. Although these r^2 values have the signs that might be expected, the relationships are weak.

The opportunity standardized earnings ratios shown in column 3 of table 7.6 indicate the relative level of earnings that Mexican Americans would have if the earnings attainment process for them were identical to that observed for Anglos, with Anglo to Mexican American differences in education and work experience remaining. In other words, these are the values that they would obtain if inequality of opportunity in the labor market were eliminated, but inequality of education and work experience did not change. They are computed by adding to the observed Mexican American mean earnings the differences in Mexican American and Anglo mean earnings attributable to differences in the parameters of the earnings functions. In each of the relevant SMSAs, the relative average earnings of Mexican Americans would improve if they were to convert their education and employment characteristics into earnings according to the "rules" that apply to Anglos. Thus, Mexican American earnings are relatively low not only because of lower educational attainment, but also because of restricted labor market opportunities.

It should be emphasized that while characteristics (education, work experience) and labor market opportunities have separate effects on earnings, they also have joint effects. The adjustment of either characteristics or opportunities will enhance the effect of changing the remaining factor. Improvements in equality of opportunity would be an appropriate means for improving the earnings of Mexican Americans who have completed their education and are already in the labor market. Younger cohorts should be encouraged to increase their educational attainment, but, of course, improvement in economic opportunities would favorably affect the earnings of Mexican Americans entering the labor market and would enhance the effects of increased educational attainment.

Educational Attainment and Mexican American Relative Earnings: Patterns of Change

The data presented in table 7.7 compare, for the years 1971 and 1977, the median incomes of Mexican American and all males aged 25 and over in terms of school years completed. In both years, the median income of Mexican Americans exceeds that of other persons with only an elementary education (8 years) or less. This indicates that Mexican Americans with only limited schooling have no difficulty in competing with other groups who have a similar number of school years completed. However, the jobs involved are in relatively low-wage, low-skill manual labor markets.

It is noteworthy that although the 1971 MO/AP median income ratio was .93 or greater at all levels of schooling except 13 years and over, the corresponding ratio for all males aged 25 and over was only .70.[10] Similarly, the 1977 MO/AP ratio was .89 or greater at all levels of schooling except 13 years and over, yet the corresponding ratio for all of the relevant males was only .75. The reason is that in both years Mexican Americans were heavily concentrated in the relatively low range of the schooling ladder.

It could be said that in 1969 "when one generalizes about Mexican American income (or other experience) in the Southwest, or in the entire United States for that matter, he is dealing largely with an average of the California and Texas experience."[11] A comparative analysis of incomes in these two states in 1959 and in 1969 indicated that 56 percent of the difference in income between Mexican Americans and Anglos in California in 1959 could be explained by the low levels of schooling of Mexican Americans. In Texas, schooling accounted for 47 percent of the difference. The 1969 data showed that schooling differences accounted for 43 percent of the differences between Mexican American and Anglo incomes in California, and for 51 percent in Texas. During the 1960s, the relative income position of Mexican Americans in California remained about the same, while their relative schooling position improved. In Texas, on the other hand, the relative income position of Mexican Americans increased faster than their relative schooling position; this meant that in 1969, schooling deficiencies explained a larger part of the smaller (relative to 1959) income difference in Texas. The labor economists who carried out this study suggest that "the California experience will become typical for most of the remainder of this century. The 'explanatory' value of schooling will fall as Chicano schooling advances more rapidly, in relative terms, than Chicano income."[12]

However, this hypothesis does not appear to be supported by evidence presented in the previous section of this chapter, where it was pointed out that the portions of the differences in Anglo and Mexican American earnings accounted for by educational differences are greater in those SMSAs where the observed levels of inequality are relatively moderate. In other words, in those SMSAs where Mexican American earnings have advanced relatively rapidly in relation to Anglo earnings, education disparities still have relatively great "explanatory" value. Nevertheless, two qualifications are in order. First, in the examination of southwestern SMSAs in 1969, the general relationship between the proportion of the mean Anglo to Mexican American earnings differential accounted for by differences in education, on the one hand, and the observed earnings ratio, on the other, was weak $(r^2=.21)$. Also, this study was cross-sectional for one point in time, whereas the California and Texas results were based on a comparative static analysis for the years 1959 and 1969.

The 1977 data shown in table 7.7 are also suggestive with respect to education and relative income. Between 1971 and 1977,

Table 7.7. Median Income of Mexican-Origin and All Males by School Years Completed, Age 25 and Over, United States, 1971 and 1977

School Years Completed	1971			1977		
	Mexican Origin	All Persons	MO/AP	Mexican Origin	All Persons	MO/AP
0–4	$3,960	$2,950	1.34	$6,461[a]	$5,402	1.20
5–7	5,650	4,240	1.33			
8	6,140	5,470	1.12	8,987	7,155	1.26
9–11	7,130	7,570	.94	9,986	10,023	1.00
12	8,420	9,090	.93	11,786	13,207	.89
13–15[b]	9,150	11,890	.77	11,347	14,247	.80
16	—	—	—	—	17,391	—

SOURCES: 1971, Vernon M. Briggs, Jr., Walter Fogel, and Fred H. Schmidt, *The Chicano Worker*, p. 54; 1977, U.S. Bureau of the Census, "Persons of Spanish Origin in the United States: March 1978," *Current Population Reports*, P-20, no. 339, table 15, p. 33; U.S. Bureau of the Census, "Money Income in 1977 of Families and Persons in the United States," *Current Population Reports*, P-60, no. 118, table 47, p. 185.

[a]Interpolated value.

[b]For 1971, this category includes all school years completed beyond 13 years.

Mexican American relative income declined for males who had completed less than eight years of school. In contrast, in three of the other four categories for which data on school years completed were available, the MO/AP ratio increased. It will be recalled that the MO/AP ratio for all males of age 25 or over rose from .70 in 1971 to .75 in 1977. A reasonable hypothesis to account for these results would be that Mexican Americans are becoming less concentrated in the lower rungs of the schooling ladder, and as their education levels advance (table 7.2), so do their earnings in relation to the rest of the population.

Per Capita Income Variation in the Borderlands

In chapter 1 (tables 1.3 and 1.4) and in chapter 4 (table 4.8) it was shown that there is a pronounced tendency for per capita income to decline from west to east along the border. In this section, variation in per capita income along the border is analyzed in relation to variation in the proportion of the population that is Mexican American. The technique employed is simple linear least squares regression analysis. The geographic units of observation are cities that both lie within the Southwest Border Regional Commission area and have a population of 25,000 or more. These cities are introduced at this point because the geographic frameworks used in previous chapters—SMSAs, BEA economic regions, and the four regional commission portions of the respective border states—provide too few units of observation for regression analysis.

At this writing, the most recent single data source that provides information on city size, per capita income, and Spanish-origin population is *County and City Data Book, 1977*. Data for these variables are given only for cities that had 25,000 or more inhabitants in 1975. All such cities located within Southwest Border Regional Commission counties are shown in table 7.8, where they are ranked according to per capita income. This ranking highlights the tendency for per capita income to decrease from west to east. The nine highest-ranking cities are all in California, while the six lowest-ranking cities are all in Texas.

The level of per capita income in a city can be influenced by many factors, among them local natural resources, climate, education and skill levels of the labor force, proximity to markets, social and economic infrastructure, and ability to attract state and federal

Table 7.8. Per Capita Income (1974) and Percent of Spanish-Origin Population (1970) in Southwest Border Regional Commission Cities Having 25,000 or More Inhabitants (1975)

City	Per Capita Income	Spanish-Origin Population
Palm Springs, CA	$7,139	8.5
La Mesa, CA	5,776	7.1
San Diego, CA	5,016	12.7
Vista, CA	4,915	15.1
El Cajon, CA	4,811	7.5
Riverside, CA	4,714	12.7
Chula Vista, CA	4,704	16.1
Escondido, CA	4,644	12.7
Oceanside, CA	4,563	15.5
Tucson, AZ	4,385	23.9
Yuma, AZ	4,351	30.5
Corona, CA	4,293	27.7
National City, CA	3,701	26.4
Las Cruces, NM	3,699	46.2
El Paso, TX	3,479	58.1
McAllen, TX	3,017	68.9
Harlingen, TX	2,951	64.3
Del Rio, TX	2,785	65.3
Laredo, TX	2,279	86.4
Brownsville, TX	2,196	85.9

SOURCE: U.S. Bureau of the Census, *County and City Data Book, 1977,* pp. 600–635, 708–719, 751–757.

financial assistance. Here, however, per capita income (Y) is analyzed solely as a function of the proportion of the population that is Mexican American (X).

The regression equation for the twenty cities shown in table 7.8 is $Y = a - 39.5X$. The value of r^2 is $-.80$, which is significant at the .01 level. This is a remarkable result in view of the fact that all factors other than proportion of Mexican American population were ignored in "explaining" per capita income variation.

A case could be made for dropping Riverside County, California, from the analysis because its "border" status is questionable. It does not belong to either the San Diego SMSA or the San Diego BEA economic region. An especially troublesome problem is posed by Palm Springs, which is in Riverside County. Palm Springs is a haven for the very rich and, as the data in table 7.8 indicate, it has relatively few Mexican Americans. It might be thought that this would bias regression analysis results in favor of a large negative r^2. In fact this is not the case because of the extremely high per capita income figure for Palm Springs; at $7,139, it is $1,363 above that in La Mesa, the second-ranking city. In view of this idiosyncratic situation, the regression equation was calculated without Palm Springs, but still including the other two cities in Riverside County, Corona and Riverside. The result for the nineteen cities is $Y=a-35.5X$. The value of r^2 in this instance is $-.93$, which is very highly significant at the .01 level!

A quite reasonable quarrel with the foregoing analyses could be made on the ground that the presence of so many cities that are either suburbs of the city of San Diego or else relatively close to San Diego unduly biases the examination of a borderlands region stretching from the Pacific Ocean to the Gulf of Mexico. Excluding the city of San Diego, seven of the cities shown in table 7.8 are suburbs of San Diego, and the three Riverside County cities are relatively close to San Diego. If these cities are excluded, only ten cities —including San Diego—remain. The regression equation for these remaining cities, which still represent all of the border states, is $Y=a-36.9X$. The value of r^2 is $-.98$; this result, which closely approaches a perfect fit, is very highly significant at the .01 level despite the fact that there are only ten pairs of observations. This equation implies that if there were no Mexican Americans $(X=0)$, per capita income would be $5,417 (the Y-intercept). Moreover, for each increase of 1 percentage point in the proportion of Mexican Americans, per capita income would be reduced by about $37. These results are similar to those obtained in the previous analysis, where Palm Springs was excluded, that is, where $n=19$. In that case, the total absence of Mexican Americans would imply a per capita income of $5,290, and each increase of 1 percentage point in the proportion of Mexican Americans would reduce per capita income by $35.50.

Attempts to account for differences in per capita income among cities almost invariably indicate that the determinants are many and that their interrelations are complex. In contrast, the results obtained here for the borderlands suggest a single explanation: the degree to which Mexican Americans are present in the local population. However, it needs to be stressed that these results should be interpreted with caution. The present evidence was obtained only within the context of Southwest Border Regional Commission counties; it does not permit inferences to be drawn concerning per capita income or Mexican Americans in other places. Also, even in the borderlands the high degree of association between per capita income and proportion of Mexican Americans does not mean that the latter variable in itself explains the former. In addressing the issue of why this association exists, such factors as education and discrimination need to be investigated.

The source from which the data in table 7.8 are taken also provides data on the number of years of school completed by persons 25 years old and older in 1970.[13] For the twenty cities shown in table 7.8, the coefficient of determination (r^2) relating the percent of population 25 years old and older with less than five years of school completed to percent of Spanish-origin population is .941. The same r^2 is obtained if the observations for Palm Springs are eliminated. If only San Diego and the non-California cities are included $(n=10)$, $r^2 = .918$. All of these r^2 values are significant at the .01 level.

For all of the cities shown in table 7.8, the coefficient of determination relating the percent of population 25 years old and older with less than five years of school completed to per capita income is $-.719$. If the observations for Palm Springs are eliminated, $r^2 = -.872$. When only San Diego and the non-California cities are included, $r^2 = -.927$. All of these r^2 values are significant at the .01 level. The regression equation for the nineteen pairs of observations excluding Palm Springs is $Y = a - 84.1X$. This implies that a 1 percentage point increase in the relatively low-education group is associated with a decline of $84 in per capita income. The regression equation for San Diego and the non-California cities is $Y = a - 78.4X$, which may be similarly interpreted.

In summation, the analyses of borderlands cities presented in this section indicate that the proportion of Mexican Americans in the total population, educational attainment, and per capita income are highly interrelated variables; and each of the last two is negatively associated with the first. However, the significance of these findings must be seen in the context of more general evidence concerning the social and economic status of Mexican Americans in the southwest. The cross-sectional nature of this study does not take into account the dynamic factors involved in the changing social and economic status of Mexican Americans. In general, the results presented earlier in this chapter suggest that they are making steady advances in terms of educational attainment and earnings in relation to the rest of the population. Moreover, although the data in table 7.8 indicate a pattern of decline in per capita income from west to east along the border, the data in table 7.5 clearly show that there has been a convergence over time among Mexican American median incomes in the border states; and data presented in chapter 4 (table 4.8) show that there has been a convergence over time with respect to mean income of the total population along the border. There is no solid evidence showing increasing relative earnings and convergence of Mexican American income along the border (the relevant data are not available for intercensal years), but all of these findings would be consistent with such an evolution.

Issues for the 1980s

Education and Economic Opportunity   Mexican Americans, like other minorities in the United States, have been the victims of discrimination in such areas as housing, public accommodations, law enforcement, and economic opportunity, which is of principal concern here. But "with the exception of Texas," discrimination "against Mexican Americans in the United States has not been as overt as it has in the case of blacks."[14] There is clear evidence that "a considerable payoff to Chicanos and to society can be gained by public efforts to develop the educational and job skills of Chicanos. Adequately trained Chicano workers are more able to overcome discriminatory job barriers than are other racial minorities."[15] It has been demonstrated that Mexican Americans with relatively little schooling—an elementary education or less—have higher earnings than other Americans with comparable schooling. But the jobs in question are generally in the disesteemed low-wage, manual-labor category. During the 1970s, Mexican Americans with less than a high school education appear to have closed the earnings gap in comparison with similar workers in the rest of the population (table 7.7). However, Mexican Americans who are high school graduates or who have at least some college education still have lower earnings than other persons with comparable educational attainments. Discrimination against Mexican Americans has decreased significantly in recent years—even in Texas. Overt discrimination in particular is much less a problem for Mexican Americans than it is for blacks, but they continue to experience the consequences of more subtle processes that involve criteria unrelated to job performance. For example, factors such as religion and kinship and friendship ties may influence hiring decisions without significantly affecting employer costs in terms of worker productivity. Most employers are Anglo, and to the extent that noneconomic bonds exist, they tend to be stronger within rather than across ethnic groups. The government can play a role in reducing this type of discrimination; in particular, the continuing efforts of the U.S. Equal Employment Opportunity Commission "to have job credentials be demonstrably related to job requirements may prove to be of extreme importance to Chicanos."[16] But in a larger sense, the struggle against discrimination must occupy all groups and persons who wish to realize in fact the stated American ideal of equality of opportunity.

Even in the absence of labor market discrimination, increased years of schooling alone would not necessarily eliminate income and employment difficulties. For one thing, the income benefits of education do not take place at once; there is a lagged response of income to education in the United States. Moreover, educational quality is variable. In relation to Anglos, a given number of school years completed by Mexican Americans may represent a lower level of actual educational achievement. The financing of public education by local school districts tends to result in relatively inferior schools in districts that have a low property tax base, a condition that characterizes many Mexican American communities.

School districts in the southwest borderlands find it especially difficult to provide high-quality education. Property tax rates often are relatively high, but the low tax base results in inadequate funds. In addition, most of the districts have large numbers of resident Mexican alien children enrolled; whether these persons are "legal" or "illegal" in practice is not determined. Many resident Mexican aliens are taxpayers, but the net effect of their presence is overcrowded schools coupled with financial inability to construct additional facilities. In Brownsville, for example, 16 percent of the pupils are children of resident Mexican aliens, and three-fourths of new enrollment is accounted for by this group. School buildings are occupied at 146 percent of capacity, and 158 portable buildings were in use recently. In Laredo, school attendance has increased by 10 percent since 1974, while the number of resident Mexican alien children has risen by 29 percent. In Rio Grande City, where the number of resident Mexican alien children has grown by 42 percent since 1975, some teachers must work in hallways or other inadequate spaces. Since 1974, average daily attendance in Calexico, California, has increased by 5 percent, whereas the number of resident Mexican alien children has risen by 75 percent; the latter now account for 43 percent of total enrollment. A similar proportion of resident Mexican alien children is enrolled in San Ysidro, where the junior high school is "functioning" at 292 percent of capacity. Over half of all borderlands school districts have permanent facilities that are occupied at a level greater than 100 percent of capacity; and many districts house children in buildings that need to be replaced due to age or poor condition. Nearly 75 percent of the districts have had to purchase or rent temporary portable facilities.[17]

To the extent that public education provides the foundation for future job skill development, the overcrowded schools of the borderlands help to perpetuate the circular process wherein lack of skills, low income, inadequate public school financing capability, and inferior schools are mutually reinforcing phenomena. It has been argued that because state and federal policies have permitted the influx of resident Mexican alien children, state and federal funds should be provided for facilities to accommodate them. The rationale is similar to that which justifies federal aid to school districts in areas that have been "impacted" by federal activities. Such support appears warranted in the borderlands so long as the federal educational bureaucracy does not place heavy burdens on already clogged administrative reporting systems or impose well-meaning but wasteful restrictions on school districts. For example, federal school aid for the education of children of migrant farm workers in the borderlands has been so categorical and the guidelines so stringent that additional space must be provided for the exclusive use of special programs. But migrants' children also must be provided regular classroom space, even if they are not in school during the whole year. The net result has been increased overcrowding when these children are in school. Thus, federal aid designed to improve educational quality for one disadvantaged group, without taking into account the total situation in the schools, has in many instances created more problems than it has solved.[18]

Farm Labor   By any standard, migrant farm workers are the poorest, the least represented, and the most abused group of workers in the United States. The vast majority of migrant workers are Mexican American, and the largest number of migrant Mexican Americans uses the Lower Rio Grande Valley of Texas as a home base. The principal migration stream fans out northward in the early spring to harvest fruits and vegetables throughout the middle west and to cultivate sugar beets and other crops in the Rocky Mountain states and the Red River Valley.[19]

Hidalgo County, in the Lower Rio Grande Valley, is the largest and most diverse agricultural county in Texas; and it ranks third in the United States in agricultural wealth. Over 80 percent of the Texas citrus crop is grown in Hidalgo County, which also leads the state in the production of cabbage, carrots, cantaloupes, and onions. Yet some of the poorest people in the United States reside in this area; in 1977, its per capita personal income was $3,859, compared with $6,827 for the state of Texas.[20] A decade ago, Hidalgo County farm workers were the least educated of any group in the country, and health statistics revealed an equally bleak picture. The federal response was to fund at least twenty-seven aid programs which during the 1970s managed to spend over a quarter of a billion dollars. By most measures with respect to income, education, health, and housing, the results have been very disappointing. As John Davidson aptly remarks, "Considering the money spent and the net results, it would seem that a great disappearing act has been performed."[21]

One reason for the poor record of federal programs in the Lower Rio Grande Valley is the nature of the Mexican American migrant worker. A person who struggles against odds faced by few other Americans simply to work for low pay is not the kind of person who would be responsive to welfare doles no matter what their guise. In the mid-1970s, trained interviewers from the Governor's Office of Migrant Affairs obtained a great deal of highly useful data from migrant and seasonal farm-worker families in the Lower Rio Grande Valley and elsewhere in Texas. It was established that many of these households did not make use of available social services for a variety of reasons, including the geographic distance between respondents and agencies; the questionable value of the services; red tape and cumbersome procedures; and rudeness on the part of welfare personnel. But a major factor for refusal to take advantage of available services was family pride. However poverty-stricken, many respondents preferred to make it on their own.[22]

Another reason for the apparent lack of success of federal programs is that the successes often are not registered in the Lower Rio Grande Valley or in other geographic sources of migrant farm labor. Given the increasing trend toward mechanization of agriculture and the movement of light industry into the Valley, these programs—oriented primarily toward education and job-skill training—have sought to divert farm workers into other occupations. Those who have in fact found employment in better-paying and more stable occupations frequently have taken jobs in other regions. Even before the advent of massive federal programs, large numbers of migrant farm workers left the migration stream to settle down in various parts of the middle west so that they could stabilize their lives, have access to more opportunities, and send their children to school for the full school year.[23] Federal programs no doubt have accelerated this movement. It also seems that some of the "slack" in the supply of migrant farm workers has been taken up by Mexicans. Over 40 percent of Hidalgo County farm-worker household heads are of Mexican birth, which implies that there is a generational turnover with children eventually moving out of farm work to employment in other activities and in other parts of the United States.[24]

In California, the traditional plight of Mexican American farm workers has been eased because of the organizing efforts of César Chávez and the United Farm Workers Union. In addition to gains that have been made with respect to wages and working conditions, the UFW has replaced the abuses of the former labor contractor system with the union hiring hall, where employment is based on seniority. Moreover, in 1975 the California legislature passed a bill giving farm workers the right to choose by secret ballot the union that should represent them.

The Texas Farm Workers Union has been pursuing essentially the same goals as those already attained by the UFW in California; but no federal or state laws protect farm-worker unionization in Texas. When TFW members picket growers in the Lower Rio Grande Valley, the growers simply fall back on the state right-to-work law and hire nonunion workers. The latter frequently are Mexicans who will accept low wages and poor working conditions, not because they deliberately seek to undermine the TFW but because they will seize any opportunity to provide something for their families. It would seem that the time is overdue for the general public and the Texas Legislature to grant Valley farm workers the rights already held by farm workers in California. One reason why Valley growers "need" cheap labor is that they manage this resource poorly. It has been demonstrated that growers could afford to pay higher wages and could attract stable work forces by hiring workers directly and implementing a standard workday. They have not done so precisely because labor is so cheap.[25] With or without unionization, the number of farm jobs will continue to decline. However, unionization would probably mean that the remaining work would be parceled out more rationally among a smaller number of professional workers. With the upgrading of farm jobs, the casual nature of the labor market would tend to disappear, and with higher family incomes, workers' children would be more able to quit the fields for better opportunities elsewhere. Improved wage scales would keep more migrants at home and perhaps lower their children's school dropout rate. A formalized system of entry into the labor market and the introduction of seniority as the basis for a first chance at jobs would also serve to discourage undocumented Mexicans from seeking farm jobs. Mexican Americans unable to find farm employment at higher wage levels would still need assistance; but those who would be employed would become taxpayers, contributing to the community and making it on their own, as most want to do but cannot under present circumstances.

Geographic Mobility Many Mexican Americans have strong cultural attachments to the borderlands, but it is clear that border areas have also served as staging grounds for migration to other parts of the United States. Surveys of the residential preferences of young Mexican Americans in the Texas borderlands indicate a high degree of mobility potential if greater economic gains can be made elsewhere.[26] There is a general lack of data on the geographic mobility of Mexican Americans since 1970, but evidence from the census of that year indicated that increasing numbers of Mexican Americans —and immigrants from Mexico—were moving to nonborder states. Migrant farm workers, exposed to better economic opportunities in states distant from the border, may have formed the nucleus of Mexican American communities in such states as Oregon, Washington, Illinois, and Michigan.[27] Chicago appears to have attracted a particularly large number of Mexican Americans, largely from Texas. Only 44 percent of the Mexican-origin persons living in Illinois in 1970 were born there; the corresponding figure for Michigan was 52 percent. Mexican American migrants to nonborder states tended to be relatively young and well educated. "In some of the states they have education and income levels equivalent to that of the state's population as a whole. It can be conjectured that the movement of Chicanos to the northern areas of the West is composed in substantial part of a younger, more upwardly mobile generation comprising those who are leaving areas of little opportunity and high discrimination for a region of greater opportunity."[28]

Despite their increasing national geographic dispersion, six out of seven Mexican Americans still lived in the southwestern states in 1978.[29] However, within these states a rising proportion of Mexican Americans has been settling away from border counties. In 1970, Los Angeles ranked first among SMSAs in terms of number of Mexican Americans (1,289,000), followed by San Antonio (385,000), San Francisco–Oakland (364,000), and Houston (212,000).[30] In the late 1960s, Walter Fogel wrote that "most immigrants from Mexico now go directly to California, and there is a good deal of interstate migration from Texas (and to a lesser extent from other states) to California. Even many of the Mexican immigrants who settle initially in Texas move on to California."[31] The flow of Mexican Americans to California was attributed to higher wages, greater chances for social acceptance, and a familiar climate.[32] During the 1950s, the Spanish-origin population of California grew by 88 percent (table 7.1), while the rate for Texas was only 37 percent; during the 1960s, these rates were 56 percent and 17 percent, respectively. But between 1970 and 1978, the rate of growth of the Spanish-origin population was about the same, 62 percent in California and 60 percent in Texas. And, whereas the median family income of the Spanish-origin population in Texas was only 66 percent of the corresponding California median in 1969, it had risen to 93 percent by 1975 (table 7.5). The evidence thus indicates that the factors that made California so attractive to Mexican Americans (and Mexican immigrants) during the postwar years, especially in relation to Texas, have not been so influential during the 1970s. The reasons for this change have not been studied in detail. However, between 1969 and 1977, per capita personal income rose by 88 percent in California; by 92 percent in the United States; and by 108 percent in Texas.[33] It would appear that in addition to migrating to distant cities in order to gain improved economic opportunities, many Mexican Americans also have been sharing in the fruits of the booming Texas economy.

Political Organization   Nevertheless, as already indicated, there is substantial room for improvement in the social and economic conditions of Mexican Americans, especially in the Texas borderlands. This relatively isolated area has long been characterized by a steady inflow of poor migrants from Mexico and Anglo political dominance. Despite the infiltration of Yankee values, Mexican cultural influences have remained strong. For example, birthrates are closer to those in Mexico than to those in the United States. In 1976, the rate of natural increase was 2.1 percent in the Lower Rio Grande Valley and 2.0 percent in the South Texas (Laredo) planning region; for Texas as a whole the corresponding rate was only 0.9 percent.[34] At the time of the 1970 census, over 40 percent of all families in the Lower Rio Grande Valley were in the poverty category; nearly half of these families had six or more children.[35]

The successes of Mexican Americans in Texas, as elsewhere, have been attained largely through the efforts of individuals and families outside of the political arena. Despite their numerical majority along the Texas-Mexico border, many Mexican Americans still do not vote, and they have formed few organizations for the purpose of dealing directly with poverty and related issues. In many communities, manipulation of the poverty population through the *patrón* system is still common.[36] Although the Democratic party traditionally has depended upon Mexican American support, campaign promises concerning political, social, and economic reforms tend to be forgotten between elections. Rudolph Gomez correctly maintains that "The greatest unresolved task confronting Chicanos desirous of using political and governmental means to improve their condition is that of mobilizing the Mexican-American population living along the Texas-Mexican border into an election-influencing voting bloc."[37] There are indications that active grassroots political groups can boost Mexican American political power. The efforts of Communities Organized for Public Service (COPS), a privately financed Mexican American activist organization that has combined the organizing tactics of the late Saul Alinsky with the influence of the Catholic Church, have been increasingly effective in bringing improved community facilities and new, relatively high-wage private sector employment to Mexican American neighborhoods in San Antonio.[38] It is noteworthy that COPS (and similar groups, formed on the COPS model, in Los Angeles, Houston, and, most recently, El Paso) has realized its greatest successes through its ability to deal effectively with elected officials and business executives in the private sector; in contrast, the federal bureaucracy has been relatively unresponsive and at times a hindrance.

Long-run social and economic improvements for Mexican Americans are more likely to come about through general economic growth and their own efforts than through government anti-poverty programs, though the efforts of the Equal Employment Opportunity Commission to eliminate all forms of labor market discrimination should continue to be valuable. Evidence in this regard is provided by the record of poverty reduction for all persons and for blacks. Between 1959 and 1967, when aggregate economic growth was relatively rapid but before the War on Poverty was in full swing, the poverty rate for all persons was reduced from 22 percent to 14 percent, while that for blacks fell from 55 percent to 39 percent. But between 1967 and 1976, the poverty rate for all persons fell by only 2 percentage points, to 12 percent. In the rapidly growing south, the poverty rate for blacks dropped from 50 percent in 1967 to 33 percent between 1967 and 1976; however, during this same period the poverty rate for blacks outside the south *increased* from 27 percent to 29 percent.[39] In view of these data, it should not be surprising that, contrary to all past experience, there is now net inmigration of blacks to the south. As Thomas Sowell has pointed out:

> For the disadvantaged ethnic minorities, it seems highly unlikely that subsidies are—on net balance—giving them more than their taxes are taking away. Even in specifically poverty-oriented programs, it is clear that the bulk of the money does not actually reach the poor but rather is paid to the predominantly middle-class suppliers of professional services designed to "fight poverty."[40]
>
> The disasters in the social reforms of recent years alone are all too apparent and painful. One need only mention Urban Renewal, public housing projects, welfare, or inner city schools to realize that the "experts" have produced more than their share of disasters.[41]

Government programs intended to help minority groups have too often attempted to achieve immediate "solutions" through job quotas, charity, subsidies, preferential treatment, and similar means. The history of American ethnic groups shows that the methods that have successfully raised minority incomes—self-reliance, work skills, education, business experience—are relatively slow in developing.[42] Mexican American political activists should continue to enlist the help of elected officials, business leaders, and even federal bureaucrats with adequate perspectives on poverty, housing, employment, and other issues of major concern to minorities. But their principal concern should be to create an overall environment within which the fundamental self-reliance and pride of achievement of the Mexican American can be relied upon to achieve long-run success.

8. Summary and Conclusions

The present-day Mexico–United States boundary resulted from the military conquest of Mexico by the United States in the War of 1846–1848. The imposition of this line of demarcation in 1848—it has been modified only slightly since then—meant that Mexico lost about half its territory to an alien people who were aggressively pushing westward under the banner of Manifest Destiny. However, few Mexicans resided north of the border; most of the hispanic population in the United States was concentrated in northern New Mexico and southern Colorado, and these people, at least today, tend to regard themselves as Spanish Americans rather than Mexican Americans. Indeed, until the coming of the railroads in the 1880s, few people lived on either side of the borderlands. Mexico had in fact deliberately ignored its northern states for fear that their development could induce further expansionist moves by the United States. In the late nineteenth and early twentieth centuries, railroad construction and the irrigation of vast tracts of land caused a large demand for Mexican labor in the southwest. The availability of these workers was assured by the completion of railroads linking the populous interior of Mexico to the distant borderlands. Since then the migration of Mexican workers has been alternately encouraged and discouraged by explicit and implicit U.S. policies, with the major determining factor being general economic conditions in the United States.

The postwar northward surge of Mexicans has been accompanied by rapid population growth in Mexican border cities. In 1921, Tijuana and Mexicali, both on the border with California, had populations of 1,000 and 7,000, respectively. In 1940, they still had modest populations of 17,000 and 19,000, respectively. But by 1970, these two cities as well as Ciudad Juárez, on the border with Texas, ranked among the ten largest cities in Mexico. In other Mexican border cities similar, if not quite as spectacular, growth has taken place. The typical pattern of urbanization along the border is international in that each Mexican city has a counterpart on the U.S.

side. With the exception of San Diego, these bicultural, bilingual border cities are relatively remote from the heartlands of their respective countries. Economic, social, and cultural relations between the twin cities have been more marked by increasing symbiosis than by the confrontation of differing systems. On both sides, formal, and perhaps even more influential informal, institutions have supported a permeable boundary.

Mexican border cities provide homes for persons who commute to work across the border, and they serve as staging areas for migration to the U.S. borderlands or, increasingly, to U.S. cities distant from the border. But depending on the location, some 20 to 25 percent of the Mexican border labor force was unemployed in 1970. The manufacturing sector, which accounted for only 12 percent of total employment, was incapable of absorbing surplus labor. An excessively large tertiary sector, heavily dependent on the U.S. market, dominated the economy; in 1970, this sector accounted for 46 percent of total Mexican border employment, whereas in Mexico as a whole the corresponding figure was only 32 percent.[1] In response to this situation the Mexican government has been attempting to attract U.S. plants to the Mexican border area. The assembly plant, or *maquiladora*, program takes advantage of U.S. tariff code provisions that allow foreign-based subsidiaries of U.S. firms to assemble products whose parts were originally made in the United States, and then export the products to the United States with duties being imposed only on the value added. In keeping with the new international division of labor, many U.S. firms have participated in this program. The advantages are the low.cost of Mexican labor, the fact that duties are paid only on these costs, and the nearness of the Mexican border area in relation to other low-labor-cost locations overseas. Mexico in turn has gained employment, foreign exchange, and an expanded industrial base for its border cities.

Critics of the *maquiladora* program point out that although it was originally conceived to provide jobs for former *braceros*, in fact over four-fifths of the workers are women. By their very nature, there are no linkages with other Mexican firms and a substantial share of the profits is repatriated to the United States. In addition, a significant proportion of the incomes of *maquiladora* workers—as well as the incomes of many other Mexicans residing on the border —is spent in U.S. border cities. The net effect of the program has thus been to increase the dependence of the Mexican border area on the United States, rather than to integrate it more closely with the

Mexican economy. Finally, it also has been argued that the program has increased unemployment in border cities because job creation has not kept pace with the number of workers who have moved from the interior in the hope of obtaining industrial employment.

On the other hand, recent data indicate that very few *maquiladora* workers have moved to the border in search of *maquiladora* employment, though the number of such migrants may be increasing. The program is currently providing over 100,000 jobs for Mexicans, and without these jobs Mexico's unemployment rate would be higher. Moreover, the incomes of these workers support many more people than the workers themselves. The Mexican border area *is* highly dependent on the United States, but it would be a mistake to blame the United States—or U.S. "monopoly capital"—for this situation. Mexicans would not be better off economically if per capita income levels in the United States were equivalent to those in Mexico. So long as per capita income in the United States is eight times that in Mexico, Mexicans will freely and willingly migrate to take advantage of the relative opportunities afforded by proximity to the United States; and still others will continue to move across the border, even if on an undocumented basis.

Whatever the attractiveness of the United States, it should be emphasized that Mexican migration northward has not been the result of a stagnant Mexican economy; rather, Mexico has been experiencing a rapid industrial revolution. Well before the confirmation of massive oil reserves, technological progress was clearly in evidence in Mexico's factories and fields. This dynamism has dislocated large numbers of uneducated and unskilled peasants who cannot yet be absorbed in nonagricultural activities. Moreover, general social and economic improvements have created a revolution of expectations. Industrial and agricultural advances have also not been fully reflected in standard of living gains because of Mexico's high rate of population growth. Despite these difficulties, "there has been a great deal of learning from policy experience, the information and skills base is much greater than it was, and the intellectual and institutional foundations of material progress are very much in evidence in many parts of the Mexican Republic."[2] It is the Mexican government's stated policy to use its new oil wealth to build the nation's industrial base; and the government's massive family planning program, begun in the early 1970s, appears to be working. Between 1973 and 1978, Mexico's annual population growth rate declined from 3.5 percent to 2.9 percent, with every indication that it would continue to decline.[3] The evidence thus clearly suggests that internal pressures promoting northward migration will be mitigated; but in the immediate future, large numbers of Mexicans will continue to migrate to the United States.

From the perspective of the United States, the most serious issue in U.S.-Mexican relations is the undocumented migration of Mexican workers to the United States, though in the past U.S. policies have varied a great deal in this regard. During the First World War and again during the 1920s Mexican workers were welcomed because of domestic labor shortages. However, the Great Depression resulted in massive deportations of Mexicans. During the Second World War Mexicans were officially encouraged to work in the United States under the *bracero* program. Then in 1954, over 1 million undocumented Mexican workers were deported. From the mid-1950s to the mid-1960s the annual deportation rate was less than 50,000, but with relatively high unemployment in the United States, the annual deportation rate has steadily increased in recent years to the current rate of over 1 million per year.

Extensive publicity has been given to the notion that there is a "time bomb in Mexico," and that there will be "no end to the invasion by the illegals."[4] Proposals for dealing with this presumed threat vary from strict curtailment of undocumented immigration to the introduction of a formal "guest worker" program. Both North American and European evidence indicates that at least for the present time neither of these approaches is warranted; either might create more problems than it would solve. The informal undocumented migration system continues to operate largely because it benefits all parties concerned, at least so long as each party looks only at its own situation and what it would be if undocumented migration were strictly curtailed. A key factor in this system is that most undocumented Mexicans are in the United States on a temporary basis. The United States gains relatively cheap labor willing to perform tasks that citizen workers are reluctant to undertake. The available evidence shows that undocumented Mexican workers do not use social services to any significant extent, though they do pay numerous taxes. For demographic reasons, in the near future fewer Americans will be available to take low-wage, entry-level jobs, so the issue of the displacement of American workers by undocumented Mexicans is likely to decline in importance. Mexico exports some of its unemployment and gains foreign exchange that workers send or bring home as well as some technical skills when workers return home. The migrants gain higher incomes and, frequently, better working conditions than in Mexico. These phenomena explain why undocumented Mexican workers have long been "a normal, functioning ingredient" of the southwest borderlands, where they have been encouraged and utilized "with the approval and support of social and cultural institutions of the region with the tacit cooperation of border control agencies and legal authorities."[5]

European experience suggests that a formal guest worker program for Mexican workers in the United States could produce disincentives for economic modernization as well as an increased rate of permanent settlement, with concomitant social problems. It also suggests that whatever the current benefits to Mexico, it may in the foreseeable future regard emigration as a drain of valuable resources. Thus, as its industrialization proceeds, Mexico can be expected to attempt to curtail emigration of its workers, just as Mediterranean countries at about the same stage of development have done.

Within the context of the United States, the southwest borderlands historically have been a relatively remote area. The great westward surge of population following the Civil War tended to bypass the borderlands. Indeed, in terms of Anglo population settlement, the area has largely grown from west to east. Once transcontinental railroads reached southern California, San Diego grew relatively rapidly because of its attractive climate. However, as recently as 1910 San Diego was still essentially an agricultural and resort community with fewer than 40,000 inhabitants. During the 1920s, California's population growth rate of 66 percent was the highest among all the states, and during the depressed 1930s its growth rate of 22 percent was still about three times the national rate. In the 1940s, California again had the highest growth rate of any state, 53 percent. Continuing rapid population increase has made California the nation's most populous state. Its 1978 population of 22.3 million was 5.5 times its 1920 population; but San Diego County's 1978 population of 1.7 million was 14 times its 1920 population.

During the 1940s, Arizona's growth rate of 50 percent was second only to California, and its 74 percent growth rate during the 1950s was exceeded only by Florida and Nevada. Arizona's growth rate between 1960 and 1970 (36 percent) was again third, behind Florida and Nevada. Between 1970 and 1978, Arizona's average annual rate of population increase was 3.4 percent, just slightly lower than the rates for Nevada (3.6 percent) and Alaska (3.5 percent). Arizona's rapid recent growth in relation to California is reflected in the Arizona borderlands. For example, during the 1960s, the Tucson SMSA grew by 32 percent, while the San Diego SMSA grew by 31 percent. However, between 1970 and 1975, the Tucson SMSA growth rate was 26 percent, compared to 17 percent for the San Diego SMSA. Similarly, between 1971 and 1976, the Tucson BEA region grew by 19 percent, while the San Diego BEA region grew by 15 percent.

Meanwhile, the westward pattern of growth clearly has been spreading to the Texas borderlands. During the 1960s, the four Texas SMSAs on the border—El Paso, Laredo, McAllen, and Brownsville— all had net outmigration of population. During the 1970s, all except Laredo have experienced net inmigration, and the rate of outmigration from Laredo has been greatly reduced. Between 1971 and 1976, the U.S. population increased by 4 percent. The three Texas borderlands BEA regions—El Paso, San Antonio, and Brownsville—had growth rates of 13 percent, 8 percent, and 22 percent, respectively, during this period. The Brownsville BEA region growth rate even exceeded the rates in the San Diego (15 percent) and Tucson (19 percent) BEA regions.

As development has moved eastward, the degree of per capita income disparities along the border has been diminishing; overall variability and the absolute gap between the poorest and richest areas have been decreasing.

In recent years there has been a general shift of population and economic activity from the northeast and north-central regions of the United States to the south and west. A number of factors have contributed to this phenomenon. New technologies have favored more decentralized location patterns, and corporate branch plants producing largely standardized outputs increasingly are located in areas with relatively plentiful low-cost labor. Climate and environmental amenities also have encouraged movement to the west and south. The elaboration of a national urban network and the diffusion of transportation (jet airplanes, the Interstate Highway System), communications, education, and other social and economic infrastructures have made it ever more feasible for persons and firms to locate in once-remote areas. Moreover, air conditioning has served to ameliorate the harsher aspects of the southern climate. Thus, a large and growing number of retired persons have been attracted to southern areas, including the borderlands. Defense spending may also have favored the south and west, though as the experience of San Diego, El Paso, and San Antonio indicates, it can have destabilizing effects on local economies. Finally, the economic growth engendered by all of these activities induces still more growth, especially in view of the fact that so much employment today is in the trade and services sectors.

Employment increases in the borderlands have been reflecting national spatial patterns of employment change. It appears that decentralization may even be leapfrogging over some areas in favor of the borderlands. For example, Bureau of Economic Analysis estimates show that employment in the border states has been growing much more rapidly than that in the nation as a whole; and the employment growth rate in Southwest Border Regional Commission counties exceeds that for other border-state counties.

The proportion of total borderlands employment accounted for by manufacturing is much less than that for the United States. This may be a result of the area's distance from major markets and the competition of *maquiladoras* across the border. However, the analyses presented in chapter 4 show that manufacturing gains are being made in each borderlands BEA region on the basis of local advantages vis-à-vis the rest of the country, and that these advantages have yet to be fully exploited. Thus, the presence of relatively cheap labor, twin-plant linkages with *maquiladoras*, and amenities (especially in San Diego and Tucson) conducive to the location of newer, diversified production activities should lead to greater manufacturing employment in the future.

In contrast to manufacturing, trade and services employment is overrepresented in the borderlands in comparison with the rest of the United States. This may result in part from tourism, but it also reflects the large number of purchases made on the U.S. side of the border by Mexicans. Average annual earnings in the large and rapidly growing trade and services sectors are relatively low. The evidence suggests that there is a high degree of turnover of female workers. It appears that many young women leave employment in trade and services—perhaps to marry or have children—but there has been an even larger number of young women taking or re-taking jobs in these sectors. This phenomenon is consistent with increasing labor force participation rates among Mexican American women. Between 1975 and 1978 alone, the proportion of Mexican American women 16 years old and over in the labor force increased from 42.1 percent to 47.0 percent.[6]

In 1972, every borderlands BEA region had a higher proportion of employment in the government sector than was the case in the United States as a whole. Military employment, which declined nationally between 1972 and 1977, also declined in the Tucson, Brownsville, and, especially, San Antonio BEA regions. Because of competitive advantages, military employment did not change substantially in the San Diego BEA region and increased significantly in the El Paso BEA region. However, overall gains in government employment in the borderlands were largely a consequence of increases in the state and local sectors.

The west to east temporal pattern of Anglo borderlands settlement has meant that the concentration of Mexican Americans in the local population increases from west to east. Moreover, per capita income and other measures of economic and social well-being also tend to decline in the same direction. The inverse correlation between per capita income and the proportion of Mexican Americans in borderlands cities having 25,000 or more inhabitants is nearly perfect. And Laredo, McAllen and Brownsville are the three poorest SMSAs in the nation.

The degree to which Mexican Americans have been sharing in the economic growth of the borderlands is not altogether clear because of limitations of the relevant data. Fortunately, the Bureau of the Census and other government agencies have been devoting more attention to them in recent years, and every effort has been made to assure that reasonably complete and accurate data concerning them will be obtained from the 1980 population census. Evidence available at this writing indicates that Mexican Americans have been moving away from the borderlands in increasing numbers. Nevertheless, in 1978 six out of seven of the nation's 7.2 million Mexican Americans still resided in the southwest. Texas had the largest proportion—21 percent—but California had by far the largest number—3.6 million.

In recent decades Mexican Americans appear to have made slow but steady relative gains with respect to education, income, and occupational position. Their occupational gains were most pronounced during the Second World War, probably because of labor shortages, and during the 1960s, when national economic growth was rapid. A number of studies agree that a substantial portion of the income differences between Mexican Americans and Anglos can be explained by differences in educational attainment, but that a considerable earnings gap remains even after educational differences are taken into account. Overt discrimination has become less a problem for Mexican Americans than it is for blacks, but Mexican Americans continue to experience the consequences of more subtle processes involving criteria unrelated to ability to perform a job. But even in the absence of labor market discrimination, increased years of schooling alone would not necessarily eliminate Mexican Americans' income and employment difficulties. The income benefits of education often do not occur immediately; there is a lagged response of income to education. In addition, educational quality is variable. The financing of public education by local school districts tends to result in relatively inferior schools in districts that have a low property tax base, a condition that characterizes many Mexican American communities in the borderlands. Moreover, large numbers of resident Mexican alien children are enrolled in most borderlands school districts; whether these children are "legal" or "illegal" is not investigated in practice. Many resident Mexican alien parents are taxpayers, but the net effect of the presence of their children is overcrowded schools coupled with financial inability—despite tax rates that are relatively high—to construct additional facilities. Some have argued that because state and federal policies allowed the influx of resident Mexican alien children, state and federal funds should be provided for facilities for them, just as federal aid to school districts is justified in areas that have been "impacted" by federal activities such as military bases. This proposal has merit so long as burdensome reporting systems and wasteful restrictions, which have characterized special federal educational programs in the borderlands in the past, are not imposed on local school districts.

The vast majority of migrant farm workers, the most disadvantaged group of workers in the United States, are Mexican Americans, most of whom use the Lower Rio Grande Valley of Texas as a home base. Federal programs appear to have been of little help to these persons, though successes may not always be realized locally: that is, recipients of education and job-skill training may find more stable and better-paying employment in other regions. However, the "slack" in the supply of migrant farm workers tends to be taken up in part by Mexicans; in Hidalgo County, which has a high concentration of migrant farm workers, over 40 percent of farm-worker household heads were born in Mexico. Without pretending that unionization is a panacea, the record in California does indicate that the traditional plight of Mexican American farm workers has been eased through the organizing efforts of César Chávez and the United Farm Workers Union. It now remains for Texas to grant farm workers the unionization rights already held by California farm workers.

During the 1950s and 1960s, the Mexican American population in California grew much more rapidly than that in Texas, but between 1970 and 1978 the respective growth rates for this group were about the same. Moreover, whereas the 1969 median family income of the Spanish-origin population in Texas was only 66 percent of the corresponding California median, it had risen to 93 percent by 1975. Between 1969 and 1977, per capita personal income rose by 88 percent in California and by 108 percent in Texas. Thus, it appears that increasing numbers of Mexican Americans have been sharing in the fruits of the booming Texas economy. Nevertheless, future gains by Mexican Americans in Texas, as elsewhere, will probably require greater political organization. Mexican Americans have had a reputation—even among themselves—for inability to organize in their own self-interest. Communities Organized for Public Service (COPS), a privately financed organization in San Antonio, has done much to dispel this notion. The history of minority achievements in the United States and the experience of COPS suggest that federal bureaucracies are not the answer to the employment, income, and housing problems of minorities. While it is important to have the active cooperation of elected officials and the private sector, in the long run a people's own efforts are its greatest resource.

From all indications, the southwest borderlands will continue to have greater population and employment growth than the United States as a whole during the decade ahead. In addition, the Texas portion is likely to grow more rapidly than the borderlands as a whole, especially in terms of per capita income. The negative aspect of this conjecture is that the area is starting from such a low base, but there also are a number of positive developments. The Texas borderlands region is less dependent on military employment than in the past, though military employment in the El Paso area has increased despite nationally declining employment in this sector. The growth of population and *maquiladora* employment on the Mexican side of the border will induce more trade and services employment on the U.S. side as in the past. The growth of *maquiladora* jobs and related manufacturing activities on the U.S. side has been especially evident in Ciudad Juárez and El Paso. "Little Detroits" are being established by General Motors and Chrysler in Ciudad Juárez, where manufacturing workers have been added at a rate of 5,000 per year since 1977, bringing the total to 37,500 at the end of 1979.[7] Moreover, we have entered an era when economic activity will be increasingly affected by energy availability. Unlike the rest of the borderlands, the Texas portion not only has sufficient energy for its own requirements, but also is expected to be a net exporter of energy in the 1980s.[8] To the extent that Mexican oil and gas are channeled northward to the border—natural gas lines already are projected to feed Reynosa and Matamoros[9]—or even beyond, there should be further stimulation of the Texas border economy. And problems arising from water shortages are less likely to affect the Texas portion of the borderlands because of the presence of the Rio Grande. Finally, belated but rapidly increasing linkages with the rest of the Texas economy will certainly be beneficial to the border area. It may be hoped that Mexican Americans, who constitute a majority of the Texas borderlands population, will have an equitable share in the growth of the area.

The U.S. and Mexican sides of the border share many common problems, yet millions of persons from both countries apparently have gained some advantages by moving freely to a region that was scarcely inhabited at the beginning of this century. Today, both sides of the border exist in a symbiotic relationship whose realities contradict both border region theory and, too frequently, the assumptions of planners in both countries.

Oil, international migration, increasing trade, and the nature of the shared border itself mean that the futures of the United States and Mexico will be more interrelated than was the case in the past. While the totality of the issues that increasingly bind these countries together clearly transcends the borderlands, this region nonetheless provides a unique laboratory for international cooperation. Success in this regard requires that the ignorance of the past concerning the borderlands be replaced by greater understanding. Chili con carne was not invented in Mexico and the cowboy was not invented in the United States.

Appendixes

A. Counties Designated for Inclusion in the Southwest Border Regional Commission as of July 1, 1980

Arizona

Cochise
Pima
Santa Cruz
Yuma

California

Imperial
Riverside
San Diego

New Mexico

Dona Ana
Grant
Hidalgo
Luna
Otero

Texas

Brewster
Cameron
Culberson
Dimmit
Edwards
El Paso
Hidalgo
Hudspeth
Jeff Davis
Jim Hogg
Kinney
La Salle
Maverick
Pecos
Presidio
Real
Starr
Terrell
Uvalde
Val Verde
Webb
Willacy
Zapata
Zavala

Note: Twenty-four Texas counties were added later in 1980. They correspond to the Alamo (San Antonio) and Coastal Bend (Corpus Christi) Councils of Government.

B. Counties in the Borderlands BEA Regions

San Diego

San Diego (core)
Imperial

Tucson

Pima (core)
Cochise
Graham
Greenlee
Santa Cruz

El Paso

El Paso (core)
Brewster
Chaves, NM
Culberson
Dona Ana, NM
Eddy, NM
Grant,NM
Hidalgo, NM
Hudspeth
Jeff Davis
Luna, NM
Otero, NM
Presidio
Sierra, NM

San Antonio

Bexar (core)
Comal (core)
Guadalupe (core)
Atascosa
Bandera
Dimmit
Edwards
Frio
Gillespie
Gonzales
Jim Hogg
Karnes
Kendall
Kerr
Kinney
La Salle
Maverick
McMullen
Medina
Real
Uvalde
Val Verde
Webb
Wilson
Zapata
Zavala

Brownsville

Cameron (core)
Hidalgo
Starr
Willacy

Note: Unless otherwise indicated the counties listed are in the same state as their metropolitan core.

C. BEA Employment Estimates by Sector, United States and Southwest Border Regional Commission Counties, by State, 1969 and 1976

The employment data used in this section are estimates of full-time and part-time wage and salary employees plus the number of proprietors of unincorporated businesses. The estimates were made by the Regional Economic Measurement Division of the Bureau of Economic Analysis, U.S. Department of Commerce. Approximately three-fourths of the total employment consists of workers covered by state unemployment insurance programs; thus most of the data are derived from administrative records of covered employment provided by state Employment Security agencies. Estimates of non-covered employment—which are less reliable than those for covered employment—are based on a variety of sources, including the Old Age and Survivors Insurance Program, the Civil Service Commission, various censuses, and information supplied by professional associations.

The widely used Bureau of Labor Statistics employment series is not used here primarily because it does not provide data at the county level; it only gives information for the United States as a whole, states, and selected labor market areas, usually SMSAs. Moreover, the BLS series is limited to nonfarm establishments and excludes household domestic workers, military personnel, and all proprietors and self-employed persons. Both the BLS and the BEA employment series are a count of jobs rather than persons—that is, a person employed by more than one establishment is counted at each place of employment.

Table C.1. BEA Employment Estimates: United States

Sector	1969		1976	
	Number	% of Total	Number	% of Total
Total employment	78,247,265	—	85,884,900	—
Agricultural services, forestry, fisheries	282,845	0.4	376,000	0.4
Mining	622,766	0.7	779,000	0.9
Contract construction	3,617,094	4.6	3,617,000	4.2
Manufacturing	20,270,000	25.9	19,041,000	22.2
Transportation, utilities, communications	4,455,000	5.7	4,560,000	5.3
Wholesale trade	3,731,825	4.8	4,570,000	5.3
Retail trade	11,204,337	14.3	13,290,000	15.5
Finance, insurance, real estate	3,597,691	4.6	4,356,000	5.1
Services	13,306,667	17.0	16,202,000	18.9
Government	15,882,583	20.3	17,690,000	20.6
Unclassified	1,276,456	1.6	1,403,900	1.6

Table C.2. BEA Employment Estimates: California Border

Sector	1969		1976	
	Number	% of Total	Number	% of Total
Total employment	728,931	—	846,183	—
Agricultural services, forestry, fisheries	6,823	0.9	17,072	2.0
Mining	2,083	0.3	2,370	0.3
Contract construction	27,646	3.8	34,097	4.1
Manufacturing	90,880	12.5	94,297	11.1
Transportation, utilities, communications	25,410	3.5	29,937	3.5
Wholesale trade	19,392	2.7	26,271	3.1
Retail trade	96,718	13.3	132,218	15.6
Finance, insurance, real estate	23,094	3.2	33,896	4.0
Services	114,854	15.8	148,875	17.6
Government	298,298	40.9	298,542	35.3
Unclassified	23,733	3.3	28,608	3.4

Table C.3. BEA Employment Estimates: Arizona Border

Sector	1969		1976	
	Number	% of Total	Number	% of Total
Total employment	171,477	—	223,087	—
Agricultural services, forestry, fisheries	1,391	0.8	1,438	0.6
Mining	7,953	4.6	8,294	3.7
Contract construction	11,974	7.0	11,423	5.1
Manufacturing	10,922	6.4	16,278	7.3
Transportation, utilities, communications	7,325	4.3	9,381	4.2
Wholesale trade	4,154	2.4	5,926	2.7
Retail trade	27,792	16.2	39,290	17.6
Finance, insurance, real estate	5,645	3.3	7,478	3.4
Services	30,577	17.8	43,026	19.3
Government	57,397	33.5	75,627	33.9
Unclassified	6,347	3.7	4,926	2.2

Table C.4. BEA Employment Estimates: New Mexico Border

Sector	1969		1976	
	Number	% of Total	Number	% of Total
Total employment	54,872	—	62,282	—
Agricultural services, forestry, fisheries	465	0.8	449	0.7
Mining	2,547	4.6	2,955	4.7
Contract construction	2,723	5.0	3,275	5.3
Manufacturing	2,942	5.4	3,513	5.6
Transportation, utilities, communications	2,144	3.9	2,279	3.7
Wholesale trade	577	1.1	1,325	2.1
Retail trade	6,570	12.0	8,891	14.3
Finance, insurance, real estate	1,254	2.3	1,593	2.6
Services	7,992	14.6	8,311	13.3
Government	24,996	45.6	27,355	43.9
Unclassified	2,662	4.9	2,336	3.8

Table C.5. BEA Employment Estimates: Texas Border

Sector	1969		1976	
	Number	% of Total	Number	% of Total
Total employment	296,248	—	364,090	—
Agricultural services, forestry, fisheries	3,123	1.1	5,003	1.4
Mining	3,237	1.1	4,537	1.2
Contract construction	13,976	4.7	15,763	4.3
Manufacturing	34,675	11.7	52,370	14.4
Transportation, utilities, communications	16,415	5.5	20,189	5.5
Wholesale trade	14,399	4.9	21,591	5.9
Retail trade	47,876	16.2	66,473	18.3
Finance, insurance, real estate	8,248	2.8	12,918	3.5
Services	43,169	14.6	54,047	14.8
Government	94,970	32.1	97,864	26.9
Unclassified	16,160	5.5	13,335	3.7

D. Nature and Limitations of the Continuous Work History Sample

The Continuous Work History Sample (CWHS) is a sample of workers' earnings records from employers' quarterly reports to the Social Security Administration (SSA). The sample is based on specific digits in workers' Social Security numbers. Because the same Social Security numbers are included in the sample for each period, work histories for workers in the sample can be assembled by linking the data files for successive periods.

In the mid-1960s the Bureau of Economic Analysis, U.S. Department of Commerce, began to develop a system for summarizing and making available through analytic tables the work force structure and migration data included in the one percent CWHS. Work histories include data on sex, race, year of birth, and, on an annual basis, place of employment, industry of employment, and an estimate of wages earned from each Social Security covered job.

The CWHS data are subject to a number of limitations, including sampling errors, incomplete coverage, lack of timeliness, and nonsampling errors arising from the reporting and processing of the data. The SSA has extensively studied the sampling variability associated with CWHS data. The approximate standard errors for estimates of workers with specific characteristics in the one percent sample are as follows:

Estimated Total	Standard Error	Relative Error
500	222	.444
1,000	315	.315
2,500	497	.199
5,000	704	.141
10,000	995	.100
50,000	2,224	.044
100,000	3,145	.031
500,000	7,018	.014
1,000,000	9,900	.010

The relative standard errors associated with estimates of average total earnings are as follows:

Population Base	
1,000	0.370
2,500	0.230
5,000	0.160
10,000	0.120
50,000	0.051
100,000	0.036
500,000	0.016
1,000,000	0.011

The CWHS does not contain information on workers not covered by the Social Security program. The largest groups in this category are federal government workers who are covered under the Civil Service Retirement System, railroad workers, certain agricultural and domestic workers, and about one-third of the employees of state and local governments. Largely because of these omissions, the first-quarter 1970 CWHS file contained approximately 80 percent of the total labor force.

The timeliness of CWHS data presents another problem. The annual SSA files are not available until about two and a half years after the end of the year in question.

Finally, perhaps the most serious difficulty with the CWHS data is the presence of reporting and processing errors in the geographic classification of workers. Some employers refuse to comply with the voluntary SSA establishment reporting plan. Moreover, changes in an employer's reporting system can produce erroneous "flows" of workers from one area to another.

Despite these limitations, the CWHS is a uniquely detailed source of information on work force characteristics and work force changes in subnational areas for intercensal years.

E. Shift-Share Analysis of Borderlands Employment Change

Classical shift-share analysis is a straightforward technique for decomposing regional employment change into three components: national growth, industry mix, and competitive position.[1] Mathematically stated, let d_{ij} be the employment growth in sector i of region j, g_{ij} the national growth effect in sector i of region j, k_{ij} the industry-mix effect in sector i of region j, and c_{ij} the competitive effect in sector i of region j. Then

$$d_{ij} = g_{ij} + k_{ij} + c_{ij}$$
$$g_{ij} = b_{ij}r_{oo}$$
$$k_{ij} = b_{ij}r_{io} - b_{ij}r_{oo} = b_{ij}(r_{io} - r_{oo})$$
$$c_{ij} = b_{ij}r_{ij} - b_{ij}r_{io} = b_{ij}(r_{ij} - r_{io}),$$

where b_{ij} = employment in sector i of region j, r_{oo} = national average rate of growth, r_{io} = national average rate of growth of sector i, and r_{ij} = growth rate of sector i of region j.

Therefore,

$$d_{ij} = b_{ij}r_{oo} + b_{ij}(r_{io} - r_{oo}) + b_{ij}(r_{ij} - r_{io}).$$

Each sector i of each region j has a standard growth, given by g_{ij}, to which has to be added the contributions to its growth (positive or negative) caused by specifically regional factors, k_{ij} and c_{ij}. The industry-mix effect, k_{ij}, represents the positive or negative effects of the specialization of regional employment in sectors where the rate of growth at the national level is more or less rapid. The competitive effect, c_{ij}, shows the contribution to growth due to the special dynamism of the given sector in that region compared with the average growth of that sector at the national level.

Because the competitive component measures the effects of region-specific influences on employment growth in a particular region, it is the most interesting of the three components of shift-share analysis. However, shift-share analysis alone reveals nothing concerning the specific nature of these influences. F. J. B. Stilwell suggested that the competitive component captures the effects of several influences: the relative attractiveness of a region to population and to employers; the effects of population migration; the effects of government-subsidized regional development policies; the nature and adequacy of public infrastructure; and multiplier effects of other local developments.[2] James A. Chalmers and Terrance L. Beckhelm found that the nature of competitive shifts in twenty-three industries in a cross section of SMSAs can be explained by spatial variations in profits.[3] Edgar S. Dunn, Jr., argued that a positive competitive component indicates that a region's access to markets and to factors "is being augmented relative to other regions engaged in the same activity."[4] John H. Cumberland maintained that the competitive component is a measure of relative regional advantages, such as levels and types of infrastructure, educational and skill levels of the labor force, and worker efficiency.[5] In the present context it is particularly noteworthy that a study of regional economic growth in West Germany suggested that the competitive component captures the effects of international influences on employment change in border regions.[6]

The classical shift-share framework has been reformulated by J. M. Esteban-Marquillas,[7] so that

$$d_{ij} = b'_{ij}r_{io} + r_{io}(b_{ij} - b'_{ij}) + b'_{ij}(r_{ij} - r_{io}) + (b_{ij} - b'_{ij})(r_{ij} - r_{io}),$$

where d_{ij} = employment growth in sector i of region j, r_{io} = national average rate of growth of sector i, b_{ij} = employment in sector i of region j, r_{ij} = growth rate of sector i of region j, and b'_{ij} = homothetic employment in sector i of region j. In classical shift-share analysis, the competitive effect is influenced by and interwoven with the industry-mix effect. In order to deal with this difficulty, Esteban-Marquillas reformulated the competitive effect by introducing the concept of homothetic employment, which is defined to be the employment that sector i in region j would have if the structure of employment in region j were identical to that for the nation. Thus,

$$b'_{ij} = b_{oj}\frac{b_{io}}{b_{oo}} = b_{io}\frac{b_{oj}}{b_{oo}},$$

where b_{io} = national employment in sector i, b_{oo} = total national employment, and b_{oj} = total employment in region j.

Tables E.1 through E.5 present shift-share analyses of employment change between 1972 and 1977 in the five respective borderlands BEA regions.[8] In each table, the four different components of

Table E.1. Shift-Share Analysis of Employment Change in the San Diego BEA Region, 1972–1977

	Distribution Effect, 1972	National Growth Effect	Industry-Mix Effect	Allocation Effect	Competitive Effect (Esteban-Marquillas)	Competitive Effect (Classical)
Total employment	−17,422	63,892	−18,275	−9,593	89,357	79,761
Proprietors	−17,113	3,473	1,008	−3,647	7,517	3,870
Farm proprietors	−309	−1,320	1,045	−3,624	4,577	953
Nonfarm proprietors	17,421	4,793	−37	−23	2,940	2,917
Total wage and salary	8,109	60,419	−19,283	−5,946	81,840	75,891
Farm	9,312	617	558	39	43	82
Nonfarm	−106,397	59,802	−19,841	−5,985	81,797	75,809
Private	−836	50,778	−6,510	−17,333	69,264	51,928
Agricultural services			D[b]			
Mining			D			
Construction	−73,847	640	−20	−233	7,599	7,366
Manufacturing	−43,100	4,656	−1,896	−12,487	24,771	12,284
Nondurables	−30,747	245	−182	−5,993	8,059	2,066
Durables	−10,003	4,411	−1,714	−6,494	16,712	10,218
Transportation	−13,264	1,353	−416	−932	3,028	2,096
Wholesale	−2,221	5,844	−2,742	−3,559	7,586	4,026
Retail	−3,015	12,853	−328	−361	14,151	13,789
F.I.R.E.[a]	−1,938	3,936	−415	−275	2,605	2,330
Services	115,709	19,294	−362	−125	6,686	6,560
Government	20,177	9,024	−13,331	11,348	12,533	23,881
Federal civilian	101,361	266	264	209	211	420
Federal military	−5,829	−2,468	−12,768	11,878	2,296	14,174
State and local		11,226	−827	−739	10,026	9,287

[a] Finance, insurance, and real estate.
[b] Federal government prohibits disclosure of data to protect confidentiality.

Table E.2. Shift-Share Analysis of Employment Change in the Tucson BEA Region, 1972–1977

	Distribution Effect, 1972	National Growth Effect	Industry-Mix Effect	Allocation Effect	Competitive Effect (Esteban-Marquillas)	Competitive Effect (Classical)
Total employment	-5,025	19,868	1,734	-12,586	14,305	1,718
Proprietors	-4,993	1,079	301	-663	727	64
Farm proprietors	-32	-411	305	-663	893	230
Nonfarm proprietors	5,023	1,490	-4		-166	-166
Total wage and salary	-775	18,789	1,433	-11,923	13,578	1,654
Farm	5,798	192	-53	276	-994	-718
Nonfarm	-16,456	18,597	1,486	-12,199	14,572	2,372
Private	8	15,790	2,141	-13,214	8,311	-4,904
Agricultural services	10,126	235	3	1	87	88
Mining	5,800	450	3,267	-4,834	-666	-5,500
Construction	-29,907	199	136	-1,113	-1,627	-2,740
Manufacturing	-13,538	1,448	-970	-7,671	11,076	3,405
Nondurables	-16,369	76	-57	-2,644	3,520	875
Durables	-2,092	1,372	-913	-5,027	7,556	2,529
Transportation	-4,316	421	-87	-169	815	646
Wholesale	3,917	1,817	-892	472	-960	-489
Retail	-2,112	3,997	579	177	1,222	1,399
F.I.R.E.[a]	2,120	1,224	-291	24	-101	-77
Services	22,254	5,999	396	-101	-1,535	-1,636
Government	3,992	2,807	-655	1,015	6,261	7,276
Federal civilian	12,313	83	52	461	730	1,191
Federal military	5,949	-767	-1,551	-890	-440	-1,331
State and local		3,491	844	1,444	5,971	7,416

[a]Finance, insurance, and real estate.

Table E.3. Shift-Share Analysis of Employment Change in the El Paso BEA Region, 1972–1977

	Distribution Effect, 1972	National Growth Effect	Industry-Mix Effect	Allocation Effect	Competitive Effect (Esteban-Marquillas)	Competitive Effect (Classical)
Total employment	25,229	25,229	-2,592	-2,286	23,440	21,152
Proprietors	-5,190	1,372	173	-423	1,165	742
Farm proprietors	-4,393	-521	268	-404	785	381
Nonfarm proprietors	-797	1,893	-95	-19	380	361
Total wage and salary	5,191	23,857	-2,765	-1,863	22,275	20,410
Farm	3,528	244	243	-648	-651	-1,299
Nonfarm	1,663	23,613	-3,008	-1,215	22,926	21,709
Private	-25,768	20,050	-1,622	-7,576	18,521	10,944
Agricultural services	77	298	27	14	150	163
Mining	4,562	571	1,472	-861	-334	-1,195
Construction	2,494	253	59	111	479	590
Manufacturing	-22,563	1,839	-1,290	-6,665	11,497	4,832
Nondurables	623	97	3	66	2,426	2,492
Durables	-23,186	1,742	-1,293	-6,731	9,071	2,340
Transportation	461	534	19	37	1,038	1,076
Wholesale	-1,860	2,307	-385	23	-140	-117
Retail	333	5,075	49	44	4,588	4,632
F.I.R.E.[a]	-3,241	1,554	-446	-197	685	488
Services	-6,031	7,619	-1,127	-82	558	475
Government	27,431	3,563	-1,386	6,361	4,405	10,765
Federal civilian	8,575	105	112	294	275	569
Federal military	15,582	-975	-1,963	5,943	2,951	8,894
State and local	3,274	4,433	465	124	1,179	1,302

[a] Finance, insurance, and real estate.

Table E.4. Shift-Share Analysis of Employment Change in the San Antonio BEA Region, 1972–1977

	Distribution Effect, 1972	National Growth Effect	Industry-Mix Effect	Allocation Effect	Competitive Effect (Esteban-Marquillas)	Competitive Effect (Classical)
Total employment	3,343	51,398	−10,035	−29,081	43,295	14,217
Proprietors	3,343	2,794	45	33	143	176
Farm proprietors	1,960	−1,062	−120	44	390	434
Nonfarm proprietors	1,383	3,856	165	−11	−247	−258
Total wage and salary	−3,344	48,604	−10,080	−29,114	43,152	14,041
Farm	2,179	497	150	−441	−1,461	−1,902
Nonfarm	−5,523	48,107	−10,230	−28,673	44,613	15,943
Private	−80,166	40,848	−4,168	−19,153	40,464	21,313
Agricultural services	−262	608	−92	−81	531	451
Mining	−256	1,164	−83	−163	2,290	2,128
Construction	1,631	515	38	128	1,721	1,848
Manufacturing	−66,816	3,746	−2,709	−16,973	24,339	7,366
Nondurables	−19,724	197	−83	−1,381	3,264	1,883
Durables	−47,092	3,549	−2,626	−15,592	21,075	5,483
Transportation	−9,520	1,088	−396	−2,105	5,783	3,678
Wholesale	−785	4,701	−162	21	−615	−593
Retail	971	10,339	144	73	5,239	5,311
F.I.R.E.ᵃ	−1,025	3,167	−141	−50	1,118	1,069
Services	−4,104	15,520	−767	−3	58	55
Government	74,643	7,259	−6,062	−9,520	4,149	−5,370
Federal civilian	31,033	214	406	−2,345	−1,237	−3,582
Federal military	47,249	−1,986	−5,952	−6,738	−2,248	−8,986
State and local	−3,639	9,031	−516	−437	7,634	7,198

ᵃFinance, insurance, and real estate.

Table E.5. Shift-Share Analysis of Employment Change in the Brownsville BEA Region, 1972–1977

	Distribution Effect, 1972	National Growth Effect	Industry-Mix Effect	Allocation Effect	Competitive Effect (Esteban-Marquillas)	Competitive Effect (Classical)
Total employment	11,895	11,895	1,649	-6,044	23,815	17,778
Proprietors	4,970	646	83	104	583	688
Farm proprietors	2,831	-246	-173	-106	-151	-257
Nonfarm proprietors	2,139	892	256	210	734	945
Total wage and salary	-4,969	11,249	1,566	-6,148	23,232	17,090
Farm	6,287	115	432	-1,003	-267	-1,269
Nonfarm	-11,256	11,134	1,134	-5,145	23,499	18,359
Private	-13,405	9,454	182	-5,945	20,267	14,327
Agricultural services	2,622	141	924	1,347	205	1,553
Mining	124	269	40	-2	-12	-13
Construction	-1	119			1,294	1,294
Manufacturing	-14,067	867	-650	-6,218	11,590	5,372
Nondurables	-2,598	46	-11	-1,256	5,216	3,960
Durables	-11,469	821	-639	-4,962	6,374	1,412
Transportation	-1,381	252	-57	-109	477	369
Wholesale	2,184	1,088	451	-112	-269	-380
Retail	2,635	2,393	389	468	2,877	3,345
F.I.R.E.ᵃ	-2,363	733	-325	-1,023	2,305	1,282
Services	-3,158	3,592	-590	-296	1,800	1,505
Government	2,149	1,680	952	800	3,232	4,032
Federal civilian	-1,216	50	-16	-167	520	353
Federal military	-1,830	-460	231	6	-12	-6
State and local	5,195	2,090	737	961	2,724	3,685

ᵃFinance, insurance, and real estate.

employment change in the Esteban-Marquillas equation are given in columns two, three, five, and four, respectively.

In each table, column one shows, by sector, the difference between actual employment in 1972 and the employment there would have been if the regional structure of employment were identical with that of the United States (homothetic employment), that is, $b_{ij} - b'_{ij}$.

The second column shows the change in regional employment that would have occurred if the region had the national structure of sectoral employment in 1972 and if each sector grew at the national rate between 1972 and 1977, that is, $b'_{ij}r_{io}$.

The third column shows the employment change that occurred because of the differential distribution of employment between the region and the nation. It is the differential structure from the first column multiplied by the national growth rate for each sector, that is, $r_{io}(b_{ij} - b'_{ij})$.

The fourth column shows the allocation effect, which is the combined effect of differential structure and differential growth rates between the region and the nation, that is, $(b_{ij} - b'_{ij})(r_{ij} - r_{io})$. If the region is not specialized in a given sector $(b_{ij} - b'_{ij} = 0)$ or if the sector does not have any competitive advantage $(r_{ij} - r_{io} = 0)$, then the allocation effect is nil and the sector does not contribute to regional growth through this effect.

The fifth column gives the employment change that would have occurred because of regional-national growth rate differences, if the regional structure of employment were identical with that of the United States in 1972, that is, $b'_{ij}(r_{ij} - r_{io})$. This is the Esteban-Marquillas competitive effect.

The sixth column shows the classical competitive effect, b_{ij} $(r_{ij} - r_{io})$, which is equivalent to the sum of the values in the fourth and fifth columns.

Although the classical and Esteban-Marquillas formulations of shift-share analysis both use the notion of a competitive effect, this is not an entirely correct description of the phenomenon in question. Most U.S. workers are not engaged in the production of interregionally traded goods; thus the competitive effect cannot simply be attributed to regional comparative advantage. However, it will be argued here that the competitive effect is influenced by border location, even where nontraded goods are concerned. But because of the ambiguity associated with the term "competitive effect," it will be replaced in the following discussion by the term "regional conditions."

The U.S. borderlands regions have a number of similarities with respect to the behavior of key sectors. For example, all regions have less employment in manufacturing than would have been the case if the regional structure of employment were identical with that of the United States (column one). In each region, change in manufacturing employment was marked by a strong regional conditions effect but a negative allocation effect. Regional conditions advantages derive from relatively cheap labor, twin plant linkages with assembly plants (maquiladoras) on the Mexican side of the border, and amenities (especially in San Diego and Tucson) conducive to the location of newer, diversified production activities. Thus, although the U.S. borderlands regions are not specialized in manufacturing, they have been benefiting from and no doubt will continue to exploit advantages related to proximity to Mexico.

The components of change in retail trade employment behave in a similar manner along the border. In every region except San Diego, the national growth, allocation, and regional conditions effects are all positive. In relation to the United States, these regions are specialized in retail trade and have a marked regional conditions advantage that is no doubt related to purchases made by residents of Mexico. San Diego has a negative allocation effect because it is not specialized in retail trade, but like the other borderlands regions it has a strongly positive regional conditions effect.

In 1972, every borderlands BEA region had a higher proportion of employment in the government sector than was the case in the United States as a whole. Military employment, which declined nationally between 1972 and 1977, also declined in the Tucson, Brownsville, and, especially, San Antonio BEA regions. Because of regional conditions, military employment did not change substantially in the San Diego BEA region and increased significantly in the El Paso BEA region. However, overall gains in government employment in the borderlands were largely a consequence of increases in the state and local sectors.

Service sector employment grew rapidly in the borderlands between 1972 and 1977, though only Tucson was relatively specialized in this sector in 1972. San Diego and Brownsville had rapid growth because of strong national growth and regional conditions effects. Tucson, El Paso, and San Antonio all had strongly positive national growth effects, but in Tucson this was offset in part by regional conditions disadvantages, while in El Paso it was partially offset by a negative industry-mix effect.

Despite variations among sectors, total employment growth in all of the borderlands regions has been mainly a result of large positive national growth and regional conditions effects. The industry-mix and allocation effects have usually been negative or, if positive, of small magnitude. Regional conditions advantages have been particularly strong in the manufacturing, retail trade, and state and local government sectors. These advantages can be explained in large part by historical and contemporary factors related to the area's proximity to Mexico. As already indicated, manufacturing activities have been attracted to the borderlands by relatively cheap labor and by opportunities to link operations on the U.S. side of the border with assembly work in the Mexican *maquiladoras.* The large and rapidly growing Mexican border population makes many of its retail purchases in U.S. stores. And problems arising from relatively poor social and economic conditions in the southwest borderlands have generated substantial state and local employment growth in agencies whose objective is to alleviate such conditions; much of this "state and local" employment has in fact been supported by some form of federal revenue sharing.

Notes

1. *Regional Development Issues in the Southwest Borderlands*

1. For information in this regard, see Niles Hansen, "Regional Policies in the United States: Experience and Prospects," in Antoni R. Kuklinski (ed.), *Regional Development and Planning: International Perspectives*, pp. 139–151.
2. Kevin F. McCarthy and Peter A. Morrison, *The Changing Demographic and Economic Structure of Nonmetropolitan Areas in the United States.*
3. The relevant issues are critically discussed in Benjamin Chinitz, "Regional Economic Development Commissions: The Title V Program," *Canadian Journal of Regional Science* 1, no. 2 (Autumn 1978): 107–127.
4. SMSAs are defined by the U.S. Bureau of the Census. An SMSA must have a central city or group of cities with at least 50,000 inhabitants. In addition to the central city or cities, the designation criteria provide that the SMSA include the county in which the central city is located and adjacent counties that are determined to be metropolitan in character and economically and socially integrated with the county of the central city. At the end of 1977 there were 281 SMSAs.
5. Riverside County, California, is an SMSA county included in the Southwest Border Regional Commission. However, the Riverside–San Bernardino–Ontario SMSA also includes San Bernardino County, which is not in the commission area. In the present study, Riverside County is considered to be a border county, but the SMSA to which it belongs is not considered to be a border SMSA. If Riverside County had been excluded, the SMSA population of the Southwest Border Regional Commission would still account for 83 percent of the region's total population.
6. Richard L. Nostrand, "The Hispanic-American Borderland: Delimitation of an American Culture Region," *Annals of the Association of American Geographers* 60, no. 4 (December 1970): 638–661.
7. Joel Garreau, "Nine Nations, Indivisible," *Austin American-Statesman*, April 29, 1979, p. C-5.

8. Steven Strasser et al., "Mexico's New Muscle," *Newsweek*, October 1, 1979, p. 32.

9. Karl A. Fox and T. Krishna Kumar, "The Functional Economic Area: Delineation and Implications for Economic Analysis and Public Policy," *Papers and Proceedings of the Regional Science Association* 15 (1965): 57–85.

10. In most instances the primary data source used in this regard was journey-to-work information from the 1960 population census; that is, counties were usually assigned to cores in accordance with commuting patterns. In cases where the commuting sheds of core areas overlapped, counties were included in the region containing the core to which most workers commuted. Where ties with two cores were exceptionally strong, the two were combined into one BEA region. In many cases the association between counties and a particular region was not based on direct commuting ties but rather on commuting linkages to noncore counties, which in turn were linked to the urban cores. In relatively remote rural areas where commuting data were not adequate, other allocation criteria were used, in particular metropolitan newspaper circulation and the advice of authorities such as state planners familiar with local conditions.

Because there was a minimum of commuting across BEA region boundaries, each region included the place of work and place of residence of its work force. Each area was also relatively self-sufficient in the output of its local service industries. The types of export activities within a particular region depend on the relative availability of the inputs required in the production process. Regions export commodities for which they have a comparative advantage and import other commodities. By this participation in interregional trade the various BEA regions resemble nations engaging in international trade, except that the regions are less affected by barriers to trade and to the movement of labor and capital.

11. U.S. Bureau of the Census, *County and City Data Book, 1977*, pp. 600, 756. Although Los Angeles has more persons of Mexican descent than any other city except Mexico City, the proportion of its total population accounted for by persons of Spanish heritage is only 18.4 percent, ibid., p. 612.

12. Governors of California, Arizona, New Mexico, and Texas, *Application for Designation as a Title V Regional Action Planning Commission*, p. i.

13. U.S. Central Intelligence Agency, *Handbook of Economic Statistics, 1978*, ER78-10365, pp. 8, 11.

14. U.S. Department of Labor, Employment and Training Administration, *Area Trends in Employment and Unemployment*, January–April, 1979, pp. 62–63.

15. U.S. Bureau of the Census, *County and City Data Book, 1972,* pp. 451, 475.
16. U.S. Department of Labor, Employment and Training Administration, *Area Trends,* pp. 42–45.
17. U.S. Bureau of the Census, *County and City Data Book, 1972,* pp. 43, 67.
18. Throughout this discussion, per capita personal income earnings within states are taken from U.S. Department of Commerce, Bureau of Economic Analysis, Regional Economic Measurement Division, "County and Metropolitan Area Personal Income," *Survey of Current Business* 59, no. 4 (April 1979). In 1975, the index of comparative costs, based on an intermediate budget for a four-person family (U.S. average urban costs = 100), was 98 for San Diego. See U.S. Department of Labor, Bureau of Labor Statistics, *Handbook of Labor Statistics 1977,* Bulletin no. 166, p. 277.
19. Manuel Vic Villalpando et al., *A Study of the Socio-economic Impact of Illegal Aliens on the County of San Diego.*
20. Joseph E. Pluta, "Urban Fiscal Strain and the Health of Large Texas Cities," *Texas Business Review* 53, no. 1 (January–February 1979): 9.
21. Ibid., p. 8.

2. The Nature of Border Regions

1. A distinction needs to be made between border regions and frontier regions. While the latter may in some cases be border regions, they are usually regarded as relatively undeveloped areas whose settlement is desirable in order to exploit natural resources. In this sense, the U.S. frontier disappeared nearly a century ago. In contrast, border area development policies in South America frequently pertain to frontier regions. See Walter Stöhr, *Regional Development Experiences and Prospects in Latin America,* pp. 156–166. Finally, in drawing on the extensive French literature on border regions, I have translated *frontière* as border or boundary because this is nearly always its sense.
2. Paul Guichonnet and Claude Raffestin, *Géographie des frontières,* pp. 11–19.
3. Ibid., pp. 20–21.
4. Niles Hansen, "Economic Aspects of Regional Separatism," *Papers of the Regional Science Association* 41 (1978): 143–152.
5. The imperialist principle also applies to France under Louis XIV and Napoleon. During the nineteenth century the central government in Paris devoted a great deal of energy to making peripheral regions more French. It was even necessary to introduce the French language to populations that spoke Catalan, Provençal, Italian, German, Flemish, Bret-

on, and Basque. In a very real sense, France was still creating the *patrie* that was allegedly already included within its borders.

6. René Gendarme, "Les problèmes économiques des régions frontières européennes," *Revue économique* 21, no. 6 (November 1970): 894.

7. Walter Christaller, *Central Places in Southern Germany*, pp. 72–76.

8. Ibid., pp. 77–80.

9. Ibid., p. 80.

10. Ibid., pp. 95–96.

11. Ibid., p. 79.

12. August Lösch, *The Economics of Location*, p. 199.

13. Ibid., p. 200.

14. Herbert Giersch, "Economic Union between Nations and the Location of Industries," *Review of Economic Studies* 17, no. 43 (1949–50): 87–97.

15. Edgar M. Hoover, *The Location of Economic Activity*, pp. 216–222, 226–237.

16. Ibid., pp. 223–224.

17. Christaller, *Central Places in Southern Germany*, p. 46.

18. Lösch, *The Economics of Location*, pp. 382–388.

19. Bertil Ohlin, *Interregional and International Trade* (revised edition), p. 207.

20. Ibid., pp. 269–270.

21. Ibid., p. 270.

22. Hoover, *The Location of Economic Activity*, pp. 224–225.

23. Ibid., p. 224.

24. See Niles Hansen (ed.), *Growth Centers in Regional Economic Development;* Antoni R. Kuklinski (ed.), *Growth Poles and Growth Centres in Regional Planning;* and Malcolm J. Moseley, *Growth Centres in Spatial Planning.*

25. Gendarme, "Les problèmes économiques," pp. 889–917.

26. Pierre Magué, "L'Alsace," in Guy Héraud (ed.), *Les régions d'Europe*, p. 43.

27. Jacques R. Boudeville, *Aménagement du territoire et polarisation*, pp. 265–267.

28. Jacques R. Boudeville, "European Integration, Urban Regions and Medium-Sized Towns," in Morgan Sant (ed.), *Regional Planning and Policy for Europe*, p. 133.

29. Jacques R. Boudeville, "Polarisation and Urbanisation (The Canadian and French Examples)," *Economie appliquée* 28, no. 1 (1975): 232.

30. See "Les régions frontière et la polarisation urbaine dans la Communauté Economique Européenne," a special number of *Economies et sociétés* 5, no. 3–4 (March–April 1971).

31. See Niles Hansen, "An Evaluation of Growth Centre Theory and

Practice," *Environment and Planning*, series A, 7, no. 7 (1975): 821–832; and Allan Pred, *The Interurban Transmission of Growth in Advanced Economies: Empirical Findings versus Regional Planning Assumptions.*

32. François Perroux, *L'économie du XXe siècle*, p. 85.
33. Ibid., p. 40.
34. Ibid., pp. 142–153.
35. Nathan Associates, *Industrial and Employment Potential of the United States–Mexico Border*, p. 17. The only source cited in support of this assertion is Inter-American Development Bank, *Hacia integración fronteriza entre Colombia y Venezuela* (Washington, D.C.: IADB, 1966). Moreover, the only case mentioned is that of the Venezuela-Colombia borderlands, but even here there is contrary evidence indicating that cooperation along this border area has been fruitful, largely because of the presence of highly favorable preconditions. See Stöhr, *Regional Development Experiences*, pp. 163–164.
36. Oscar J. Martínez, *Border Boom Town: Ciudad Juárez since 1848*, p. 8.
37. Ibid., p. 5.
38. Ibid.
39. Bill Enriquez, "International Legal Implications of Industrial Development along the Mexican-U.S. Border," in Albert E. Utton (ed.), *Pollution and International Boundaries*, p. 90.
40. *Journal officiel de la République Française*, December 26, 1975, p. 683.
41. Koren T. Sherrill, "Economic Growth in West German Border Regions: An Empirical Study of Sub-national Regions Directly Affected by International Influences," University of Texas at Austin, 1979.
42. Harry W. Richardson, "Regional Development Policy in Spain," *Urban Studies* 8, no. 1 (February 1971): 41; Hansen, "Economic Aspects of Regional Separatism," p. 148.
43. Despite the large geographic size of Canada, most of its population lives relatively close to the United States, and issues related to this propinquity are frequently discussed in Canada. These issues take on different dimensions depending on whether they are viewed from the Vancouver region, the plains and prairies, Ontario, Quebec, or the Maritimes.
44. Governors of California, Arizona, New Mexico, and Texas, *Application for Designation as a Title V Regional Action Planning Commission*, cover letter to the Secretary of Commerce.
45. Ibid., p. i.
46. Ibid.
47. Ibid.
48. Ibid., p. 15.
49. Ibid., cover letter.
50. Ibid., p. 5. The emphasis is in the original text.

51. Vernon M. Briggs, Jr., "Illegal Aliens: The Need for a More Restrictive Border Policy," *Social Science Quarterly* 56, no. 3 (December 1975): 482.

3. Subregions of the Southwest Borderlands

1. James R. Mills, *San Diego: Where California Began*, pp. 15, 20–22, 26–27, 47–51.
2. "San Diego Overview," *The Union-Tribune's Annual Review of San Diego Business Activity 1978*, pp. 4–5, 27–33.
3. John A. Price, *Tijuana: Urbanization in a Border Culture*, p. 3.
4. Oscar J. Martínez, *Border Boom Town: Ciudad Juárez since 1848*, p. 161.
5. Jean Revel-Mouroz, "Les migrations vers la frontière Mexique–Etats-Unis," *Cahiers des Amériques Latines* 12 (1975): 322.
6. Price, *Tijuana*, p. xiii.
7. Tore Tjersland and Dan Greenblat, "Baja California," *San Diego Economic Profile 1977*, p. 7.
8. "Border Crossing Statistics," *The Union-Tribune's Annual Review of San Diego Business Activity 1978*, p. 42.
9. Ibid.
10. Tjersland and Greenblat, "Visitor," *San Diego Economic Profile 1977*, pp. 25–26.
11. Tjersland and Greenblat, "Trade," *San Diego Economic Profile 1977*, pp. 8, 13.
12. San Diego OEDP General Committee, *San Diego Region Overall Economic Development Program: Direction '80*, p. 6.
13. Ibid.
14. U.S. Bureau of the Census, *County and City Data Book, 1977*, pp. 65, 77.
15. Governors of California, Arizona, New Mexico, and Texas, *Application for Designation as a Title V Regional Action Planning Commission*, p. B-24.
16. U.S. Bureau of the Census, *County and City Data Book, 1977*, pp. 42, 600.
17. Barry Goldwater, *Arizona*, p. 103.
18. Ibid., p. 114.
19. City of Tucson, *Overall Economic Development Program*, pp. 1–4.
20. Ibid., p. 14.
21. William E. Blundell, "Colorado River, Vital to Southwest, Travels Ever-Rockier Course," *Wall Street Journal*, February 12, 1979, p. 1.
22. For example, farmers in the Imperial Valley of California pay $4.50 per 326,000 gallons of water that has been stored behind federal dams and

piped to them at enormous cost, whereas San Francisco residents pay the same amount for only 2,460 gallons of unsubsidized water. Richard Boeth et al., "Western Water Fight," *Newsweek*, June 12, 1978, p. 51.

23. Francisco Oyarzabal-Tamargo and Robert A. Young, "International External Diseconomies: The Colorado River Salinity Problem in Mexico," *Natural Resources Journal* 18, no. 1 (January 1978): 78–79; Myron B. Holburt, "International Problems," in Dean F. Peterson and A. Berry Crawford (eds.), *Values and Choices in the Development of the Colorado River Basin*, pp. 220–225.

24. Judy Wiessler, "Mexico Was Offered Pay But Did Not Bill U.S. for Salt Water Damages," *Houston Chronicle*, October 7, 1979, p. 6, sec. 1.

25. Ibid.

26. Blundell, "Colorado River, Vital to Southwest, Travels Ever-Rockier Course," p. 1.

27. City of Tucson, *Overall Economic Development Program*, p. 7.

28. Price, *Tijuana*, pp. 13–14.

29. Southwest New Mexico Council of Governments, *Overall Economic Development Plan Update 1978–1979*, pp. 13–15.

30. Southern Rio Grande Council of Governments, *Southern Rio Grande Economic Development District Overall Economic Development Plan*, book I, pp. 13–14, 27, 38–40.

31. Martínez, *Border Boom Town*, p. 22. An excellent account of the historic development of the entire Rio Grande Valley is given in Paul Horgan, *Great River: The Rio Grande in North American History*.

32. Martínez, *Border Boom Town*, pp. 4–5.

33. In 1973, legal commuters from Mexico accounted for 9 percent of the El Paso labor force, ibid., p. 139.

34. Arthur Young and Company, *An Economic and Demographic Study of U.S. Border Cities*, p. 322.

35. Ellwyn R. Stoddard and Jonathan P. West, *The Impact of Mexico's Peso Devaluation on Selected U.S. Border Cities*, p. 62.

36. West Texas Council of Governments, *District Overall Economic Development Plan 1978–1979*, pp. 69–71, 77.

37. Middle Rio Grande Development Council, *Overall Economic Development Program*, pp. 80–84.

38. Ibid., pp. 83–84, 91.

39. Ibid., pp. 83, 89.

40. U.S. Bureau of the Census, "Estimates of the Population of Texas Counties and Metropolitan Areas: July 1, 1976 (Revised) and 1977 (Provisional)," *Current Population Reports*, P-25, no. 798, pp. 4, 6.

41. South Texas Development Council, *Overall Economic Development Program (Revised) 1977–1979*, vol. 1, pp. 24–25, 167.

42. Gilbert Cardenas, *The Manpower Impact of Mexico's Peso Devaluation of 1976 on Border Labor Markets in Texas*, p. 21.

43. South Texas Development Council, *Overall Economic Development Program*, pp. 69–72, 95.
44. Charles P. Zlatkovich, *The Identification of Functional Regions Based on Highway Traffic Flow Data*.
45. Alamo Area Council of Governments, *AACOG District Overall Economic Development Program 1976*, p. 24.
46. U.S. Bureau of the Census, "Estimates of the Population of Texas Counties and Metropolitan Areas: July 1, 1976 (Revised) and 1977 (Provisional)," *Current Population Reports*, p. 7.
47. Charles P. Zlatkovich and Carol T. F. Bennett, "The Lower Rio Grande Valley: An Area of Rapid Growth," *Texas Business Review* 51, no. 5 (September–October 1977): 205.
48. Michael V. Miller and Robert Lee Maril, *Poverty in the Lower Rio Grande Valley of Texas: Historical and Contemporary Dimensions*, pp. 23–27.
49. Ibid., p. 27.
50. Ibid., p. 29.
51. Ibid., p. 5.
52. Lower Rio Grande Development Council, *Overall Economic Development Program*, p. 34.
53. Lower Rio Grande Valley Policy Research Project, *Colonias in the Lower Rio Grande Valley of South Texas: A Summary Report*.
54. Lower Rio Grande Development Council, *Overall Economic Development Program*, p. 72.
55. Zlatkovich and Bennett, "The Lower Rio Grande Valley," pp. 205–208.
56. Lower Rio Grande Development Council, *Overall Economic Development Program*, pp. 88–89, 93.

4. Regional Development

1. A 10 percent CWHS is available only for the years 1971, 1973, and, on a preliminary basis, 1975, a recession year.
2. The Bureau of Economic Analysis does not publish its employment series, but data for individual counties are available upon request. The data presented in this section were specially processed from BEA-supplied tapes by James P. Miller, Regional Analysis Program Area, Economic Development Division, U.S. Department of Agriculture.
3. U.S. Department of Commerce, Bureau of Economic Analysis, *Regional Work Force Characteristics and Migration Data*; David W. Cartwright, "Major Limitations of CWHS Files and Prospects for Improvement," paper presented at the National Bureau of Economic Research Workshop on Policy Analysis with Social Security Research Files, Washington, D.C., March 17, 1978.

4. Oakah L. Jones, Jr., *Los Paisanos: Spanish Settlers on the Northern Frontier of New Spain*, p. 250.
5. U.S. Bureau of the Census, *Statistical Abstract of the United States: 1979*, p. 397.
6. U.S. Department of Commerce, Bureau of Economic Analysis, *Regional Work Force Characteristics and Migration Data*, p. 87.
7. Ellwyn R. Stoddard, *Patterns of Poverty along the U.S.-Mexico Border.*
8. Dun and Bradstreet data on *manufacturing* unit starts, closures, relocations, and continuing operations in Southwest Border Regional Commission counties were processed for this study by James P. Miller, U.S. Department of Agriculture. The results indicate that 385 manufacturing units were present in the borderlands in both 1969 and 1975. In this interval, 299 units closed and 312 units opened; 3 units relocated outside the area and 6 units relocated into the area. There were 209 borderlands units that were covered in 1975 but not in 1969; of these, 124 are probably new branch plants. Detailed breakdowns by two-digit SIC code were processed for each category of manufacturing unit. Unfortunately, the 912 units covered in 1975 had total employment of 42,193, whereas the BEA estimate for borderlands manufacturing employment in 1976 is 167,088. I originally intended to make extensive use of the Dun and Bradstreet manufacturing data I have for the borderlands. However, because of the severe degree of underreporting—which is not typical at the national level—I have limited my discussion to this note. The detailed Dun and Bradstreet manufacturing data set for the borderlands is available from me on request.
9. Niles Hansen, "Employment Patterns in the Southwest Borderlands," *Texas Business Review* 54, no. 1 (January–February 1980): 20–24.
10. Kenneth Horowitz of the BEA was especially helpful in the task of data processing.

5. The Role of Mexican Labor in Southwestern Economic Development

1. David J. Weber (ed.), *Foreigners in Their Native Land.*
2. Rodolfo Alvarez, "The Psycho-Historical and Socioeconomic Development of the Chicano Community in the United States," *Social Science Quarterly* 53, no. 4 (March 1973): 920.
3. Joe B. Frantz, "The Borderlands: Ideas on a Leafless Landscape," in Stanley R. Ross (ed.), *Views across the Border*, p. 47.
4. Leo Grebler, Joan W. Moore, and Ralph C. Guzman, *The Mexican-American People: The Nation's Second Largest Minority*, pp. 43–44.
5. Gilberto López y Rivas, *The Chicanos*, p. 38.
6. Américo Paredes, "The Problem of Identity in a Changing Culture: Popular Expressions of Culture Conflict along the Lower Rio Grande

Border," in Stanley R. Ross (ed.), *Views across the Border*, p. 74.

7. Vernon M. Briggs, Jr., *Mexican Migration and the U.S. Labor Market*, p. 5.

8. Arthur F. Corwin, "Early Mexican Labor Migration: A Frontier Sketch, 1848–1900," in Arthur F. Corwin (ed.), *Immigrants—and Immigrants*, pp. 34–35.

9. Oscar J. Martínez, "On the Size of the Chicano Population: New Estimates, 1850–1900," *Aztlán* 6, no. 1 (Spring 1975): 48, 56.

10. Rivas, *The Chicanos*, pp. 33–36.

11. John A. Price, *Tijuana: Urbanization in a Border Culture*, p. 12.

12. Oscar J. Martínez, *Border Boom Town: Ciudad Juárez since 1848*, p. 161.

13. Briggs, *Mexican Migration and the U.S. Labor Market*, p. 6.

14. Martínez, *Border Boom Town*, p. 110.

15. Peter N. Kirstein, *Anglo over Bracero: A History of the Mexican Worker in the United States from Roosevelt to Nixon*.

16. Ibid., p. 103.

17. Briggs, *Mexican Migration and the U.S. Labor Market*, p. 11.

18. Kirstein, *Anglo over Bracero*, p. 104.

19. U.S. Bureau of the Census, *Statistical Abstract of the United States: 1978*, p. 91.

20. Kenneth Roberts et al., "Counting Illegal Mexican Aliens: Myths and Misconceptions," *Texas Business Review* 52, no. 6 (June 1978): 101–105.

21. Ellwyn R. Stoddard, "Illegal Mexican Labor in the Borderlands: Institutionalized Support of an Unlawful Practice," *Pacific Sociological Review* 19, no. 2 (April 1976): 175–210.

22. Arthur F. Corwin and Johnny M. McCain, "Wetbackism since 1964: A Catalogue of Factors," in Arthur F. Corwin (ed.), *Immigrants—and Immigrants*, p. 69.

23. Briggs, *Mexican Migration and the U.S. Labor Market*, p. 10.

24. U.S. Bureau of the Census, *Current Population Reports*, P-20, no. 329, "Persons of Spanish Origin in the United States: March 1977," p. 2.

25. Ibid., p. 19.

26. Rivas, *The Chicanos*, p. 38.

27. Ibid.

28. Raul A. Fernandez, *The United States–Mexico Border: A Politico-Economic Profile*, p. 156.

29. V. S. Pritchett, *The Myth Makers*, p. 41.

30. Fernandez, *The United States–Mexico Border*, p. 70.

31. Ibid., pp. 70–71.

32. U.S. Bureau of the Census, *Statistical Abstract of the United States: 1978*, p. 865.

33. Paul S. Taylor, "The Future of Mexican Immigration," in Arthur F. Corwin (ed.), *Immigrants—and Immigrants*, p. 349.
34. Fernandez, *The United States–Mexico Border*, p. 99. See also Rivas, *The Chicanos*, p. 40.
35. Wayne A. Cornelius, "Illegal Migration to the United States: Recent Research Findings, Policy Implications, and Research Priorities," mimeographed, MIT Center for International Studies, p. 20.
36. Martínez, *Border Boom Town*, p. 161.
37. Víctor Urquidi and Sofía Méndez Villareal, "Economic Importance of Mexico's Northern Border Region," in Stanley R. Ross (ed.), *Views across the Border*, pp. 141–143.
38. Michael J. Greenwood, "An Econometric Model of Internal Migration and Regional Economic Growth in Mexico," *Journal of Regional Science* 18, no. 1 (April 1978): 28–29.
39. James L. Schlagheck, *The Political, Economic, and Labor Climate in Mexico*, pp. 73–76.
40. Greenwood, "An Econometric Model of Internal Migration," p. 18.
41. John M. Crewdson, "Border Region Is Almost a Country unto Itself, Neither Mexican Nor American," *New York Times*, February 14, 1979, p. A-22.
42. Ellwyn R. Stoddard, "A Conceptual Analysis of the 'Alien Invasion': Institutionalized Support of Illegal Mexican Aliens," *International Migration Review* 10, no. 2 (Summer 1976): 162.
43. Corwin and McCain, "Wetbackism since 1964," p. 75.
44. C. D. Dillman, "Urban Growth along Mexico's Northern Border and the Mexican National Border Program," *Journal of Developing Areas* 4, no. 4 (July 1970): 492.
45. Martínez, *Border Boom Town*, pp. 139–141.
46. Jerry R. Ladman and Mark O. Paulsen, *Economic Impact of the Mexican Border Industrialization Program: Agua Priete, Sonora*, p. 40.
47. Urquidi and Villareal, "Economic Importance of Mexico's Northern Border Region," p. 155.
48. Martínez, *Border Boom Town*, p. 141.
49. Dillman, "Urban Growth along Mexico's Northern Border," p. 501.
50. Wilbur R. Thompson, "The Economic Base of Urban Problems," in Neil W. Chamberlain (ed.), *Contemporary Economic Issues*, p. 8.
51. Rodney A. Erickson and Thomas R. Leinbach, "Characteristics of Branch Plants Attracted to Nonmetropolitan Areas," in Richard E. Lonsdale and H. L. Seyler (eds.), *Nonmetropolitan Industrialization*, pp. 57–59; Werner Hirsch, *Location of Industry and International Competitiveness*, p. 16.
52. Joseph Persky, "Dualism, Capital-Labor Ratios and the Regions of the U.S.," *Journal of Regional Science* 18, no. 3 (December 1978): 381.

53. Ibid.
54. Peter M. Allaman and David L. Birch, "Components of Employment Change for Metropolitan and Rural Areas in the United States by Industry Group, 1970–1972," WP-8, MIT-Harvard Joint Center for Urban Studies, Inter-Area Migration Project; Carol L. Jusenius and Larry C. Ledebur, *Documenting the "Decline" of the North.*
55. James P. Miller, "Research with Dun and Bradstreet Data," Working Paper no. 7903, Economic Development Division, U.S. Department of Agriculture, p. 5.
56. Rodney A. Erickson, "The New Wave of Nonmetropolitan Industrialization," *Earth and Mineral Sciences* 48, no. 3 (December 1978): 17.
57. Ibid., p. 19.
58. Philippe Aydalot, "L'aménagement du territoire en France: une tentative de bilan," *L'Espace Géographique* 7, no. 4 (October 1978): 251.
59. Niles Hansen, *The Future of Nonmetropolitan America,* pp. 165–166.
60. Urquidi and Villareal, "Economic Importance of Mexico's Northern Border Region," p. 148.
61. Martínez, *Border Boom Town,* p. 133.
62. C. D. Dillman, "Maquiladoras in Mexico's Northern Border Communities and the Border Industrialization Program," *Tijdschrift voor Economisch en Sociaal Geografie* 67, no. 3: 148.
63. Ibid.
64. "GM Expanding South of the Border," *Austin American-Statesman,* March 5, 1980, p. G-6.
65. Fernandez, *The United States–Mexico Border,* p. 125.
66. Mitchell A. Seligson and Edward J. Williams, *Maquiladoras and Migration: A Study of Workers in the Mexican–United States Border Industrialization Program,* pp. 4–5.
67. Thomas J. Murray, "American Boom in Mexico," *Dun's Review* 112, no. 4 (October 1978): 127.
68. Ibid., p. 123.
69. Dillman, "Maquiladoras in Mexico's Northern Border Communities," p. 147.
70. Harry W. Ayer and M. Ross Layton, "The Border Industry Program and the Impacts of Expenditures by Mexican Border Industry Employees on a U.S. Border Community: An Empirical Study of Nogales," *Annals of Regional Science* 8, no. 2 (June 1974): 105–117.
71. Martínez, *Border Boom Town,* pp. 199–200.
72. Ellwyn R. Stoddard and Jonathan P. West, *The Impact of Mexico's Peso Devaluation on Selected U.S. Border Cities.*
73. Charles J. Ellard and Gilbert Cardenas, "The Effects of the Mexican Peso Devaluation of 1976 on Employment and Unemployment in the Texas-Mexico Border Area," mimeographed, Pan American University, Edinburg, Texas, 1978.

74. Stuart Greenfield, "Texas Border Communities and the Peso Devaluation," *Texas Business Review* 53, no. 2 (March–April 1979): 54–56.
75. Wendell Gordon, "A Case for a Less Restrictive Border Policy," *Social Science Quarterly* 56, no. 3 (December 1975): 490.

6. Undocumented Mexican Immigration

1. Workers who "lend" their Social Security numbers to undocumented Mexicans can file for reimbursement of "excess" Social Security and income tax payments. Some undocumented Mexicans even receive kickbacks (15 percent seems to be a common figure) for playing their part in this practice.
2. Kenneth Roberts et al., "Counting Illegal Mexican Aliens: Myths and Misconceptions," *Texas Business Review* 52, no. 6 (June 1978): 101–105; Ellwyn R. Stoddard, "A Conceptual Analysis of the 'Alien Invasion': Institutionalized Support of Illegal Mexican Aliens in the U.S.," *International Migration Review* 10, no. 2 (Summer 1976): 164.
3. U.S. Bureau of the Census, *Statistical Abstract of the United States: 1978*, p. 91.
4. Numerous citations to this effect are contained in Vernon M. Briggs, Jr., "Illegal Aliens: The Need for a More Restrictive Border Policy," *Social Science Quarterly* 56, no. 3 (December 1975): 477–484; his "Mexican Workers in the United States Labour Market: A Contemporary Dilemma," *International Labour Review* 112, no. 5 (November 1975): 351–368; and Paul R. Ehrlich, Loy Bilderback, and Anne H. Ehrlich, *The Golden Door: International Migration, Mexico, and the United States*, pp. 175–236.
5. Tad Szulc, "Foreign Policy Aspects of the Border," in Stanley R. Ross (ed.), *Views across the Border*, pp. 227–228. The reference to a "rate of migration around the three million level" implicitly means an annual immigration rate. This is an excessive estimate and it takes no account of return migration to Mexico.
6. Arthur F. Corwin and Johnny M. McCain, "Wetbackism since 1964: A Catalogue of Factors," in Arthur F. Corwin (ed.), *Immigrants—and Immigrants*, p. 99. The authors add that "The ghost of Santa Anna must have grinned" (ibid).
7. Briggs, "Illegal Aliens: The Need for a More Restrictive Border Policy," p. 482.
8. David North and Marion Houstoun, *The Characteristics and Role of Illegal Aliens in the U.S. Labor Market: An Exploratory Study*, p. 12.
9. Alejandro Portes, "Return of the Wetback," *Society* 11, no. 1 (March–April 1974): 40–46.
10. "LDC Debt: The Load Eases," *Newsweek*, February 27, 1978, p. 73.

11. Julian Samora, *Los Mojados*, pp. 96–97.
12. Richard Mines, "Riding the Tide of Migration," *Daily Texan* (University of Texas at Austin), January 18, 1978, p. 5.
13. Michael V. Miller and Robert Lee Maril, *Poverty in the Lower Rio Grande Valley of Texas: Historical and Contemporary Dimensions*, pp. 35–57.
14. Michael J. Piore, *Birds of Passage: Migrant Labor and Industrial Societies*, p. 61. The emphasis is Piore's.
15. Ibid., p. 52.
16. Charles Hirschman, "Prior U.S. Residence among Mexican Immigrants," *Social Forces* 56, no. 4 (June 1978): 1198.
17. These phenomena are described in rich detail in Ellwyn R. Stoddard, "Illegal Mexican Labor in the Borderlands: Institutionalized Support of an Unlawful Practice," *Pacific Sociological Review* 19, no. 2 (April 1976): 194–202.
18. Gilbert Cardenas, "Mexican Illegal Aliens in the San Antonio Labor Market," *Texas Business Review* 53, no. 6 (November–December 1979): 188.
19. Stoddard, "Illegal Mexican Labor in the Borderlands," p. 199.
20. Harvey M. Choldin and Grafton D. Trout, *Mexican Americans in Transition: Migration and Employment in Michigan Cities*; Arthur F. Corwin, "¿Quien Sabe? Mexican Migration Statistics," in Arthur F. Corwin (ed.), *Immigrants—and Immigrants*, p. 123.
21. Ellwyn R. Stoddard, Oscar J. Martínez, and Miguel Angel Martínez Lasso, *El Paso–Ciudad Juárez Relations and the "Tortilla Curtain": A Study of Local Adaptation to Federal Border Policies*, pp. 23–30.
22. Ibid., p. 30.
23. Ibid. A leading planner in San Diego told me in an interview that the high level of apprehensions of undocumented Mexicans in San Diego does not mean that these persons intended to stay in San Diego, which they tend to regard as a relatively inhospitable place. Once they clear the San Diego border area, most undocumented Mexicans head out for other cities, principally Los Angeles.
24. Ehrlich, Bilderback, and Ehrlich, *The Golden Door*, p. 281.
25. There is general evidence that employment growth and migration are mutually dependent. Richard F. Muth, "Migration: Chicken or Egg?" *Southern Economic Journal* 37, no. 3 (January 1971): 295–306; Lee D. Olvey, "Regional Growth and Interregional Migration: Their Pattern of Interaction," *Review of Regional Studies* 2, no. 2 (Winter 1972): 139–163.
26. Cardenas, "Mexican Illegal Aliens in the San Antonio Labor Market," pp. 189–191.
27. Allan G. King, "Unemployment Consequences of Illegal Aliens from

Mexico," *Texas Business Review* 53, no. 2 (March–April 1979): 43–45.

28. Dual labor market theory maintains that workers in the primary labor market make their decisions about where to work in terms of the progression of jobs they can expect to hold during their employment. If they pass screening, they enter the firm's "internal labor market," which is characterized by specific training, relatively high wages, employment stability, and reasonable opportunity for advancement. In contrast, the secondary labor market is characterized by absenteeism, tardiness, high job turnover, and antisocial behavior, such as thievery. Employers simply find it easier to adjust to such conditions, perhaps by paying lower wages, than to try to change them. Workers who enter the secondary labor market tend to become habituated to behavior which permanently excludes them from later employment opportunities in the primary market: F. Ray Marshall, Allan M. Cartter, and Allan G. King, *Labor Economics*, 3rd ed., pp. 276–277.

29. *Texas Observer*, March 25, 1977, p. 12.

30. Michael L. Wachter, "Second Thoughts about Illegal Immigrants," *Fortune*, May 22, 1978, pp. 80–87.

31. Barton Smith and Robert Newman, "Depressed Wages along the U.S.-Mexico Border: An Empirical Analysis," *Economic Inquiry* 15, no. 1 (January 1977): 63.

32. Wayne A. Cornelius, "Illegal Mexican Migration to the United States: Recent Research Findings, Policy Implications, and Research Priorities," p. 12; Ehrlich, Bilderback, and Ehrlich, *The Golden Door*, pp. 190–196; North and Houstoun, *The Characteristics and Role of Illegal Aliens*; Cardenas, "Mexican Illegal Aliens in the San Antonio Labor Market," p. 190.

33. Manuel Vic Villalpando et al., *A Study of the Socio-economic Impact of Illegal Aliens on the County of San Diego.*

34. Mines, "Riding the Tide of Migration"; North and Houstoun, *The Characteristics and Role of Illegal Aliens*; Roberts et al., "Counting Illegal Mexican Aliens"; Cornelius, "Illegal Mexican Migration to the United States," pp. 7–8; Miller and Maril, *Poverty in the Lower Rio Grande Valley of Texas*, p. 47.

35. Cornelius, "Illegal Mexican Migration to the United States," p. 8.

36. Cardenas, "Mexican Illegal Aliens in the San Antonio Labor Market," p. 188.

37. Mines, "Riding the Tide of Migration."

38. Roberts et al., "Counting Illegal Mexican Aliens," p. 105.

39. Jean Revel-Mouroz and Claude Bataillon, "Les migrations Mexicaines vers les Etats-Unis et la frontière nord du Mexique," *Tiers-Monde* 18, no. 69 (January–March 1977): 61, 64.

40. Barry R. Chiswick, "Immigrants and Immigration Policy," in William

Fellner (ed.), *Contemporary Economic Problems, 1978*, pp. 311–314.

41. Piore, *Birds of Passage*, p. 183. See also Cardenas, "Mexican Illegal Aliens in the San Antonio Labor Market," p. 190.

42. Tracy Cortese, "Alien Labor Used in Austin," *Austin American-Statesman*, September 1, 1979, p. B-1.

43. Bruce Koon, "Instead of Turning In Illegal Aliens, Some Unions Try Signing Them Up," *Wall Street Journal*, November 13, 1979, p. 19.

44. Cornelius, "Illegal Mexican Migration to the United States," pp. 14–15.

45. Carrol Norquest, *Rio Grande Wetbacks: Mexican Migrant Workers*.

46. Revel-Mouroz and Bataillon, "Les migrations Mexicaines," pp. 67–68.

47. Piore, *Birds of Passage*, pp. 123–131. Piore's source for the Jalisco case study is Juan Diez-Canedo's doctoral dissertation research in progress in the Department of Economics, MIT.

48. Revel-Mouroz and Bataillon, "Les migrations Mexicaines," pp. 67–68.

49. Edwin P. Reubens, "Illegal Immigration and the Mexican Economy," *Challenge* 21, no. 5 (November–December 1978): 19. At this writing a guest worker program for the United States is being considered by the prestigious Select Commission on Immigration and Refugee Policy, whose members include four Cabinet officers and eight members of Congress.

50. The adjective "northern" is used loosely here and includes such countries as France and Austria. The international labor migration discussed in this section essentially refers to movements from the Mediterranean area to more northerly countries.

51. A labor-availability interpretation of postwar economic expansion in Western Europe has been most cogently argued in Charles P. Kindleberger, *Europe's Postwar Growth: The Role of Labor Supply*. Current opinion tends toward the view that industrial growth generated demand for labor, not the converse, but Kindleberger recognized (pp. 14 and 154–155) that excess labor is permissive rather than growth-initiating.

52. In West Germany, for example, unemployed aliens have the same right as local citizens to claim unemployment benefits. They may claim other welfare benefits as long as they have a valid work permit and residence visa: *German Tribune*, January 16, 1975, p. 4.

53. George Hoffman, *A Geography of Europe*, 4th edition, p. 90; Philip L. Martin and Marion F. Houstoun, "The Future of International Labor Migration," paper prepared for the Select Commission on Immigration and Refugee Policy, Washington, D.C., November 1979; Ehrlich, Bilderback, and Ehrlich, *The Golden Door*, p. 40; Hilde Wander, "The Role of International Migration in the Changing Pattern of Economic, Social and Demographic Structure in Europe," in Milos Macura (ed.), *The Effect of Current Demographic Change in Europe on Social Structure*, p. 31. European authorities have customarily assumed that illegal for-

eign workers represent about 10 percent of the legal foreign worker population: "Slamming the Door on Europe's Guest Workers," *Economist,* August 9, 1975, p. 24.

54. Philip L. Martin, "Guestworker Programs: Lessons from Europe," paper prepared for the Joint Economic Committee, U.S. Congress, June 1979, p. 2.

55. Detailed restrictive measures are given in "Slamming the Door on Europe's Guest Workers," *Economist,* August 9, 1975, p. 24. Common Market countries that formerly received large numbers of guest workers have been imposing ever-stricter penalties on employers and middlemen, though most also continue to impose penalties on the workers themselves. For details, see Donald F. Heisel and Ellen Brennan, "Policies for Dealing with Illegal-Undocumented International Migration," Population Division, Department of International Economic and Social Affairs, United Nations, 1979, pp. 8–15.

56. Hoffman, *A Geography of Europe,* p. 94.

57. Robert Ball, "How Europe Created Its 'Minority Problem,'" *Fortune,* December 1973, p. 132.

58. These problems tended to be especially acute in relatively few industrial areas. During the middle 1970s in West Germany, foreign workers accounted for 25 percent of Stuttgart's labor force and for 17 percent of Munich's. In Cologne's large Ford plant 40 percent of the workers were foreigners, mostly unskilled Turks. In France the foreign workers were concentrated in the Paris region and two other regional departments: Hoffman, *A Geography of Europe,* p. 91. "Schools in the host countries were suddenly faced with large numbers of pupils who were unable to understand the language and whose previous schooling ranged from barely adequate to nonexistent" (Ball, "How Europe Created Its 'Minority Problem,'" p. 136).

59. W. R. Böhning, "Some Thoughts on Emigration from the Mediterranean Basin," *International Labour Review* 111, no. 3 (March 1975): 251–277; Ball, "How Europe Created Its 'Minority Problem,'" p. 134.

60. Douglas Brown, "Europe's Migrant Workers," *Optima* 24, no. 1 (1974): 35–46; Wander, "The Role of International Migration," p. 21.

61. W. R. Böhning, *Basic Aspects of Immigration and Return Migration in Western Europe.*

62. Piore, *Birds of Passage,* p. 33.

63. Ibid., p. 32.

64. Ibid., pp. 53–55.

65. Philip L. Martin and Mark Miller, "Regulating Alien Labor in Industrial Societies," paper presented to the 32nd Annual Meeting of the Industrial Relations Research Association, Atlanta, Georgia, December 30, 1979, pp. 6–7.

66. Ibid., p. 10.

67. Cardenas, "Mexican Illegal Aliens in the San Antonio Labor Market," p. 187.
68. Ehrlich, Bilderback, and Ehrlich, *The Golden Door*, p. 350.
69. Dan Meyers, "Bracero Revival Seen as End to Alien Problems," *Austin American-Statesman*, August 19, 1979, p. A-14.
70. Martin, "Guestworker Programs: Lessons from Europe," p. 61.
71. Martin and Miller, "Regulating Alien Labor," p. 8; Wander, "The Role of International Migration," p. 29.
72. U.S. Central Intelligence Agency, *Handbook of Economic Statistics, 1977*, p. viii.

7. Mexican Americans

1. "Chicanos on the Move," *Newsweek*, January 1, 1979, p. 22.
2. U.S. Bureau of the Census, "Persons of Spanish Origin in the United States: March 1978," *Current Population Reports*, P-20, no. 399, pp. 1, 15, 54–56.
3. Vernon M. Briggs, Jr., Walter Fogel, and Fred H. Schmidt, *The Chicano Worker*, p. 59. Anglos are all white persons, as defined by the U.S. Bureau of the Census, who are not Mexican American.
4. U.S. Bureau of the Census, "Persons of Spanish Origin in the United States: March 1976 (Advance Report)," *Current Population Reports*, P-20, no. 302, table 9, p. 11.
5. Ibid., table 10, p. 11.
6. U.S. Bureau of the Census, "Money Income and Poverty Status of Families and Persons in the United States: 1978 (Advance Report)," *Current Population Reports*, P-60, no. 120, table 22, p. 35.
7. U.S. Bureau of the Census, "Persons of Spanish Origin in the United States: March 1978," table 31, p. 50.
8. Dudley L. Poston, Jr., and David Alvirez, "On the Cost of Being a Mexican American Worker," *Social Science Quarterly* 53, no. 4 (March 1973): 697–709; Dudley L. Poston, Jr., David Alvirez, and Marta Tienda, "Earnings Differences between Anglo and Mexican American Male Workers in 1960 and 1970: Changes in the 'Cost' of Being Mexican American," *Social Science Quarterly* 57, no. 3 (December 1976): 618–631; Leo Grebler, Joan W. Moore, and Ralph C. Guzman, *The Mexican American People*, pp. 180–204.
9. This section is adapted from Mark Fossett, "Local Differences in Anglo–Mexican American Earnings Inequality: A Consideration of the Role of Education in the Metropolitan Southwest," Southwest Borderlands Regional Economic Development Project, Mexican–United States Border Research Program, University of Texas, Austin, 1979.
10. Briggs, Fogel, and Schmidt, *The Chicano Worker*, p. 55.
11. Ibid., p. 47.

12. Ibid., p. 56.
13. U.S. Bureau of the Census, *County and City Data Book, 1977*, pp. 602, 614, 626, 710, 758.
14. Julian Samora and Patricia Vandel Simon, *A History of the Mexican-American People*, p. 165.
15. Briggs, Fogel, and Schmidt, *The Chicano Worker*, p. 101.
16. Ibid., p. 102.
17. Susan Hartman and Leticia Chavez, *Impact of Resident Aliens and Migrant School Children on Border Public School Districts*.
18. Ibid., pp. 20, 64–65.
19. Tony Dunbar and Linda Kravitz, *Hard Traveling: Migrant Farm Workers in America*, p. 4.
20. U.S. Department of Commerce, Bureau of Economic Analysis, Regional Economic Measurement Division, "County and Metropolitan Area Personal Income," *Survey of Current Business* 59, no. 4 (April 1979): 44–45.
21. John Davidson, "A Harvest of Poverty," *Texas Observer*, February 3, 1978, p. 5.
22. Governor's Office of Migrant Affairs, *Migrant and Seasonal Farmworkers in Texas*, pp. 64–66.
23. Samora and Simon, *A History of the Mexican-American People*, p. 149.
24. Michael V. Miller and Robert Lee Maril, *Poverty in the Lower Rio Grande Valley of Texas: Historical and Contemporary Dimensions*, p. 55.
25. Davidson, "A Harvest of Poverty," p. 8.
26. Niles Hansen and William C. Gruben, "The Influence of Relative Wages and Assisted Migration on Locational Preferences: Mexican Americans in South Texas," *Social Science Quarterly* 52, no. 1 (June 1971): 103–114.
27. Miller and Maril, *Poverty in the Lower Rio Grande Valley of Texas*, p. 55.
28. Briggs, Fogel, and Schmidt, *The Chicano Worker*, pp. 17–18.
29. U.S. Bureau of the Census, "Persons of Spanish Origin in the United States: March 1978," *Current Population Reports*, P-20, no. 339, table 1, p. 17.
30. Briggs, Fogel, and Schmidt, *The Chicano Worker*, p. 19.
31. Walter Fogel, *Mexican Americans in Southwest Labor Markets*, p. 108.
32. Ibid., p. 109.
33. U.S. Department of Commerce, "County and Metropolitan Area Personal Income," pp. 27, 42.
34. Thomas R. Plaut, *Net Migration into Texas and Its Regions: Trends and Patterns*, pp. 37, 43, 44.
35. Miller and Maril, *Poverty in the Lower Rio Grande Valley of Texas*, p. 7.

36. Ibid., p. 63.
37. Rudolph Gomez, "The Politics of the Mexican–United States Border," in Stanley R. Ross (ed.), *Views across the Border: The United States and Mexico*, p. 388.
38. "Chicanos on the Move," *Newsweek*, January 1, 1979, p. 23; Paul Burka, "The Second Battle of the Alamo," *Texas Monthly*, December 1977, pp. 139–143.
39. Niles Hansen, "Does the South Have a Stake in Northern Urban Poverty?" *Southern Economic Journal* 45, no. 4 (April 1979): 1220–1224.
40. Thomas Sowell, *Race and Economics*, p. 197.
41. Ibid., p. 204.
42. Ibid., p. 238.

8. Summary and Conclusions

1. Jean Revel-Mouroz, "Les migrations vers la frontière Mexique–Etats-Unis," *Cahiers des Amériques Latines* 12 (1975): 315–350.
2. William P. Glade, "Prospects for Mexico's Socioeconomic Growth," *Texas Business Review* 53, no. 2 (March–April 1979): 49.
3. "Report Notes Dramatic Reversal in Mexico's Population Growth," *Austin American-Statesman*, December 15, 1978, p. H-1.
4. "Time Bomb in Mexico: Why There'll Be No End to the Invasion by 'Illegals,'" *U.S. News and World Report*, July 4, 1977, p. 27.
5. Ellwyn R. Stoddard, "Illegal Mexican Labor in the Borderlands: Institutionalized Support of an Unlawful Practice," *Pacific Sociological Review* 19, no. 2 (April 1976): 175.
6. U.S. Bureau of the Census, *Statistical Abstract of the United States: 1979*, p. 397.
7. "GM Expanding South of the Border," *Austin American-Statesman*, March 5, 1980, p. G-6.
8. D. P. Vogt et al., *Energy Availabilities for State and Local Development: Projected Energy Patterns for 1985 and 1990*, pp. 291–293, 310, 312.
9. H. Smith Hylton, "Oil Boom Means Boost to Industry on Border," *Austin American-Statesman*, November 13, 1978, p. A-1.

Appendix E. Shift-Share Analysis of Borderlands Employment Change

1. Employment data are typically used in shift-share studies, but the same technique also can be used to analyze other kinds of regional data such as output, population, or income. The terminology found in shift-share studies is not consistent. For example, the national growth effect is

sometimes referred to as the regional share component. The industry-mix effect has been termed the structural component, the composition component, and the proportionality shift. The competitive effect has been termed the growth or regional component as well as the differential shift.

2. F. J. B. Stilwell, "Regional Growth and Structural Adaptation," *Urban Studies* 6, no. 2 (June 1969): 166.

3. James A. Chalmers and Terrance L. Beckhelm, "Shift and Share and the Theory of Industrial Location," *Regional Studies* 10, no. 1 (1976): 21.

4. Edgar S. Dunn, Jr., "A Statistical and Analytical Technique for Regional Analysis," *Papers and Proceedings of the Regional Science Association* 6 (1960): 101.

5. John H. Cumberland, "Current Issues in Regional Development Theory and Practice," *Economie Appliquée* 28, no. 2 (1975): 370.

6. Koren T. Sherrill, "Economic Growth in West German Border Regions: An Empirical Study of Sub-national Regions Directly Affected by International Influences," University of Texas at Austin, 1979.

7. J. M. Esteban-Marquillas, "A Reinterpretation of Shift-Share Analysis," *Regional and Urban Economics* 2, no. 3 (October 1972): 249–261.

8. These analyses were carried out, in cooperation with the author, at the Bureau of Economic Analysis, U.S. Department of Commerce.

Bibliography

UNPUBLISHED MATERIAL

Allaman, Peter M., and Birch, David L. "Components of Employment Change for Metropolitan and Rural Areas in the United States by Industry Group, 1970–1972." Cambridge: MIT-Harvard Joint Center for Urban Studies, Inter-Area Migration Project, WP-8, 1975.

Cartwright, David W. "Major Limitations of CWHS Files and Prospects for Improvement." Paper presented at the National Bureau of Economic Research Workshop on Policy Analysis with Social Security Research Files, Washington, D.C., March 17, 1978.

Cornelius, Wayne A. "Illegal Mexican Migration to the United States: Recent Research Findings, Policy Implications, and Research Priorities." Cambridge, Mass.: MIT Center for International Studies, May 1977.

Ellard, Charles J., and Cardenas, Gilbert. "The Effects of the Mexican Peso Devaluation of 1976 on Employment and Unemployment in the Texas-Mexico Border Area." Mimeographed. Edinburg, Tex.: Pan American University, 1978.

Fossett, Mark. "Local Differences in Anglo–Mexican American Earnings Inequality: A Consideration of the Role of Education in the Metropolitan Southwest." Austin: Southwest Borderlands Regional Economic Development Project, Mexico–United States Border Research Program, University of Texas, 1979.

Heisel, Donald F., and Brennan, Ellen. "Policies for Dealing with Illegal-Undocumented International Migration." New York: Population Division, Department of International Economic and Social Affairs, United Nations, 1979.

Martin, Philip L. "Guestworker Programs: Lessons from Europe." Paper prepared for the Joint Economic Committee, U.S. Congress, June 1979.

Martin, Philip L., and Houstoun, Marion F. "The Future of International Labor Migration." Paper prepared for the Select Commission on Immigration and Refugee Policy, Washington, D.C., November 1979.

Martin, Philip L., and Miller, Mark. "Regulating Alien Labor in Industrial Societies." Paper presented at the 32nd Annual Meeting of the Industrial Relations Research Association, Atlanta, Georgia, December 30, 1979.

Miller, James P. "Research with Dun and Bradstreet Data." Washington,

D.C.: Economic Development Division, U.S. Department of Agriculture, Working Paper no. 7903, 1979.

Sherrill, Koren T. "Economic Growth in West German Border Regions: An Empirical Study of Sub-national Regions Directly Affected by International Influences," Ph.D. dissertation, Department of Economics, University of Texas at Austin, 1979.

U.S. GOVERNMENT DOCUMENTS

Jusenius, Carol L., and Ledebur, Larry C. *Documenting the "Decline" of the North*. Washington, D.C.: Economic Development Administration, U.S. Department of Commerce, 1978.

Seligson, Mitchell A., and Williams, Edward J. *Maquiladoras and Migration: A Study of Workers in the Mexican–United States Border Industrialization Program*. Report no. DLMA 21-04-78-1. Springfield, Va.: National Technical Information Service, January 19, 1980.

U.S. Bureau of the Census. *County and City Data Book, 1972*. Washington, D.C.: U.S. Government Printing Office, 1973.

———. *County and City Data Book, 1977*. Washington, D.C.: U.S. Government Printing Office, 1978.

———. "Estimates of the Population of Texas Counties and Metropolitan Areas: July 1, 1976 (Revised) and 1977 (Provisional)." *Current Population Reports*. P-25, no. 798. Washington, D.C.: U.S. Government Printing Office, March 1979.

———. "Money Income and Poverty Status in 1975 of Families and Persons in the United States and the South Region, by Divisions and States." *Current Population Reports*. P-60, no. 112. Washington, D.C.: U.S. Government Printing Office, June 1978.

———. "Money Income and Poverty Status in 1975 of Families and Persons in the United States and the West Region, by Divisions and States." *Current Population Reports*. P-60, no. 113. Washington, D.C.: U.S. Government Printing Office, July 1978.

———. "Money Income and Poverty Status of Families and Persons in the United States: 1978 (Advance Report)." *Current Population Reports*. P-60, no. 120. Washington, D.C.: U.S. Government Printing Office, November 1979.

———. "Money Income in 1977 of Families and Persons in the United States." *Current Population Reports*. P-60, no. 118. Washington, D.C.: U.S. Government Printing Office, March 1979.

———. "Persons of Spanish Origin in the United States: March 1976 (Advance Report)." *Current Population Reports*. P-20, no. 302. Washington, D.C.: U.S. Government Printing Office, November 1976.

———. "Persons of Spanish Origin in the United States: March 1977." *Current Population Reports*. P-20, no. 329. Washington, D.C.: U.S. Government Printing Office, June 1978.

———. "Persons of Spanish Origin in the United States: March 1978." *Current Population Reports.* P-20, no. 339. Washington, D.C.: U.S. Government Printing Office, June 1979.

———. "Persons of Spanish Origin in the United States: March 1979 (Advance Report)." *Current Population Reports.* P-20, no. 347. Washington, D.C.: U.S. Government Printing Office, October 1979.

———. *Statistical Abstract of the United States: 1978.* Washington, D.C.: U.S. Government Printing Office, 1978.

———. *Statistical Abstract of the United States: 1979.* Washington, D.C.: U.S. Government Printing Office, 1979.

U.S. Central Intelligence Agency. *Handbook of Economic Statistics, 1977.* Washington, D.C.: CIA, 1977.

———. *Handbook of Economic Statistics, 1978.* Washington, D.C.: CIA, 1978.

U.S. Department of Commerce. Bureau of Economic Analysis. *Local Area Personal Income 1971–1976.* Volume 1. Summary. Washington, D.C.: U.S. Department of Commerce, August 1978.

———. *Regional Work Force Characteristics and Migration Data.* Washington, D.C.: U.S. Government Printing Office, 1976.

———. Regional Economic Measurement Division. "County and Metropolitan Area Personal Income." *Survey of Current Business* 59, no. 4 (April 1979).

U.S. Department of Labor. Bureau of Labor Statistics. *Handbook of Labor Statistics 1977.* Bulletin no. 1966. Washington, D.C.: U.S. Department of Labor, 1977.

———. Employment and Training Administration. *Area Trends in Employment and Unemployment.* Washington, D.C.: U.S. Department of Labor, January–April 1979.

SOUTHWEST AGENCY AND ORGANIZATION REPORTS

Alamo Area Council of Governments. *AACOG District Overall Economic Development Program 1976.* San Antonio: Alamo Area Council of Governments, July 1976.

City of Tucson. *Overall Economic Development Program.* Tucson: City of Tucson, 1979.

Governors of California, Arizona, New Mexico, and Texas. *Application for Designation as a Title V Regional Action Planning Commission,* submitted to the U.S. Department of Commerce, July 1976.

Governor's Office of Migrant Affairs. *Migrant and Seasonal Farmworkers in Texas.* Austin: Governor's Office of Migrant Affairs, 1976.

Hartman, Susan, and Chavez, Leticia. *Impact of Resident Aliens and Migrant School Children on Border Public School Districts.* El Paso: Organization of U.S. Border Cities and Counties, 1979.

Lower Rio Grande Development Council. *Overall Economic Development*

Program. McAllen, Tex.: Lower Rio Grande Development Council, November 1977.

Middle Rio Grande Development Council. *Overall Economic Development Program*. Del Rio, Tex.: Middle Rio Grande Development Council, 1977.

San Diego OEDP General Committee. *San Diego Region Overall Economic Development Program: Directions '80*. San Diego: OEDP General Committee, 1979.

Southern Rio Grande Council of Governments. *Southern Rio Grande Economic Development District Overall Economic Development Plan*. Book 1. Las Cruces: SRGCOG, 1977.

South Texas Development Council. *Overall Economic Development Program (Revised) 1977–1979*. Vol. 1. Laredo, Tex.: South Texas Development Council, May 1977.

Southwest New Mexico Council of Governments. *Overall Economic Development Plan 1978–1979*. Silver City, N.M.: SNMCG, 1979.

Stoddard, Ellwyn R., Martínez, Oscar J., and Lasso, Miguel Angel Martínez. *El Paso–Ciudad Juárez Relations and the "Tortilla Curtain": A Study of Local Adaptation to Federal Border Policies*. El Paso: El Paso Council on the Arts and Humanities, September 1979.

Stoddard, Ellwyn R., and West, Jonathan P. *The Impact of Mexico's Peso Devaluation on Selected U.S. Border Cities*. El Paso: Organization of U.S. Border Cities, 1977.

Villalpando, Manuel Vic, et al. *A Study of the Socioeconomic Impact of Illegal Aliens on the County of San Diego*. San Diego: County of San Diego Human Resources Agency, January 1977.

West Texas Council of Governments. *District Overall Economic Development Plan 1978–1979*. El Paso: West Texas Council of Governments, 1978.

Young, Arthur, and Company. *An Economic and Demographic Study of U.S. Border Cities*. El Paso: Organization of U.S. Border Cities, 1978.

BOOKS AND ARTICLES

Alvarez, Rodolfo. "The Psycho-Historical and Socioeconomic Development of the Chicano Community in the United States." *Social Science Quarterly* 53, no. 4 (March 1973): 920–942.

Aydalot, Philippe. "L'aménagement du territoire en France: une tentative de bilan." *L'Espace Géographique* 7, no. 4 (October 1978): 245–253.

Ayer, Harry W., and Layton, M. Ross. "The Border Industry Program and the Impacts of Expenditures by Mexican Border Industry Employees on a U.S. Border Community: An Empirical Study of Nogales." *Annals of Regional Science* 8, no. 2 (June 1974): 105–117.

Ball, Robert. "How Europe Created Its 'Minority Problem,'" *Fortune*, December 1973, pp. 130–142.

Blundell, William E. "Colorado River, Vital to Southwest, Travels Ever-Rockier Course." *Wall Street Journal*, February 12, 1979, pp. 1, 18.

Boeth, Richard, et al. "Western Water Fight." *Newsweek*, June 12, 1978, pp. 49–55.

Böhning, W. R. *Basic Aspects of Immigration and Return Migration in Western Europe.* Geneva, Switzerland: World Employment Project, International Labour Office, 1975.

——. "Some Thoughts on Emigration from the Mediterranean Basin." *International Labour Review* 111, no. 3 (March 1975): 251–277.

Boudeville, Jacques R. *Aménagement du territoire et polarisation.* Paris: Génin, 1972.

——. "European Integration, Urban Regions and Medium-Sized Towns." In *Regional Planning and Policy for Europe*, edited by Morgan Sant, pp. 129–156. Lexington, Mass.: D. C. Heath, 1974.

——. "Polarisation and Urbanisation (The Canadian and French Examples)." *Economie Appliqueé* 28, no. 1 (1975): pp. 215–241.

Briggs, Vernon M., Jr. "Illegal Aliens: The Need for a More Restrictive Border Policy." *Social Science Quarterly* 56, no. 3 (December 1975): pp. 477–484.

——. *Mexican Migration and the U.S. Labor Market.* Austin: Bureau of Business Research, University of Texas, 1975.

——. "Mexican Workers in the United States Labour Market: A Contemporary Dilemma." *International Labour Review* 112, no. 5 (November 1975): 351–368.

Briggs, Vernon M., Jr., Fogel, Walter, and Schmidt, Fred H. *The Chicano Worker.* Austin: University of Texas Press, 1977.

Brown, Douglas. "Europe's Migrant Workers." *Optima* 24, no. 1 (1974): 35–46.

Burka, Paul. "The Second Battle of the Alamo." *Texas Monthly*, December 1977, pp. 139–143.

Cardenas, Gilbert. *The Manpower Impact of Mexico's Peso Devaluation of 1976 on Border Labor Markets in Texas.* Edinburg, Tex.: School of Business Administration, Pan American University, 1979.

——. "Mexican Illegal Aliens in the San Antonio Labor Market." *Texas Business Review* 53, no. 6 (November–December 1979): 187–191.

Chalmers, James A., and Beckhelm, Terrance L. "Shift and Share and the Theory of Industrial Location." *Regional Studies* 10, no. 1 (1976): 15–23.

"Chicanos on the Move." *Newsweek*, January 1, 1979.

Chinitz, Benjamin. "Regional Economic Development Commissions: The Title V Program." *Canadian Journal of Regional Science* 1, no. 5 (Autumn 1978): 107–127.

Chiswick, Barry R. "Immigrants and Immigration Policy." In *Contemporary Economic Problems, 1978,* edited by William Fellner, pp. 285–326. Washington, D.C.: American Enterprise Institute for Public Policy Research, 1978.

Choldin, Harvey M., and Trout, Grafton D. *Mexican Americans in Transition: Migration and Employment in Michigan Cities.* East Lansing, Mich.: Rural Manpower Center, Michigan State University, 1969.

Christaller, Walter. *Central Places in Southern Germany.* Translated by Carlisle W. Baskin. Englewood Cliffs, N.J.: Prentice-Hall, 1966. (The original German edition was published as *Die zentralen Orte in Süddeutschland* [Jena: Gustav Fischer, 1933].)

Cortese, Tracy. "Alien Labor Used in Austin." *Austin American-Statesman,* September 1, 1979, p. B-1.

Corwin, Arthur F. "Early Mexican Labor Migration: A Frontier Sketch: 1848–1900." In *Immigrants—and Immigrants: Perspectives on Mexican Labor Migration to the United States,* edited by Arthur F. Corwin, pp. 25–37. Westport, Conn.: Greenwood Press, 1978.

————. "¿Quien Sabe? Mexican Migration Statistics." In *Immigrants—and Immigrants,* edited by Arthur F. Corwin, pp. 108–135. Westport, Conn.: Greenwood Press, 1978.

Corwin, Arthur F., and McCain, Johnny M. "Wetbackism since 1964: A Catalogue of Factors." In *Immigrants—and Immigrants,* edited by Arthur F. Corwin, pp. 67–107. Westport, Conn.: Greenwood Press, 1978.

Crewdson, John M. "Border Region Is Almost a Country unto Itself, Neither Mexican Nor American." *New York Times,* February 14, 1979, p. A-22.

Cumberland, John H. "Current Issues in Regional Development Theory and Practice." *Economie Appliquée* 28, no. 2 (1975): 361–377.

Davidson, John. "A Harvest of Poverty." *Texas Observer,* February 3, 1978.

Dillman, C. D. "Maquiladoras in Mexico's Northern Border Communities and the Border Industrialization Program." *Tijdschrift voor Economisch en Sociaal Geografie* 67, no. 3: 138–150.

————. "Urban Growth along Mexico's Northern Border and the Mexican National Border Program." *Journal of Developing Areas* 4, no. 4 (July 1970): 487–508.

Dunbar, Tony, and Kravitz, Linda. *Hard Traveling: Migrant Farm Workers in America.* Cambridge, Mass.: Ballinger, 1976.

Dunn, Edgar S., Jr. "A Statistical and Analytical Technique for Regional Analysis." *Papers and Proceedings of the Regional Science Association* 6 (1960): 97–109.

Ehrlich, Paul R., Bilderback, Loy, and Ehrlich, Anne H. *The Golden Door: International Migration, Mexico, and the United States.* New York: Ballantine Books, 1979.

Enriquez, Bill. "International Legal Implications of Industrial Development along the Mexican–U.S. Border." In *Pollution and International*

Boundaries, edited by Albert E. Utton, pp. 88–98. Albuquerque: University of New Mexico Press, 1973.

Erickson, Rodney A. "The New Wave of Nonmetropolitan Industrialization." *Earth and Mineral Sciences* 48, no. 3 (December 1978): 17–20.

Erickson, Rodney A., and Leinbach, Thomas R. "Characteristics of Branch Plants Attracted to Nonmetropolitan Areas." In *Nonmetropolitan Industrialization,* edited by Richard E. Lonsdale and H. L. Seyler, pp. 57–78. New York: Halsted Press, 1979.

Esteban-Marquillas, J. M. "A Reinterpretation of Shift-Share Analysis." *Regional and Urban Economics* 2, no. 3 (October 1972): 249–261.

Fernandez, Raul A. *The United States–Mexico Border: A Politico-Economic Profile.* Notre Dame, Ind.: University of Notre Dame Press, 1977.

Fogel, Walter. *Mexican Americans in Southwest Labor Markets.* Los Angeles: UCLA Graduate School of Business Administration, Mexican-American Study Project. Advance Report no. 10, October 1967.

Fox, Karl A., and Kumar, T. Krishna. "The Functional Economic Area: Delineation and Implications for Economic Analysis and Public Policy." *Papers and Proceedings of the Regional Science Association* 15 (1965): 57–85.

Frantz, Joe B. "The Borderlands: Ideas on a Leafless Landscape." In *Views across the Border,* edited by Stanley R. Ross, pp. 33–49. Albuquerque: University of New Mexico Press, 1978.

Garreau, Joel. "Nine Nations, Indivisible." *Austin American-Statesman,* April 29, 1979.

Gendarme, René. "Les problèmes économiques des régions frontières européennes." *Revue Economique* 21, no. 6 (November 1970): 889–917.

German Tribune, January 16, 1975.

Giersch, Herbert. "Economic Union between Nations and the Location of Industries." *Review of Economic Studies* 17, no. 43 (1949–50): 87–97.

Glade, William P. "Prospects for Mexico's Socioeconomic Growth." *Texas Business Review* 53, no. 2 (March–April 1979): 47–49.

"GM Expanding South of the Border." *Austin American-Statesman,* March 5, 1980, p. G-6.

Goldwater, Barry. *Arizona.* Chicago: Rand McNally, 1978.

Gomez, Rudolph. "The Politics of the Mexican–United States Border." In *Views across the Border,* edited by Stanley R. Ross, pp. 386–389. Albuquerque: University of New Mexico Press, 1978.

Gordon, Wendell. "A Case for a Less Restrictive Border Policy." *Social Science Quarterly* 56, no. 3 (December 1975): 485–491.

Grebler, Leo, Moore, Joan W., and Guzman, Ralph C. *The Mexican American People: The Nation's Second Largest Minority.* New York: Free Press, 1970.

Greenfield, Stuart. "Texas Border Communities and the Peso Devaluation."

Texas Business Review 53, no. 2 (March–April 1979): 54–56.

Greenwood, Michael J. "An Econometric Model of Internal Migration and Regional Economic Growth in Mexico." *Journal of Regional Science* 18, no. 1 (April 1978): 17–31.

Guichonnet, Paul, and Raffestin, Claude. *Géographie des frontières.* Paris: Presses Universitaires de France, 1974.

Hansen, Niles. "Does the South Have a Stake in Northern Urban Poverty?" *Southern Economic Journal* 45, no. 4 (April 1979): 1220–1224.

———. "Economic Aspects of Regional Separatism." *Papers of the Regional Science Association* 41 (1978): 143–152.

———. "Employment Patterns in the Southwest Borderlands." *Texas Business Review* 54, no. 1 (January–February 1980): 20–24.

———. "An Evaluation of Growth Centre Theory and Practice." *Environment and Planning*, series A, 7, no. 7 (1975): 821–832.

———. *The Future of Nonmetropolitan America.* Lexington, Mass.: D.C. Heath, 1973.

———, ed. *Growth Centers in Regional Economic Development.* New York: Free Press, 1972.

———. "International Labor Migration: Europe's Guest Worker Policies and Mexicans in the United States." *Growth and Change* 10, no. 2 (April 1979): 2–8.

———. "Regional Policies in the United States: Experience and Prospects." In *Regional Development and Planning: International Perspectives*, edited by Antoni R. Kuklinski, pp. 139–151. Leyden, The Netherlands: Sijthoff, 1973.

Hansen, Niles, and Gruben, William C. "The Influence of Relative Wages and Assisted Migration on Locational Preferences: Mexican Americans in South Texas." *Social Science Quarterly* 52, no. 1 (June 1971): 103–114.

Hirsch, Werner. *Location of Industry and International Competitiveness.* Oxford: Clarendon Press, 1967.

Hirschman, Charles. "Prior U.S. Residence among Mexican Immigrants." *Social Forces* 56, no. 4 (June 1978): 1179–1201.

Hoffman, George. *A Geography of Europe.* 4th edition. New York: Ronald Press, 1977.

Holburt, Myron B. "International Problems." In *Values and Choices in the Development of the Colorado River Basin*, edited by Dean F. Peterson and A. Berry Crawford, pp. 220–237. Tucson: University of Arizona Press, 1978.

Hoover, Edgar M. *The Location of Economic Activity.* New York: McGraw-Hill, 1948.

Horgan, Paul. *Great River: The Rio Grande in North American History.* New York: Holt, Rinehart, and Winston, 1954.

Hylton, H. Smith. "Oil Boom Means Boost to Industry on Border." *Austin American-Statesman*, November 13, 1978, p. A-1.

Jones, Oakah L., Jr. *Los Paisanos: Spanish Settlers on the Northern Frontier of New Spain.* Norman: University of Oklahoma Press, 1979.

Journal officiel de la République Française. 1975.

Kindleberger, Charles P. *Europe's Postwar Growth: The Role of Labor Supply.* Cambridge, Mass.: Harvard University Press, 1967.

King, Allan G. "Unemployment Consequences of Illegal Aliens from Mexico." *Texas Business Review* 53, no. 2 (March–April 1979): 43–45.

Kirstein, Peter N. *Anglo over Bracero: A History of the Mexican Worker in the United States from Roosevelt to Nixon.* San Francisco: R and E Research Associates, 1977.

Koon, Bruce. "Instead of Turning In Illegal Aliens, Some Unions Try Signing Them Up." *Wall Street Journal*, November 13, 1979, p. 19.

Kuklinski, Antoni R., ed. *Growth Poles and Growth Centres in Regional Planning.* Paris and The Hague: Mouton, 1972.

Ladman, Jerry R., and Paulsen, Mark O. *Economic Impact of the Mexican Border Industrialization Program: Agua Priete, Sonora.* Tempe, Ariz.: University of Arizona, Center for Latin American Studies, 1972.

"LDC Debt: The Load Eases." *Newsweek*, February 27, 1978, p. 73.

López y Rivas, Gilberto. *The Chicanos.* New York: Monthly Review Press, 1973.

Lösch, August. *The Economics of Location.* Translated by W. H. Woglom and Wolfgang W. Stolper. New Haven, Conn.: Yale University Press, 1954. (The original German edition was published as *Die räumliche Ordnung der Wirtschaft* [Jena: Gustav Fischer, 1940].)

Lower Rio Grande Valley Policy Research Project. *Colonias in the Lower Rio Grande Valley of South Texas: A Summary Report.* Austin: Lyndon B. Johnson School of Public Affairs Policy Research Project Report no. 18, University of Texas at Austin, 1977.

Magué, Pierre. "L'Alsace." In *Les régions d'Europe*, edited by Guy Héraud, pp. 35–46. Paris and Nice: Presses d'Europe, 1973.

Marshall, F. Ray, Cartter, Allan M., and King, Allan G. *Labor Economics.* 3rd ed. Homewood, Ill.: Richard D. Irwin, 1976.

Martínez, Oscar J. *Border Boom Town: Ciudad Juárez since 1848.* Austin: University of Texas Press, 1978.

———. "On the Size of the Chicano Population: New Estimates, 1850–1900." *Aztlán* 6, no. 1 (Spring 1975): 43–67.

McCarthy, Kevin F., and Morrison, Peter A. *The Changing Demographic and Economic Structure of Nonmetropolitan Areas in the United States.* Santa Monica, Ca.: Rand Corporation, 1979.

Meyers, Dan. "Bracero Revival Seen as End to Alien Problems." *Austin American-Statesman*, August 19, 1979, p. A-14.

Miller, Michael V., and Maril, Robert Lee. *Poverty in the Lower Rio Grande Valley of Texas: Historical and Contemporary Dimensions.* College Station, Tex.: Department of Rural Sociology Technical Report no. 78-2, Texas A&M University, 1979.

Mills, James R. *San Diego: Where California Began.* San Diego: San Diego Historical Society, 1976.

Mines, Richard. "Riding the Tide of Migration." *Daily Texan* (University of Texas at Austin), January 18, 1978, p. 5.

Moseley, Malcolm J. *Growth Centres in Spatial Planning.* Oxford: Pergamon Press, 1974.

Murray, Thomas J. "American Boom in Mexico." *Dun's Review* 112, no. 4 (October 1978): 119–127.

Muth, Richard F. "Migration: Chicken or Egg?" *Southern Economic Journal* 37, no. 3 (January 1971): 295–306.

Nathan, Robert R., Associates. *Industrial and Employment Potential of the United States–Mexico Border.* Washington, D.C.: U.S. Department of Commerce, 1968.

National Journal, February 10, 1979, p. 212.

Norquest, Carrol. *Rio Grande Wetbacks: Mexican Migrant Workers.* Albuquerque: University of New Mexico Press, 1972.

North, David, and Houstoun, Marion. *The Characteristics and Role of Illegal Aliens in the U.S. Labor Market: An Exploratory Study.* Washington, D.C.: Linton and Company, 1976.

Nostrand, Richard L. "The Hispanic-American Borderland: Delimitation of an American Culture Region." *Annals of the Association of American Geographers* 60, no. 4 (December 1970): 638–661.

Ohlin, Bertil. *Interregional and International Trade.* Revised edition. Cambridge, Mass.: Harvard University Press, 1967.

Olvey, Lee D. "Regional Growth and Interregional Migration: Their Pattern of Interaction." *Review of Regional Studies* 2, no. 2 (Winter 1972): 139–163.

Oyarzabal-Tamargo, Francisco, and Young, Robert A. "International External Diseconomies: The Colorado River Salinity Problem in Mexico." *Natural Resources Journal* 18, no. 1 (January 1978): 77–89.

Paredes, Américo. "The Problem of Identity in a Changing Culture: Popular Expressions of Culture Conflict along the Lower Rio Grande Border." In *Views across the Border,* edited by Stanley R. Ross, pp. 68–96. Albuquerque: University of New Mexico Press, 1978.

Perroux, François. *L'économie du XXe siècle.* Paris: Presses Universitaires de France, 1964.

Persky, Joseph. "Dualism, Capital-Labor Ratios and the Regions of the U.S." *Journal of Regional Science* 18, no. 3 (December 1978): 373–382.

Piore, Michael J. *Birds of Passage: Migrant Labor and Industrial Societies.* Cambridge: Cambridge University Press, 1979.

Plaut, Thomas R. *Net Migration into Texas and Its Regions: Trends and Patterns.* Austin: Bureau of Business Research, University of Texas, 1979.

Pluta, Joseph E. "Urban Fiscal Strain and the Health of Large Texas Cities." *Texas Business Review* 53, no. 1 (January–February 1979): 8–12.

Portes, Alejandro. "Return of the Wetback." *Society* 11, no. 1 (March–April 1974): 40–46.

Poston, Dudley L., Jr., and Alvirez, David. "On the Cost of Being a Mexican American Worker." *Social Science Quarterly* 53, no. 4 (March 1973): 697–709.

Poston, Dudley L., Jr., Alvirez, David, and Tienda, Marta. "Earnings Differences between Anglo and Mexican American Male Workers in 1960 and 1970: Changes in the 'Cost' of Being Mexican American." *Social Science Quarterly* 57, no. 3 (December 1976): 618–631.

Pred, Allan. *The Interurban Transmission of Growth in Advanced Economies: Empirical Findings versus Regional Planning Assumptions.* Laxenburg, Austria: International Institute for Applied Systems Analysis, 1976.

Price, John A. *Tijuana: Urbanization in a Border Culture.* Notre Dame, Ind.: University of Notre Dame Press, 1973.

Pritchett, V. S. *The Myth Makers.* New York: Random House, 1979.

"Les régions frontière et la polarisation urbaine dans la Communauté Economique Européenne." A special number of *Economies et Sociétés* 5, no. 3–4 (March–April 1971).

"Report Notes Dramatic Reversal in Mexico's Population Growth." *Austin American-Statesman*, December 15, 1978, p. H-1.

Reubens, Edwin P. "Illegal Immigration and the Mexican Economy." *Challenge* 21, no. 5 (November–December 1978): 13–19.

Revel-Mouroz, Jean. "Les migrations vers la frontière Mexique–Etats-Unis." *Cahiers des Amériques Latines* 12 (1975): 315–350.

Revel-Mouroz, Jean, and Bataillon, Claude. "Les migrations Mexicaines vers les Etats-Unis et la frontière nord du Mexique." *Tiers-Monde* 18, no. 69 (January–March 1977): 55–76.

Richardson, Harry W. "Regional Development Policy in Spain." *Urban Studies* 8, no. 1 (February 1971): pp. 39–54.

Roberts, Kenneth, Conroy, Michael E., King, Allan G., and Rizo-Patron, Jorge. "Counting Illegal Mexican Aliens: Myths and Misconceptions." *Texas Business Review* 52, no. 6 (June 1978): 101–105.

Samora, Julian. *Los Mojados.* Notre Dame, Ind.: University of Notre Dame Press, 1971.

Samora, Julian, and Simon, Patricia Vandel. *A History of the Mexican-American People.* Notre Dame, Ind.: University of Notre Dame Press, 1977.

Schlagheck, James L. *The Political, Economic, and Labor Climate in Mex-*

ico. Philadelphia: Industrial Research Institute, Wharton School, University of Pennsylvania, 1977.

"Slamming the Door on Europe's Guest Workers." *Economist*, August 9, 1975, p. 24.

Smith, Barton, and Newman, Robert. "Depressed Wages along the U.S.-Mexico Border: An Empirical Analysis." *Economic Inquiry* 15, no. 1 (January 1977): 50–66.

Sowell, Thomas. *Race and Economics.* New York: David McKay, 1975.

Stilwell, F. J. B. "Regional Growth and Structural Adaptation." *Urban Studies* 6, no. 2 (June 1969): 162–178.

Stoddard, Ellwyn R. "A Conceptual Analysis of the 'Alien Invasion': Institutionalized Support of Illegal Mexican Aliens in the U.S." *International Migration Review* 10, no. 2 (Summer 1976): 157–187.

———. "Illegal Mexican Labor in the Borderlands: Institutionalized Support of an Unlawful Practice." *Pacific Sociological Review* 19, no. 2 (April 1976): 175–210.

———. *Patterns of Poverty along the U.S.-Mexico Border.* El Paso: Center for Inter-American Studies, University of Texas at El Paso, 1978.

Stöhr, Walter. *Regional Development Experiences and Prospects in Latin America.* Paris and The Hague: Mouton, 1975.

Strasser, Steven, et al. "Mexico's New Muscle." *Newsweek*, October 1, 1979.

Szulc, Tad. "Foreign Policy Aspects of the Border." In *Views across the Border*, edited by Stanley R. Ross, pp. 226–240. Albuquerque: University of New Mexico Press, 1978.

Taylor, Paul S. "The Future of Mexican Immigration." In *Immigrants—and Immigrants*, edited by Arthur F. Corwin, pp. 347–352. Westport, Conn.: Greenwood Press: 1978.

Texas Observer, March 25, 1977.

Thompson, Wilbur R. "The Economic Base of Urban Problems." In *Contemporary Economic Issues*, edited by Neil W. Chamberlain, pp. 1–48. Homewood, Ill.: Richard D. Irwin, 1969.

"Time Bomb in Mexico: Why There'll Be No End to the Invasion by 'Illegals.'" *U.S. News and World Report*, July 4, 1977, pp. 27–34.

Tjersland, Tore, and Greenblat, Dan. *San Diego Economic Profile 1977.* San Diego: Economic Research Bureau of the San Diego Chamber of Commerce, 1977.

The Union-Tribune's Annual Review of San Diego Business Activity 1978. San Diego: Union-Tribune Publishing Company, 1978.

Urquidi, Víctor, and Villareal, Sofía Méndez. "Economic Importance of Mexico's Northern Border Region." In *Views across the Border*, edited by Stanley R. Ross, pp. 141–162. Albuquerque: University of New Mexico Press, 1978.

Vogt, D. P., Rice, P. L., Corey, T. A., and Pai, V. P. *Energy Availabilities for State and Local Development: Projected Energy Patterns for 1985 and 1990.* Oak Ridge, Tenn.: Oak Ridge National Laboratory, 1979.

Wachter, Michael L. "Second Thoughts about Illegal Immigrants." *Fortune,* May 22, 1978, pp. 80–87.

Wander, Hilde. "The Role of International Migration in the Changing Pattern of Economic, Social and Demographic Structure in Europe." In *The Effect of Current Demographic Change in Europe on Social Structure,* edited by Milos Macura, pp. 21–31. Belgrade, Yugoslavia: Ekonomski Institut, 1979.

Weber, David J., ed. *Foreigners in Their Native Land.* Albuquerque: University of New Mexico Press, 1973.

Weintraub, Sidney, and Ross, Stanley R. *The Illegal Alien from Mexico: Policy Choices for an Intractable Issue.* Austin: Mexico–United States Border Research Program, University of Texas at Austin, 1980.

Wiessler, Judy. "Mexico Was Offered Pay But Did Not Bill U.S. for Salt Water Damages." *Houston Chronicle,* October 7, 1979, p. 6, sec. 1.

Zlatkovich, Charles P. *The Identification of Functional Regions Based on Highway Traffic Flow Data.* Austin: Bureau of Business Research, University of Texas, 1977.

Zlatkovich, Charles P., and Bennett, Carol T. F. "The Lower Rio Grande Valley: An Area of Rapid Growth." *Texas Business Review* 51, no. 5 (September–October 1977): 204–209.

Index

Agua Prieta, Mexico, 91
Ajo, Arizona, 40
Albuquerque, New Mexico, 137–138
Anaheim, California, 137
Anglos: colonization of Texas by, 78–79; definition of, x; education and earnings of, compared to Mexican Americans, 132–142
Arizona borderlands. See Borderlands, Southwest U.S.
Austin, Texas, 114
Austria, 32
Austro-Hungarian Empire, 20

Baja California, Mexico, 36–38, 52
BEA regions. See Bureau of Economic Analysis regions
Beaumont, Texas, 8
Beckhelm, Terrance, 175
Benelux nations, 32
Böhning, W. R., 121
Borderlands, Southwest U.S.: definition of, in terms of BEA regions, 8–10, 168; definition of, in terms of Southwest Border Regional Commission counties, 7–8, 167; and MexAmerica, 8
Border trade. See Trade, border
Boudeville, Jacques, 28–30
Bracero program: abuses of, 83; evolution of, 82–84, 101, 158; and maquiladoras, 156; rationale for, 82, 101; and undocumented migration, 82–84, 101, 105, 114
Brawley, California, 39
Briggs, Vernon M., Jr., 104
Brownsville BEA region: definition of, 168; employment in, 72–74, 162, 180, 182; growth of, 14, 16, 160; income in, 15–16; rationale for use of, 9. See also Brownsville SMSA; Brownsville, Texas
Brownsville SMSA: defined, 49; employ-

ment in, 52; income in, 14–15, 162; population change in, 13–15, 50, 160; unemployment in, 12. See also Brownsville BEA region; Brownsville, Texas
Brownsville, Texas: growth of, 50–51; and Matamoros, Mexico, 11, 50; Mexican Americans in, 50–51, 143; and peso devaluation, 99; schools in, 147. See also Brownsville BEA region; Brownsville SMSA
Bureau of Economic Analysis regions: definition of, 9–10, 186. See also Brownsville BEA region; El Paso BEA region; San Antonio BEA region; San Diego BEA region; Tucson BEA region

Calexico, California, 39, 147
California borderlands. See Borderlands, Southwest U.S.
Canada, 21, 25, 31, 87, 189
Cardenas, Gilbert, 107, 113, 123
Central Arizona Project, 42
Chalmers, James, 175
Chávez, César, 111, 163
Chicago, Illinois, 108, 130, 151
Chicanos. See Mexican Americans
Christaller, Walter, 22–25, 30
Chula Vista, California, 143
Cochise County, Arizona, 17, 40
Colonias, 51
Colorado River, 36, 39, 40–43
Colorado River Interstate Compact, 42
Communities Organized for Public Service (COPS), 153, 164
Commuter workers, 12, 39, 46, 89–92
Cooperation, trans-border, 3, 8, 11, 38, 46
Cornelius, Wayne, 113
Corona, California, 143–144
Corpus Christi, Texas, 10, 49, 137–138, 167
Cumberland, John, 175

Dallas, Texas, 8, 17, 137
Davidson, John, 149
Decentralization in U.S., 160–161
Del Rio, Texas, 48, 143
Denver, Colorado, 41, 137
Detroit, Michigan, 108, 130
Dona Ana County, New Mexico, 17, 44
Douglas, Arizona, 91
Dunn, Edgar S., Jr., 175

Eagle Pass, Texas, 48
Earnings: in borderlands BEA regions,
  72–76; of Mexican Americans,
  136–143, 146–151, 162–163; in the
  Middle Rio Grande region, 47–48; in
  Southwest Border Regional Commis-
  sion counties, 64–71; of undocu-
  mented Mexican workers, 37, 114.
  See also Income
Echeverría, President Luis, 43
Edwards Plateau, 47
El Cajon, California, 143
El Centro, California, 39
El Paso BEA region: definition of, 168;
  employment in, 44–47, 73, 162, 178,
  182–183; growth of, 14–16, 44–46,
  160, 162; income in, 15–16; and
  Juárez, Mexico, 44–46; and New
  Mexico, 44, 46; rationale for use of, 9;
  and west Texas, 46–47. See also El
  Paso SMSA; El Paso, Texas
El Paso SMSA: income in, 14–15; Mex-
  ican Americans in, 12; population
  change in, 13–15, 160. See also El
  Paso BEA region; El Paso, Texas
El Paso, Texas: commuter workers in,
  91; defense spending in, 160; and
  Juárez, Mexico, 11, 45–46, 52, 91, 99,
  108; local revenues of, 17; and maquiladoras, 99, 164; Mexican Americans in, 137, 143, 153; and peso
  devaluation, 99. See also El Paso BEA
  region; El Paso SMSA
Employment: in borderlands BEA regions, 72–76, 174–183; in the El Paso
  BEA region, 44–47, 73, 162, 178,
  182–183; in the Imperial Valley, 39;
  in the Lower Rio Grande Valley,
  51–52; of Mexican Americans,
  131–133, 146–151, 162–163; of Mexican commuters, 90–92; in San Diego
  SMSA, 36; in the South Texas region,
  48–49; in Southwest Border Regional
  Commission counties, 53–72,

161–162, 169–172; in Tucson SMSA,
  41. See also International division of
  labor; Maquiladora program; Undocu-
  mented Mexican workers
Energy, 165
Ensenada, Mexico, 37
Equal Employment Opportunity Com-
  mission, 147, 153
Escondido, California, 143
Esteban-Marquillas, J. M., 175, 181
European Economic Community, 21, 25

Fernandez, Raul, 86–87
Fort Worth, Texas, 8
Fox, Karl, 8
France, 27–30, 32, 95–96, 118
Functional economic areas, 8–9. See
  also Bureau of Economic Analysis
  regions

Gadsen Purchase, 40
Gary, Indiana, 130
Gendarme, René, 27–29
Germany, 20, 25, 27–28, 30, 32, 118
Giersch, Herbert, 24–26
Gomez, Rudolph, 153
Grant County, New Mexico, 17, 44
Greece, 117, 119, 125
"Green Carders." See Commuter
  workers
Growth pole theory, 26–30
"Guest worker" programs, 116–126,
  159

Harlingen, Texas, 49–50, 143
Hidalgo County, New Mexico, 17, 44
Hidalgo County, Texas, 149–150, 163
Hidalgo, Texas, 99
Hirschman, Charles, 107
Hoover, Edgar, 24, 26
Horton, Alonzo, 35
Houston, Texas, 8, 17, 112, 137,
  152–153

Illegal Mexican immigration. See Undocumented Mexican workers
Immigration and Naturalization Service,
  82, 114–115
Imperial Valley, California, 38–39
Income: in borderlands SMSAs, 14–15;
  in the Lower Rio Grande Valley, 51; of
  Mexican Americans, 132–137,
  142–151, 162–164; Mexico-U.S. difference in, 12; in Southwest Border

Regional Commission counties, 16–17, 160. *See also* Earnings
International division of labor, 92–96, 122–123
International trade theory, 21–22
Italy, 119

Jalisco, Mexico, 107
Juárez, Mexico: as border city, 31; and El Paso, Texas, 11, 45–46, 52, 91, 99, 108; growth of, 81, 89, 155; *maquiladoras* in, 164; tertiary sector in, 36

Kansas City, Missouri-Kansas, 130
King, Allan, 110

La Mesa, California, 143–144
Laredo SMSA: definition of, 48; employment in, 48–49; income in, 14–15, 162; Mexican Americans in, 12, 48–49; population change in, 13–14, 160; and the San Antonio BEA region, 10, 49. *See also* Laredo, Texas
Laredo, Texas, 99, 143, 147. *See also* Laredo SMSA
Las Cruces, New Mexico, 44, 143
Location theory, 22–26, 92–94
López Portillo, President José, 42
López y Rivas, Gilberto, 86
Los Angeles, California, 8, 137, 152–153
Lösch, August, 22–26, 30
Lower Rio Grande Valley, 49–52, 148–153, 163
Luna County, New Mexico, 17, 44

Manifest Destiny, 20, 31, 155
Maquiladora program, 77; advantages of, 98–100, 157; criticisms of, 97–99, 156–157; growth of, 97, 100, 164; and "twin plants," 98–99, 161, 183. *See also* International division of labor
Martínez, Oscar, 31
Matamoros, Mexico, 11, 50, 165
McAllen SMSA: definition of, 49; employment in, 52; income in, 14–15, 162; population change in, 13–14, 50, 160; unemployment in, 12. *See also* Brownsville BEA region; Lower Rio Grande Valley
Mexicali, Mexico: commuters from, to Imperial Valley, 39; growth of, 36–37, 81, 89, 155; shoppers from, in U.S., 91

Mexicali Valley, Mexico, 42–43
Mexican American Legal Defense and Education Fund, 124
Mexican Americans: *barrios* of, 51; as conquered minority, 77–78; discrimination against, 78, 139, 146–148, 152–154, 162–163; educational attainment of, 131, 136–142, 146–148, 162–163; geographic mobility of, 151–152; income and earnings of, 112, 132–146, 162–164; labor force participation of, 76, 161; and Mexico, 3, 13, 79, 127; occupational distribution of, 131–133; political organization of, 152–154, 164; as population, 10, 12–13, 49, 79–80, 85–86, 127–130, 162, 164; and undocumented Mexican workers, 13, 51, 79, 99, 107, 111–112. *See also* Migrant farm workers
Mexicans: deportation of, from U.S., 81–82, 84; migration of, to U.S., 79–82, 86–89, 100–102; in U.S. in 1850, 79, 85–86, 155. *See also* Bracero program; Commuter workers; *Maquiladora* program; Trade, border; Undocumented Mexican workers
Mexican–United States War, 77–79, 155
Mexico: attitude of, to northern border regions, 31; attitude of, to undocumented migration, 115; and Colorado River water, 42–44; dependency of, on U.S., 31–32, 86–87, 97–98, 125, 157; economic progress of, 105–106, 116, 125, 157; oil reserves of, 105, 125, 157, 165; population growth in, 157–158; urbanization of northern border area, 89–90, 101, 155–157. *See also* Bracero program; Commuter workers; *Maquiladora* program; Mexicans; Mexican–United States War; Trade, border; Undocumented Mexican workers
Mexico City, 105, 116
Michigan, 151
Michoacán, Mexico, 107
Middle Ages, 19
Middle Rio Grande region of Texas, 47–48
Migrant farm workers, 49, 51, 148–151, 163
Migration: to borderlands SMSAs, 13–14, 160; of Mexican Americans,

151–152, 162; in Mexico, 89–90, 101, 155–157; to the Southwest, 159–160; of workers in Southwest Border Regional Commission counties, 65–67. *See also* Mexicans; Undocumented Mexican workers
Mines, Richard, 113
Monterrey, Mexico, 8, 10, 116

National City, California, 143
National Labor Relations Board, 115
Newman, Robert, 112
New Mexico borderlands. *See* Borderlands, Southwest U.S.
Nogales, Arizona, 44, 99
Nogales, Mexico, 99
North Africa, 117
Nuevo Laredo, Mexico, 52, 81

Oakland, California, 152
Oceanside, California, 143
Ohlin, Bertil, 25
Otero County, New Mexico, 17, 44

Palm Springs, California, 143–145
Perroux, François, 30
Persky, Joseph, 94–95
Peso devaluation of 1976, 99–100
Phoenix, Arizona, 8–10, 42, 137
Pima County, Arizona, 17, 40–41
Piore, Michael, 106–107, 114, 121
Portolá, Gaspár de, 35
Portugal, 117, 119

Real County, Texas, 7, 47
Regional development legislation, 5–7. *See also* Southwest Border Regional Commission
Reubens, Edwin, 117
Reynosa, Mexico, 50, 165
Rio Grande City, Texas, 147
Riverside, California, 143–144

Salton Sea, 38–39
San Angelo, Texas, 9–10
San Antonio BEA region: definition of, 168; employment in, 72–74, 162, 179, 182; growth of, 14–16, 160; income in, 15–16; and Laredo, Texas, 49; rationale for use of, 9–10, 49. *See also* San Antonio, Texas
San Antonio, Texas: defense spending in, 160; Mexican Americans in, 137, 153; undocumented Mexican workers

in, 107, 113, 123–124. *See also* San Antonio BEA region
San Bernardino, California, 137
San Diego BEA region: definition of, 168; employment in, 72–74, 162, 176, 182; growth of, 14–16, 160; income in, 14–16; rationale for use of, 9. *See also* San Diego, California; San Diego SMSA
San Diego, California: defense spending in, 160; growth of, 35–38, 159–161; Mexican Americans in, 137, 142–145; and peso devaluation, 99; and Tijuana, Mexico, 11, 36–38, 52, 108, 155–156; undocumented Mexican workers in, 37, 108, 112; unionization of commuters in, 91; water needs of, 41. *See also* San Diego BEA region; San Diego SMSA
San Diego County, California, 16–17
San Diego SMSA: employment in, 36; income in, 14–15; Mexican Americans in, 13; population change in, 13–15, 160; unemployment in, 13. *See also* San Diego BEA region; San Diego, California
San Francisco, California, 137–138, 152
San Jose, California, 137
Santa Cruz County, Arizona, 17, 40
Santa Fe, New Mexico, 8, 79
San Ysidro, California, 147
School districts, 147–148
Secondary labor market, 120–123, 199
Serra, Junípero, 35
Smith, Barton, 112
SMSAs. *See* Standard Metropolitan Statistical Areas
Sonoran Desert, 40
South Padre Island, Texas, 52
South Texas region, 48–49
Southwest Border Regional Commission, 3–5, 7–8, 10–18, 33, 53, 144–145, 161, 167
Sowell, Thomas, 154
Spain, 32, 78, 117, 119
Spatial-industrial filtering, 92–96
Standard Metropolitan Statistical Areas: definition of, 185; population of, in borderlands, 6–7. *See also* Brownsville SMSA; El Paso SMSA; Laredo SMSA; McAllen SMSA; San Diego SMSA; Tucson SMSA
Starr County, Texas, 17, 48

Stilwell, F. J. B., 175
Switzerland, 25, 29, 32, 118
Szulc, Tad, 103

Taos, New Mexico, 79
Tecate, Mexico, 37
Terrell County, Texas, 17, 47
Texas borderlands. See Borderlands, Southwest U.S.
Texas Farm Workers Union, 150
Texas Governor's Office of Migrant Affairs, 149
Texas Rangers, 78
Tijuana, Mexico: growth of, 37, 81, 89, 155; and San Diego, California, 11, 36–38, 52, 108, 155–156; tertiary sector in, 36–37
Tombstone, Arizona, 40
"Tortilla Curtain" incident, 108
Tourism, 11, 25, 36–37, 45, 47, 49, 52, 100
Trade, border: between Arizona and Mexico, 43–44, 75, 91, 99, 182–183; between California and Mexico, 36–38, 75, 91, 99, 182; between Texas and Mexico, 46, 48–49, 52, 75, 91, 99–100, 182–183
Tucson, Arizona: growth of, 40–41, 161; Mexican Americans in, 143; Mexican visits to, 44; and peso devaluation, 99; water scarcity in, 41–42. See also Tucson BEA region; Tucson SMSA
Tucson BEA region: definition of, 168; employment in, 72–74, 162, 177, 182–183; growth of, 14–16, 160; income in, 15–16; rationale for use of, 9. See also Tucson, Arizona; Tucson SMSA
Tucson SMSA: definition of, 17; income in, 14–17; Mexican Americans in, 13; population change in, 13–15, 40–41, 160; unemployment in, 13, 41. See also Tucson, Arizona; Tucson BEA region

Undocumented Mexican workers: in Austin, Texas, 114; and the bracero program, 88, 105, 114, 158; case against, 109–110; and European "guest worker" experience, 88–89, 116–126; location of, in U.S., 84, 106–107, 123; Marxist view of, 88–89, 100–101; number of, 3, 84, 101, 103; permanency of, in U.S., 112–113, 123, 126, 158; positive aspects of, 111–116; problems associated with, 103–104; reasons for migration of, 104–109; in San Antonio, 107, 113, 123–124; in San Diego, 37, 108, 112, 198; tacit support of, in U.S. borderlands, 84, 100, 107–108, 159; and unemployment in U.S., 11–12, 84, 100, 110–112, 158. See also Mexican Americans; Mexicans; Mexico
Unemployment, 12–13, 110–111
United Farm Workers, 111, 114, 151, 163

Vienna, Austria, 23
Vista, California, 143

Water scarcity, 41–43, 47
Webb, Walter Prescott, 78
Wellton-Mohawk Project, 43

Yugoslavia, 117, 125
Yuma, Arizona, 40, 43, 143
Yuma County, Arizona, 17, 40